THE
DISAPPEARING

THE DISAPPEARING

FUTURE EVENTS THAT WILL ROCK THE WORLD

TERRY JAMES & PETE GARCIA

Foreword by Jan Markell

DEFENDER

CRANE, MO

The Disappearing: Future Events That Will Rock the World
By Terry James & Pete Garcia

Unless otherwise indicated, Bible quotations are taken from the King James Version and the New King James Version of Scripture.

Cover design by Jeffrey Mardis

ISBN: 9781948014571

Dedicated to our friend and brother in Christ, Jack Kinsella,
From whom we both learned so much.
Till we meet again.

ACKNOWLEDGMENTS

First and foremost, I would like to thank my Lord and Savior, Jesus Christ, for dying in my place and taking the full wrath of God upon Himself, conquering death and hell, and giving me eternal life. I am also eternally thankful to God for my wife and children, who graciously tolerate my writing addiction and keep me grounded. I am also indebted to the many faithful supporters of my writing endeavors, both with the *Omega Letter* and now with Rev310. Thank you for your prayers and support. Lastly, to Jack and Kari, for taking a chance on me many years ago. Maranatha!
—Pete Garcia

To my wife Margaret, my deepest love and thanks for allowing hours spent in almost complete isolation, which is required for those engaged in the writing life—at least it is for me.

To Terry Jr., Nathan, and Kerry, my love and fatherly prayers, asking for the very best the Lord has for each.

To my daughter-close editor, Angie, my love and profound appreciation for many years of devoted attention to correcting my writing missteps.

To my daughter-associate Dana, my deep love for always being there to take care of writing and research business whenever they pop up.

To Tom Horn and his associates at Defender Publishing and Sky-Watch TV, my warmest affection and grateful acknowledgment for their wonderful work on the books and for their brotherly and sisterly friendship in Christ.

To my coauthor, Pete, my thanks for faithfully using his marvelous writing talents in the service of our Lord in working with me on this book.

To the readers who will hopefully be edified by this volume, our sincerest prayerful thanks and God-blessed best wishes.

To the Lord Jesus Christ, without Whom there would be nothing of value in life, now or in the future: my eternal love and devotion.

—Terry James

CONTENTS

Foreword ix

Prologue 1

Chapter 1: The Genesis of the Rapture Mystery 9

Chapter 2: Perilous Times 17

Chapter 3: Why Rapture? 29

Chapter 4: The Decline of Western Civilization 49

Chapter 5: The Disappearing 81

Chapter 6: Children and the Rapture 91

Chapter 7: Mind the Gap 107

Chapter 8: The Satanic Trinity/Antichrist Zeitgeist 135

Chapter 9: The Seal Judgments 159

Chapter 10: The Trumpet Judgments 177

Chapter 11: The Bowl Judgments 199

Chapter 12: The Armageddon Campaign 211

Chapter 13: The Millennial Age 227

Chapter 14: Rules for Remnant 239

Appendix A: Seals, Trumpets, and Bowls. 251

Appendix B: Living in Biblical Times 259

Appendix C: The Environmental Impacts of the Tribulation
            Upon the Earth 269

Notes 281

FOREWORD

By Jan Markell

was in junior high when I first learned about end-time events and our wonderful "blessed hope." My mother was hoping that when we moved, we might be in close proximity to a Bible-believing church. At the time of our move, we found ourselves but a few steps from a prominent Baptist church in south Minneapolis in walking distance to our new home.

It was more than Bible-believing: *It was prophecy-believing.* We had regular sermons based on the hope of Christ's soon return.

When I was thirty years old, I took my first trip to Israel. When I returned, an organization called Jews for Jesus made a presentation in my church. What timing! They taught about the importance of Israel and the Jewish people. I would later join their staff.

Things were all coming together. It was starting to make so much sense. At the same time, I was handed Hal Lindsey's *Late-Great Planet Earth.* Suddenly, the complicated made so much sense!

That began my life-long journey of studying and teaching Bible prophecy. In 2001, I began a radio and conference outreach, and I was privileged to either interview, or become good friends with, some prophecy icons. They included Hal Lindsey, Ron Rhodes, Dave Reagan, Mark Hitchcock, Jack Hibbs, J.D. Farag, Amir Tsarfati, Chuck Missler, Tim LaHaye, and two-dozen more.

And I would eventually discover the wonderful writings of Terry James. I am not sure there is anyone I quote more than Terry, just because his writing and thinking are consistent and I don't have to worry that he might go off the reservation theologically speaking. *Over the years, many have!*

When I learned of his book project with Pete Garcia on the coming disappearance, I was enthused and honored to write a few paragraphs. Not a day goes by in the office of Olive Tree Ministries that several do not write us about this topic. However, it is not always in the happiest of contexts.

Rather, it is often that they are seeking a church or even a fellowship of like-minded believers who are looking up and listening for a trumpet and a shout. And they often come away empty-handed, so to speak. *There are few such believers out there anymore.* What a contrast to my growing-up years!

I'm not certain why the pulpits have dropped this glorious topic in the last thirty years. Perhaps the Harold Campings scared solid people away from Bible prophecy. Perhaps the date-setters have caused too much wreckage. Perhaps the topic doesn't fit into "your best life now" scenario that the church loves to talk about. Perhaps the church has started a twenty-five year building program and the Rapture would be bad for their fundraising efforts.

Or maybe Bible prophecy is just a casualty of the predicted great falling away from sound doctrine.

All I know for sure is that believers must have hope, and with the world crumbling all around us, we are left with only the predicted "blessed hope." This world has nothing to offer the Bible-believing Christian. Our focus must be eternity, and that is likely soon for many reading this book—not because readers will face an untimely demise, but rather because Christ's return is at the door.

So I hope you'll keep some of this in mind as you read this book. How privileged we are to be a part of a few remnant believers who actually know the road map to the future. That road map is found in eschatology, or Bible prophecy!

The King is coming, perhaps today!

PROLOGUE

CLARISSA SAT DOWN WITH HER PARENTS AT THE KITCHEN TABLE for a quick breakfast and pulled out her iPhone. She wanted to look up something she heard at church the Wednesday prior, but had forgotten about until this morning.

"What are you reading?" her dad asked.

"Something called the 'Bema Judgment,'" she responded. "Matt [her youth minister] said, as believers, we will go through it."

"I've read that as well," her dad replied. "It's in 3rd Corinthians I think," he added with a wink.

"Dad, there is no 3rd Corinthians. Quit pulling my leg."

"I know, just testing ya," he said jokingly. "That was your final test; glad you passed."

Clarissa was in her senior year of high school, planning to start college the next fall to become a teacher like her mom.

"You still hanging out with Marcie these days?" her mother asked.

"Yeah, not as much as we should. She's busy with track, and since she doesn't go to church, we kind of run in different crowds. But, she's going to college with me, so we've promised to make up for lost time there."

"She doesn't go to church anymore?"

"Nah, not since her parents divorced a few years ago. She kind of just gave up on believing in God."

"Oh no, well, we will keep her in our prayers. Maybe God has plans for her yet," her mother replied.

"I hope so. She's such a sweet soul." Her eyes were drawn back to the screen of her phone as it signaled a message. "Oh, here it is."

"What?" her dad asked.

"This article on the Bema. Matt sent it to me; he said it explains it very understandably."

"Read it; inquiring minds want to know," her dad said with a raised eyebrow.

"Ugh. I hate reading out loud," Clarissa said. "But okay, here goes. It's by a guy named Jack Kinsella."

"Who's that?" her mom asked.

"I don't know, never heard of him," the teen replied. "It's called, 'And After This, the Judgment.'"

She continued:

Judgment is a central theme of Scripture. The entire Old Testament is filled with accounts of divine judgment. The judgment on Adam and Eve, the Flood judgment, the judgment against the unfaithful generation during the Exodus, Sodom and Gomorrah, the various judgments against Israel, the ultimate judgment at Calvary, just to name a few. Some in this generation will face the twenty-one judgments outlined in the book of Revelation during the Tribulation Period.

The writer of Hebrews tells us, "It is appointed unto man once to die, but after this the judgment" (Hebrews 9:27).

There are five separate judgments identified in Scripture that differ in five general aspects: the subjects, the time, the place, the basis and the result.

There are two judgments for believers. The subjects of the first judgment are sinners. The time of this judgment was roughly AD 33. The place was Calvary. The basis for the judgment was the finished work of Christ. And the result was justification for the believer.

This first judgment is in three parts; as a sinner, as a son, and as a servant.

The "sin" question is settled at the Cross. The "son" question is an ongoing series of personal judgments that the Bible calls "chastisement."

When a believer steps outside God's permissive will, it brings about judgments designed to bring that believer back into line.

"If ye endure chastening, God dealeth with you as with sons; for what son is he whom the father chasteneth not? But if ye be without chastisement, whereof all are partakers, then are ye bastards, and not son." (Hebrews 12:7–8).

Now we come to the question posed about the Bema Seat. The Bema Seat is where we are judged as servants. The only ones at this judgment are believers. This judgment takes place after the Rapture. The basis for this judgment is not grace, but works. Now this is critical to understanding the whole scene: what is at stake is not salvation, but rewards.

"For we must all appear before the judgment seat of Christ; that every one may receive the things done in his body, according to that he hath done, whether it be good or bad" (2 Corinthians 5:10).

The Scriptures say that every one of us will give an account of ourselves before the Lord, either as a sinner before the Great White Throne, or as a servant at the Bema Seat. When the Scriptures promise that God will forget our sins, it isn't that God develops amnesia. What it really means is that God no longer counts it as sin—it has been covered by the blood of Christ.

"But I say unto you, That every idle word that men shall speak, they shall give account thereof in the day of judgment" (Matthew 12:36).

The Scripture is clear: One day I will stand before the Lord at the Bema Seat where I will also be called to give account for every idle word spoken. I will not be punished for it but I've no doubt I will suffer great shame.

There will be the Lord, with the nail holes in His hands and feet, with the spear wound in His side, all five wounds received by Him on my behalf.

And there I will stand, explaining why it was too hard for me...yes, there will be great shame. And judgment. But no punishment. That is the part that the Lord "forgets." The Bema Seat judgment is not for sin, but for service. How well did you serve? There is no way to determine that outside of the context of one's life, so by definition, those sins for which were are forgiven must still be presented before the Judgment Seat of Christ.

"So then every one of us shall give account of himself to God" (Romans 14:12).

We will be judged for EVERY idle word we speak. And for every idle deed. Again, it is not a judgment for sin. It is a judgment of your service.

"Every man's work shall be made manifest: for the day shall declare it, because it shall be revealed by fire; and the fire shall try every man's work of what sort it is."

Think about that for a moment! Everything you ever did will be analyzed and scrutinized openly by the Lord Jesus Christ. Every good thing...and every bad thing. We'll be called on to give account of every word, every deed, every thought.

For most believers, the Judgment Seat of Christ will be an excruciating experience. "Knowing therefore the terror of the Lord, we persuade men," Paul wrote.

But, the result isn't heaven—that is already assured. The result is reward. That is where a believer's works come into play. Rewards. Or loss of them.

"If any man's work abide which he hath built thereupon, he

shall receive a reward. If any man's work shall be burned, he shall suffer loss: but he himself shall be saved; yet so as by fire." (1 Corinthians 3:13–15)

Assessment

There are five possible rewards a believer can receive at the Bema Seat. The Bible calls them "crowns."

The first is the crown of life. This is the martyr's crown. You get this one the hard way: "Be thou faithful unto death, and I will give thee a crown of life" (Revelation 2:10).

Then is the crown of glory. This is the "pastor's crown" given by the Chief Shepherd when He shall appear to those who serve, "willingly; not for filthy lucre, but of a ready mind; Neither as being lords over God's heritage, but being ensamples to the flock."

It is important to understand both the distinction and the difference between judgment for salvation and judgment for rewards. Salvation is a gift of grace through faith, and that not of yourselves. Crowns, on the other hand, well, them you have to work for.

"And when the chief Shepherd shall appear, ye shall receive a crown of glory that fadeth not away" (1 Peter 2:4).

I'm working to earn this particular crown. It is a spiritual goal of mine.

The crown of rejoicing is the one I am working to help YOU earn.

This is the soul-winners' crown. Those whom we've led to Christ WILL be our crown of rejoicing.

"For what is our hope, or joy, or crown of rejoicing? Are not even ye in the presence of our Lord Jesus Christ at His coming?" (1 Thessalonians 2:19).

The crown of righteousness is reserved for those of us of every generation who wait patiently for His return, the watchmen on the wall who give the warning of the soon appearance of the Lord.

"Henceforth there is laid up for me a crown of righteousness, which the Lord, the righteous Judge, shall give me at that day: and not to me only, but unto all them also that love His appearing" (2 Timothy 4:8).

The incorruptible crown is a tough one to earn. This is the "victor's crown," which is set aside for those who master temperance in this lifetime.

Those who don't yield to the lusts of the flesh, saturate themselves with alcohol and drugs, and keep themselves separate from the world can expect to be rewarded with the incorruptible crown.

There are, altogether, five judgments outlined by Scripture. The first two are believer's judgments: the judgment at the cross and the Bema Seat judgment.

The third judgment is reserved for the Jews. We call it the Tribulation period. The prophet Jeremiah calls it "the time of Jacob's Trouble."

"Alas! for that day is great, so that none is like it: it is even the time of Jacob's trouble; but he shall be saved out of it" (Jeremiah 30:7). The basis for this judgment is Israel's continued rejection of the Messiah, and the end result is the national redemption of Israel.

The fourth divine judgment also takes place during the Tribulation. The subjects are the Gentile nations. The place is the Valley of Jehoshaphat. The basis for this judgment will be their treatment of the Jews.

"And before Him shall be gathered all nations: and He shall separate them one from another, as a shepherd divideth His sheep from the goats" (Matthew 25:32).

The nations will be divided into the "sheep nations" and the "goat nations." The result is the sheep nations will be permitted to enter into the Millennial Kingdom. The "goat nations" will be destroyed.

This judgment takes place at the conclusion of the Tribulation period. The fifth and final judgment takes place at the Great White Throne. It will take place at the close of the Millennium, a thousand years after the judgment of the nations, and before the Great White Throne.

This is the judgment for sin. All the righteous (saved) dead arose at the first resurrection, or the Rapture. But what about the Tribulation saints?

The words "whosoever was not found written in the Book of Life" imply there will be some saved who will be present at the Great White Throne. There will be some whose names will be found in the Book of Life, but they are post-Church Age believers.

Those who are saved and die between the first resurrection and the second resurrection, (like the Tribulation saints), will rise with the wicked at the second resurrection. The Bible identifies five judgments and five crowns. The judgments are as I've outlined them, by those who are subject to them, when, where, why, and how.

Clarissa looked up from the phone screen.

"Wow, that was pretty thorough and understandable," her dad said.

"Yeah," his daughter replied. "Also, it's a very heavy topic. I don't like the idea of being judged."

"But, like he said, it's not for our sins, but for our work in the Lord. We aren't working for our salvation, but because of it. Don't you want to be rewarded for all the good things you've done for Him?"

"Yeah, but if this Bema Judgment sounds intimidating, even for us believers, imagine how scary the judgment will be for the lost who don't know Him as Lord and Savior after the Rapture."

"It will be terrifying no doubt. Best keep that Marcie girl close, and in your prayers. The Lord will use you to bring her to salvation one day."

"I hope so."

"Better get to school; only a few months to go and you will be graduated!"

"Love ya'll, I'll see you later!" Clarissa yelled as she walked out the door.

1

THE GENESIS OF THE RAPTURE MYSTERY

Bible prophecy foretells a specific event that will disrupt human history in a way like no other experienced by mankind. It will take place in a fraction of a second, at a time totally unexpected by most who are alive at that stunning instant.

Millions across the planet will suddenly vanish before the astonished eyes of those left behind. This mass Disappearing will involve taking from planet earth those within the Church, which is described by Jesus Christ in the following prophecy:

When Jesus came into the coasts of Caesarea Philippi, he asked his disciples, saying, Whom do men say that I the Son of man am? And they said, Some say that thou art John the Baptist: some, Elias; and others, Jeremias, or one of the prophets. He saith unto them, But whom say ye that I am? And Simon Peter answered and said, Thou art the Christ, the Son of the living God. And Jesus answered and said unto him, Blessed art thou, Simon Bar-jona: for flesh and blood hath not revealed it unto thee, but my Father which is in heaven. And I say also unto thee, That thou art

Peter, and upon this rock I will build my church; and the gates of hell shall not prevail against it. (Matthew 16:13–18)

Jesus prophesied that He will build His Church. He said that the gates of Hell will not defeat it. It will not only survive, but will overcome the world of evil and Hell itself. It is, as described elsewhere, the Church triumphant!

Most Christian theologians of the fundamentalist sort hold that the Church was birthed during the astonishing time described in the biblical book of Acts. It happened not long after the death, burial, and resurrection of Jesus.

The birth described in the following passage of the entity Jesus called the Church was itself a stupendous event, yet it wasn't as dramatic as that future Disappearing event will be.

And when the day of Pentecost was fully come, they were all with one accord in one place. And suddenly there came a sound from heaven as of a rushing mighty wind, and it filled all the house where they were sitting. And there appeared unto them cloven tongues like as of fire, and it sat upon each of them. And they were all filled with the Holy Ghost, and began to speak with other tongues, as the Spirit gave them utterance. And there were dwelling at Jerusalem Jews, devout men, out of every nation under heaven.

Now when this was noised abroad, the multitude came together, and were confounded, because that every man heard them speak in his own language. And they were all amazed and marvelled, saying one to another, Behold, are not all these which speak Galilaeans? And how hear we every man in our own tongue, wherein we were born? Parthians, and Medes, and Elamites, and the dwellers in Mesopotamia, and in Judaea, and Cappadocia, in Pontus, and Asia, Phrygia, and Pamphylia, in Egypt, and in the parts of Libya about Cyrene, and strangers of Rome, Jews and proselytes, Cretes and Arabians, we do hear them speak in our tongues the wonderful works of God. And they were all amazed, and were in doubt, saying one to another, What meaneth this? Others mocking said, These men are full of new wine.

But Peter, standing up with the eleven, lifted up his voice, and said unto them, Ye men of Judaea, and all ye that dwell at Jerusalem, be this known unto you, and hearken to my words: For these are not drunken, as ye suppose, seeing it is but the third hour of the day. But this is that which was spoken by the prophet Joel; And it shall come to pass in the last days, saith God, I will pour out of my Spirit upon all flesh: and your sons and your daughters shall prophesy, and your young men shall see visions, and your old men shall dream dreams: And on my servants and on my handmaidens I will pour out in those days of my Spirit; and they shall prophesy:

And I will shew wonders in heaven above, and signs in the earth beneath; blood, and fire, and vapour of smoke: The sun shall be turned into darkness, and the moon into blood, before that great and notable day of the Lord come: And it shall come to pass, that whosoever shall call on the name of the Lord shall be saved. Ye men of Israel, hear these words; Jesus of Nazareth, a man approved of God among you by miracles and wonders and signs, which God did by him in the midst of you, as ye yourselves also know: Him, being delivered by the determinate counsel and foreknowledge of God, ye have taken, and by wicked hands have crucified and slain: Whom God hath raised up, having loosed the pains of death: because it was not possible that he should be holden of it. (Acts 2:1–24)

One of the first preachers of the Christian faith was a man named Stephen. The Scripture says the following about his ministry in and around Jerusalem:

And Stephen, full of faith and power, did great wonders and miracles among the people. Then there arose certain of the synagogue, which is called the synagogue of the Libertines, and Cyrenians, and Alexandrians, and of them of Cilicia and of Asia, disputing with Stephen. And they were not able to resist the wisdom and the spirit by which he spake. Then they suborned men, which said, we have heard him speak blasphemous words against Moses, and against God. And they stirred up the people, and the elders, and the scribes, and came upon him, and caught him, and brought him to the council, And set up false witnesses, which said, This man ceaseth not to speak blasphemous words against this holy place, and the law: For we have heard him say, that this Jesus of Nazareth shall destroy this place, and shall change the customs which Moses delivered us. (Acts 6:8–14)

Like they chose to deal with the Builder of the Church, Jesus, the Judaizers—the religious hierarchy of the Jewish religious system—were determined to kill Stephen, who preached about this new faith system we now call Christianity.

There was a young religious zealot among them named Saul. When the Judaizers pulled Stephen out of the city and prepared to stone him to death, Saul was placed in charge of the cloaks of those who hurled the large rocks at Stephen until he died.

Saul, filled with self-righteous anger against Christians, watched while Steven, just before dying, said he saw Jesus standing at the right hand of the throne of God. Stephen then asked Jesus to receive his spirit, and died.

The exuberant zealot Saul was commissioned by the Jewish authorities to go to Damascus and capture all who had adopted the new religion based upon their martyred—and, as they believed, resurrected—Lord. He was to bring them to Jerusalem in chains.

While on the road to Damascus, Saul was struck down by the very Lord he persecuted to the fullest extent of his authority and ability. Jesus Christ spoke to Saul, who was blinded by supernatural light.

And he fell to the earth, and heard a voice saying unto him, Saul, Saul, why persecutest thou me? And he said, Who art thou, Lord? And the Lord said, I am Jesus whom thou persecutest: it is hard for thee to kick against the pricks. And he trembling and astonished said, Lord, what wilt thou have me to do? And the Lord said unto him, Arise, and go into the city, and it shall be told thee what thou must do. And the men which journeyed with him stood speechless, hearing a voice, but seeing no man. And Saul arose from the earth; and when his eyes were opened, he saw no man: but they led him by the hand, and brought him into Damascus. And he was three days without sight, and neither did eat nor drink. (Acts 9:4–9)

From the moment the Lord intervened in Saul's evil purge of all who had become Christians, the zealot's life was transformed. Saul's name was changed to Paul, and from that experience on, he became arguably the greatest of all apostles—even though he called himself the "least" of them. He was sent by Heaven to the Gentile (non-Jewish) world and established churches throughout his missionary journeys.

Paul became the great apostle who laid out God's grace gospel and who was given the commission from Christ to take that message to the Gentile world. He was the prophet who foretold a great mystery, which is the prime topic of this book: God's astonishing plan that would bring the Church Age to its inevitable and preordained end.

From the founding of the Church at Pentecost (the start of the Church Age) to the end of that time—also called the Age of Grace—those saved by belief in the death, burial, and resurrection of Christ—Gentiles and Jews alike—are considered the Bride of Christ. They are forever in God's family and are destined for their eternal homes in heaven.

Just before His crucifixion, Jesus made this promise to His disciples who were surrounding Him at the time (He also was speaking to all believers who would come to Him for salvation throughout the Age of Grace):

Let not your heart be troubled: ye believe in God, believe also in me. In my Father's house are many mansions: if it were not so, I would have told you. I go to prepare a place for you. And if I go and prepare a place for you, I will come again, and receive you unto myself; that where I am, there ye may be also. (John 14:1–3)

Paul's experience on the road to Damascus created in him a zeal even more fervent than when he had been a persecutor of Jewish believers in Christ before his conversion. He eagerly taught all who would listen the truth of, more often than not, startling and eternal importance. The Lord revealed to him amazing prophetic utterances, the most profound of which was that of how the Lord would one day, in a millisecond, fulfill Jesus' promise recorded in John 14:1–3.

Paul had taught the believers at Thessalonica that Jesus Christ would come to take them away to their heavenly homes before God's judgment and wrath would fall upon the rebellious world of unbelievers. At this point, many among the believers had died, and they were particularly concerned that those who had died would miss being a part of being taken away to Heaven.

So it was that Paul sat writing from Corinth, Achaea, composing a letter to the believers in Thessalonica addressing their fears.

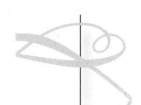

THE REVELATION OF
THE RAPTURE

WHEN HE SAT ON THE ROUGHLY HEWN CHAIR, A WOMAN HANDED him a cup made of hardened clay slightly glazed to assure its nonporous integrity. He smiled while looking into her eyes, nodded his thanks, and sipped the cool water.

Paul saw in his mind's eye—while he read their fearful letter and prepared to write his reply—the worried looks on the faces of the people he envisioned staring at him.

A man with a thick, black beard stood in the imaginary scene and said, "Those rabbis who claim faith in Jesus are saying that we are now in that time of great trouble you told us about. They say that all is lost. Those we loved and who have died are gone and that is the end of it. They have no chance of going to Heaven."

Paul, in his imagination, listened while the voices in the room comingled in agreement that the speaker was telling the truth. He envisioned setting the cup on the little table and standing, holding his hands out, palms-down, asking for calm.

"My children—" his words would begin in an effort to alleviate their fears. "These are troubled times, it is true. But I don't want you to be ignorant, brethren, concerning them which are asleep, that you are not full of sorrow, even as others which have no hope. For if, we believe that Jesus died and rose again, even so them also which sleep in Jesus God will bring with him. For this we say unto you by the word of the Lord, that we which are alive and remain unto the coming of the Lord will not precede them which are asleep. For the Lord himself shall descend from heaven with a shout, with the voice of the archangel, and with the trump of God. And the dead in Christ shall rise first. Then we which are alive and remain will be caught up together with them in the clouds, to meet the Lord in the air. And so shall we ever be with the Lord. Wherefore comfort one another with these words."[1]

Another man in the scene Paul was contemplating stood and said, "But teacher, we look around and nothing changes. Our conditions remain the same. When will these things happen?"

Again, in Paul's thoughts while he was writing to those in Thessalonica, mumbles of agreement to the man's questions amidst nodding of heads met his ears and eyes while he scanned the men and women in the room.

Like before, Paul could see himself putting his hands out for calm, while he again began to speak.

"It is hard to be patient, I know," he would tell them. "But of the times and the seasons, brethren, you have no need that I write unto you. For you all know perfectly that the day of the Lord will come like a thief in the night. For when they will then say, Peace and safety; then sudden destruction will come upon them, as travail upon a woman with child; and they will not escape. But you, brethren, are not in darkness, that that day should overtake you as a thief. You are all the children of light, and the children of the day: we are not of the night, nor of darkness.

Therefore let us not sleep, as do others; but let us watch and be sober. For they that sleep sleep in the night; and they that be drunken are drunken in the night. But let us, who are of the day, be sober, putting on the breastplate of faith and love; and for an helmet, the hope of salvation. For God has not appointed us to wrath, but to obtain salvation by our Lord Jesus Christ, Who died for us, that, whether we wake or sleep, we should live together with him. Wherefore comfort yourselves together, and edify one another, even as also you do."[2]

2

PERILOUS TIMES

The same Paul who recorded the words we discussed in the preceding narrative went on throughout his preaching and teaching journey to lay out exactly what the world would be like at the time this stupendous vanishing event would take place. His most profound and detailed prophetic writings in this regard are recorded in two biblical books, the first of which is Romans.

While he sat in Corinth somewhere between AD 57–59, Paul addressed the believers in Rome by letter about twenty-five years following the crucifixion, burial, and resurrection of the Lord Jesus Christ. He laid out for his readers the characteristics of sinful mankind that, ultimately, inevitably, bring God's judgment. His examples of ungodly living were obviously based upon the debauched ungodliness of previous generations, like those during Noah's time before the Flood and when Lot lived in Sodom.

Like in addressing those in Thessalonica, the apostle must have poured his soul into the writing, with full concentration on every word he chose, while he received direct revelation from the Holy Spirit.

Those words are now recorded in the first chapter of the book of

Romans. We will look closely at those condemning declarations from the mind of God a bit later.

Paul, no doubt, while he wrote to the Roman believers, was inspired to think about the days of Lot in Sodom, as now recorded in Genesis chapter 19. The society and culture of Sodom and its twin sister city, Gomorrah, were saturated with every sort of debauchery. God, Himself, it is intimated, came down to speak with Abraham about the desperate evil that had singed his holy nostrils. The cities were so steeped in evil that angels, in the form of men, were sent into Sodom to remove the only righteous people who could be found. Lot and several of his family members were taken out to the city of Zoar. That very day, the Scripture says, fire of judgment fell from Heaven and destroyed everyone in Sodom and Gomorrah.

The story in Genesis 19 makes it blatantly clear that the primary sin of Sodom involved sexual perversion of every sort. Homosexuality, in particular, was at the center of the sin-saturated activity by Sodom's people.

The point was finally reached in the anti-God, in-your-face evil that the Lord's cup of wrath was full. He removed the only righteousness still left in the cities. Destruction was then the only thing left to be done with the rebels whose sin infection had totally corrupted society and culture.

THE REMOVAL FROM MODERN SODOM

Paul's words to the Romans made it clear that the sin-saturated comportment found in that earlier time inevitably brings God's judgment and wrath. He soon would expand upon the forewarning to all throughout human history yet to unfold. He wrote of how mankind would repeat the sins people have committed since the fall in the Garden of Eden. He prophesied of how things will be in our own time in the following Scripture passage, which consists of a letter to his spiritual son/protégé, Timothy.

Paul wrote by divine inspiration in what is thought to be his last epistle from his imprisonment in Rome in AD 66 or 67. (His death was said to be in either May or June of AD 68.) He outlined what would be the characteristics of man as the end of the Church Age nears.

With this detailed description, the soon-to-be martyred apostle foretold the anti-godliness that would mark the end of the Age of Grace.

He had, in his earlier letter to the Roman believers, given what happens to a people that have turned their backs on God:

And even as they did not like to retain God in their knowledge, God gave them over to a reprobate mind, to do those things which are not convenient. (Romans 1:28)

There are coming, in the last days, perilous times—that is, times that are unusually dangerous to people who will be living on earth. Paul writes that this will be the condition of mankind, because people will be turned over to a reprobate mind. They will have a cognitive problem: upside-down thinking. All of this will stem from having turned their backs on God and His prescription for properly conducting themselves. They will have, it is implied, both mental and spiritual dementia.

It doesn't take a doctorate in sociology, psychology, or psychiatry to understand that a large portion of this generation has now been infected with thinking that is reprobate. Analysis of today's issues and events overlaid by the biblical template presented by Paul's perilous-times prophecy makes clear these are the last days.

Peering into the characteristics of end-times people through Paul's prophetic presentation in 2 Timothy chapter 3 brings forth the reality of the nearness of the next biblically promised catastrophic event in human history: the removal from modern Sodom.

Paul gives a stunning overview of how the world will be just before Christ's return. Gary Stearman, host of the *Prophecy Watchers* television program, further enlightens in this regard:

Years ago, I noticed something in Paul's Second Letter to Timothy. It struck home in a big way, and to this day directs my thinking about Bible prophecy. In the third chapter, there is an intriguing statement: "This know also, that in the last days, perilous times shall come." Probably most serious Christians have noticed this warning, and then have continued to read the long list of character deficiencies that follow:

"For men shall be lovers of their own selves, covetous, boasters, proud, blasphemers, disobedient to parents, unthankful, unholy, Without natural affection, trucebreakers, false accusers, incontinent, fierce, despisers of those that are good, Traitors, heady, high-minded, lovers of pleasures more than lovers of God; Having a form of godliness, but denying the power thereof: from such turn away. For of this sort are they which creep into houses, and lead captive silly women laden with sins, led away with divers lusts, Ever learning, and never able to come to the knowledge of the truth" (2 Timothy 3:2–7).

This description of latter-day societal shortcomings rings with a surprising familiarity to those of us who observe the daily media parade. As I read this, it occurred to me that I needed to do a deeper study of what the term "perilous times" really meant. Looking it up, I found that the word "perilous" came from the Greek word, *chalepos*.

Looking further, I discovered that in the New Testament, this word was used only twice, the other time being in Matthew, chapter 8, in which Jesus and His disciples had sailed across the Sea of Galilee. A windstorm had risen and swamped their sailboat, until He spoke and calmed the waters:

"But the men marvelled, saying, What manner of man is this, that even the winds and the sea obey him! And when he was come to the other side into the country of the Gergesenes, there met him two possessed with devils, coming out of the tombs, exceeding fierce, so that no man might pass by that way" (Matthew 8:27, 28).

To my amazement, I discovered that the Greek word *chalepos* was used in the phrase, "exceedingly fierce!"

And fierce they were...so strong that in this territory of the beach and its cliffs, no one could pass. Their strength came from demonic possession.

I was immediately struck with the thought that when Paul wrote those prophetic words to Timothy, his exhaustive description of latter-day humanity was constructed around the idea of madness...raging insanity empowered by dark forces! Suddenly, I was deeply impressed with Paul's true intent: to show Timothy—and us, in the twenty-first century—that the days before Christ's return would be marked by a growing social insanity.

And not just that; it would be an insanity driven by the same dark forces encountered by Jesus and His disciples on the shores of Galilee on that day so long ago.[3]

Indeed, the characteristic Paul termed "fierce" is most appropriate for the chief evil manifestation of those opposed to God in these times. Not in all of modern history has there been a more concerted hatred targeted at any one person because of animosity toward attempts to turn a people back to a godlier comportment.

And it is all done because that comportment, established by the Lord of Heaven and set into the US Constitution by America's founding fathers, constrains the desires and efforts of Ephesians 6:12 in their drive to establish a neo Tower of Babel—a New World Order that the supernatural powers and principalities are in an absolute rage to bring forth as a platform for launching their Antichrist regime.

CONSTRUCTING LUCIFER'S TOWER

Groundwork has been set in motion by unseen hands. Erecting the edifice that will be the reconstruction of an anti-God tower of evil is well underway.

Anxiety is palpable while this generation makes its way through each waking hour. National—indeed, worldwide—schizophrenia marks the last half-decade, in America in particular, as being split irreparably with regard to the most relevant facets of life.

No matter which direction the angst-ridden turn to understand the times, the reconnaissance comes back with reports that are increasingly unsettling. The most comfort the leaders of nations can offer is that we are facing a future fraught with "new normals." These will require, we are informed, that a "reset" be instituted in order to reestablish societal, cultural, and—especially—economic equilibrium.

For what seems to be half of the nation, there is an acceptance of the so-called cancel culture. That rampage to establish new norms includes the violent tearing down of old values and traditions—in effect, ripping down the institutions and statuary that define America's founding. The globalist elite whose scheming is at the heart of this deconstruction speciously vow to "Build Back Better." At the heart of the cancel culture is the redefining of what constitutes humanity itself.

No longer are individuals required to identify with the gender on their birth certificate. No longer is the definition valid that pronounces that marriage is to be between one man and one woman. Perhaps, it is supposed by some sociologists, psychologists, and other such arbiters, same-sex marriages are even preferable to heterosexual unions.

Now we are to begin considering that sexual relations between children—even the very young—and adults should no longer be forbidden. To that effect, those formerly thought deviant, such as transvestites, are now applauded with smiles of approval while they teach kindergarteners and first graders the "normalcy" of the transvestite lifestyle in this new age of tolerance.

Any disagreement with the half of America that is all in for establishing the new normality is immediately branded. "Homophobic," "transphobic," "xenophobic," and other "phobic" words now in the American vernacular are accusatorial terms that mark those who hold to the traditions that made America, well, America. As a matter of fact, to want to "Make America Great Again" and to say "America First" is to invite violence that is, at the very least, tacitly condoned by those in the highest echelons of government, mainstream news media, and the entertainment agglomerate.

Words and phrases like "sovereignty" and "national borders" are anathema to these purveyors of one-worldism who are obsessed with what can be termed the "Babel Syndrome."

And who can deny that violence born of that obsession has been rampant in the years leading up to the 2020 presidential elections? Cities were burned and small businesses were destroyed (many of them minority businesses), along with the lives of those who struggled to build them. All was done for the purpose of, the rioters say, showing that "Black Lives Matter" (BLM).

Meanwhile, the most violent of all acts—shedding the blood of the most innocent among us, the highest percentage of which were black babies killed in their mothers' wombs—is considered a good thing by those who approve of the BLM actions.

Taking the lives of millions of black, aborted babies seems to the progressive mind to be okay, even though they go to war over one black adult who resists arrest and dies in the process. All the while, many of our elected officials, who have taken oaths to uphold the Constitution of the United States, look the other way as anarchists of BLM and Antifa, organizations that are avowed communist, fight to destroy our constitutional government and bring to the nation Soviet-like, Marxist-style socialism.

The national schizophrenia was made undeniably clear with the coming of the presidency of Donald J. Trump. It is as if the election of 2016 opened a gaping wound in the American psyche. Half of the nation now seems to want the country to remain as founded, with governance conceived and implemented by the founding fathers, steeped in Judeo-Christian precepts. The other half, many of whom care only about not having to be concerned with principles of morality, eagerly embrace ideology of the globalist elite, those who wield the power in the "high places" of wickedness outlined in Ephesians 6:12.

Those one-world-order builders, with the all-out complicity of the mainstream news and entertainment conglomerate, have assaulted the very God of Heaven in their effort to establish global government. They have been restrained for the most part to the time of this writing. It is as if this is the precise moment in human history for which God, through the psalmist, wrote God's great, scathing condemnation of the rebels of earth. He added the only God-ordained prescription for curing what ails this judgment-doomed sphere:

> Why do the heathen rage, and the people imagine a vain thing? The kings of the earth set themselves, and the rulers take counsel together, against the LORD, and against his anointed, saying, Let us break their bands asunder, and cast away their cords from us. He that sitteth in the heavens shall laugh: the Lord shall have them in derision. Then shall he speak unto them in his wrath, and vex them in his sore displeasure.
>
> Yet have I set my king upon my holy hill of Zion. I will declare the decree: the LORD hath said unto me, Thou art my Son; this day have I begotten thee. Ask of me, and I shall give thee the heathen for thine inheritance, and the uttermost parts of the earth for thy possession. Thou shalt break them with a rod of iron; thou shalt dash them in pieces like a potter's vessel. Be wise now therefore, O ye kings: be instructed, ye judges of the earth. Serve the LORD with fear, and rejoice with trembling. Kiss the Son, lest he be angry, and ye perish from the way, when his wrath is kindled but a little. Blessed are all they that put their trust in him. (Psalm 2:1–12)

The minions, both human and demonic, continue to push forward despite the numerous times their efforts to accomplish their devilish plan to bring America down have been thwarted—we believe by God's own restraining hand. Theirs is a rage that defies all psychological models, according to psychiatric findings. Rage at such a level, according to those who study such things, cannot be sustained for long periods of time—certainly not for years, such as has been the case for the hatred of President

Donald Trump. Yet the strange phenomenon of Trump hatred long since has reached such a level that it has been termed the "Trump Derangement Syndrome" and is now part of our lexicon.

God's Word has an explanation for the unbridled hatred we've witnessed these past few years:

> For the wrath of God is revealed from heaven against all ungodliness and unrighteousness of men, who hold the truth in unrighteousness; Because that which may be known of God is manifest in them; for God hath showed it unto them For the invisible things of him from the creation of the world are clearly seen, being understood by the things that are made, even his eternal power and Godhead; so that they are without excuse: Because that, when they knew God, they glorified him not as God, neither were thankful; but became vain in their imaginations, and their foolish heart was darkened....
>
> And even as they did not like to retain God in their knowledge, God gave them over to a reprobate mind, to do those things which are not convenient; Being filled with all unrighteousness, fornication, wickedness, covetousness, maliciousness; full of envy, murder, debate, deceit, malignity; whisperers, Backbiters, haters of God, despiteful, proud, boasters, inventors of evil things, disobedient to parents, Without understanding, covenant breakers, without natural affection, implacable, unmerciful: Who knowing the judgment of God, that they which commit such things are worthy of death, not only do the same, but have pleasure in them that do them. (Romans 1:18–21, 28–32)

The "wicked" in "high places" of Ephesians 6:12 have fomented anti-God rage. This is not meant to say that Donald Trump is in any way God-like. Quite the contrary, in our view. He was, however, we are convinced, a man chosen by God to be in the most powerful office in the world at a time that is bumping up against the end of this age. He has been used to help implement the Almighty's restraint in Heaven's delaying action against the enraged, anti-God minions, both human and supernatural.

Those who have observably come against God in their enragement and with unbridled sophistry, determined to do what is right in their own eyes, have been turned over to the "reprobate mind" that Paul mentions in the Scripture passage above. They call good evil and evil good. They cannot and/or will not see things as they are or should be. Their thinking is upside-down. How else can they champion the murder of more than sixty million babies in the womb, many of them black, while in a rage against one man being killed because of perceived racial injustice? How can they condone agreeing, and making a law by which we must all abide, that a girl born a girl can be a boy, if she wants—or that a boy born a boy can be a girl? How can they strive to force everyone to agree that same-sex unions are as appropriate as heterosexual ones? This thinking, of course, defies all logic biologically, physiologically, spiritually, and in every other way. It is madness.

And the madness is scheduled to get worse...much worse.

We've heard much about and witnessed fraud in ways and at levels that are mind-bending. It has been and continues to be so blatant that only the completely oblivious to reason could miss the level of deception taking place recently. First the lies and distortions took place on a daily basis from the moment of the Trump nomination for president. The media were arrayed totally against one man they continue to want removed so their global agenda can move forward.

With the voting fraud in our faces constantly in the aftermath of the presidential campaign, deceit so rampant cannot be ignored. This truth should not be missed by the spiritually attuned among God's people.

Deception is the first prophetic forewarning Jesus gave when His disciples asked: "What will be the sign of your coming, and of the end of the age?"

The Lord indicated in His answer that the first sign to look for will be that deception will be prevalent. Paul the apostle said that, in the last days, "evil men and seducers" will get "worse and worse, deceiving and being deceived" (2 Timothy 3:13).

Lying and deceit saturate our culture and society at every level at this late hour. To confirm that, we have only to remember the Russian collusion of which Mr. Trump was accused. Perhaps $40 million or more of taxpayer money was used to investigate the lies that were ultimately shown to be perpetrated in a political witch hunt by Trump's opponents. The Deep State—the intelligence services of the US—were almost certainly complicit in the phony Russian collusion matter. All was done to serve the masters in the wicked, high places of globalism, it is believed. America must be brought down so that national borders across the world can be erased and the neo-Babel tower can be raised.

All this portends bad news for inhabitants of planet earth, it seems. Things are scheduled to get worse—infinitely worse, according to Heaven's pronouncements found in the Revelation and other apocalyptic portions of God's Word.

This dire outlook is only partially true, however, according to that same Holy Word.

Millions of people will face quite a different experience. That experience will be glorious beyond all imagination, God has promised.

Read on and be comforted. We will explain all about the magnificent prospects that await you in what looks to be in the very near future.

3

WHY RAPTURE?

Adversity is always unexpected and unwelcomed. It is an intruder and a thief, and yet in the hands of God, adversity becomes the means through which His supernatural power is demonstrated.[4]
—Charles Stanley

t didn't matter where you lived or what you were doing that day, everyone alive and of age reading this remembers where they were when the events of 9/11 happened. It didn't matter who you talked to or what news channel you were watching it on, there were really only three shades of emotion that day: shock, disbelief, and anger as we all watched the tragedy unfolding before our eyes.

Though the majority of Americans didn't know anyone personally killed in the attacks in New York City; Shanksville, Pennsylvania; or Washington, DC, we collectively grieved as a nation at the sudden and staggering loss of life. It was hard to wrap our minds around the magnitude of the events on that fateful day.

Let's bring this closer to home, though. As individuals, most of us have experienced this same sense of shock when tragedy personally visits our doorstep. It could have been the sudden death of a loved one due to a car crash or heart attack, or even an expected one caused by old age or cancer. Perhaps it was even a natural disaster such as a tornado or a flood that cut a life too short. Regardless of how it comes, death always manages to reverberate both the finality and frailty of our mortal frames. Nevertheless, tragedies happen, all day, every day, and yet the world loves to live in a September 10 world.

We mortals continually live on the razor-thin edge of life, always with death lingering about like an unwanted guest. In fact, nothing but a heartbeat separates this corporeal, temporal existence from the next. We are but fragile beings in a harsh world, with nothing but a hope and a prayer to guide us from moment to moment. For those who do not hope or do not pray, life and what comes after can certainly be a terrifying prospect. We are not promised tomorrow. We're not even promised our next breath. The Bible is quite clear that our lives are but a vapor; we're here one moment and gone the next. Even still, most people never think about how quickly our lives can change, or about our eternal destination once we depart our earthly lives.

However, it is not all doom and gloom. The Holy Bible promises, unapologetically, that eternal life is free for those who seek it. Not only can we be redeemed here and now, but we are promised redemption from the bondage of sin and death, as well as deliverance from the wrath to come. In addition, for one generation of believers, deliverance will come in the form of a Disappearing from this present reality and an appearing in the next, bypassing death altogether. This is what makes the theological doctrine of the Rapture of the Church ridiculous, intriguing, and yet, absolutely true. It is the fantastical exception to the rule that many (even many theologians) simply will not accept. The Rapture is the ultimate *black-swan event*, the divine game-changer in the human story.

But what if the validity of the Rapture depended on how fantastical it appeared? Why do many reject it for that very reason, when in the same breath, they defend a six-day Creation? What do they do with Adam, Eve, and a talking serpent? Noah and the global Flood? Israel's supernatural Exodus out of Egyptian bondage? David and Goliath? Jonah and the whale? Jesus raising Lazarus from the dead? Jesus' own resurrection?

You see, if you discount one thing, you would pretty much have to discount the rest, since they are all quite bizarre and are intertwined into a singular story. If the Rapture is not true simply due to how irrational it sounds, then none of the aforementioned can be true either. The Rapture highlights Christ's crowning achievement of not only conquering sin, death, and Hell by His death, burial, and resurrection, but in creating (and taking) the Church that He Himself built.

> Jesus answered and said to him, "Blessed are you, Simon Bar-Jonah, for flesh and blood has not revealed this to you, but My Father who is in heaven. And I also say to you that you are Peter, **and on this rock I will build My church,** and the gates of Hades shall not prevail against it. And I will give you the keys of the kingdom of heaven, and whatever you bind on earth will be bound in heaven, and whatever you loose on earth will be loosed in heaven." (Matthew 16:17–19, emphasis added)

Some think the Rapture is not true because of how they interpret the Bible. They either smoosh the Church into Israel or they replace Israel with the Church altogether and then try to cram it all into the Olivet Discourse (Matthew 24, Mark 13, Luke 21). Either way, hermeneutical consistency goes out the window. Israel cannot be the Church, because Jesus stated in Matthew 16:19, "I will build it" (future tense), meaning this new body of believers did not, could not, exist until Him. That pretty much rules out anyone in the Old Testament.

Furthermore, Hebrews 9:16–17 states that this New Testament (or new covenant) could not even exist until He (the testator) dies. So if some believe the Church to be the new and improved Israel, a) it could not have existed until after Jesus' death, burial, and resurrection; and b) it could not be built until Christ built it. Hypothetically speaking, if He were implying that He intended to transfer both the covenant (Exodus 19–23) and the blessings to this new, hybrid body of believing Jews and Gentiles, He would have stated something to the effect that He was either replacing, or improving upon, the failures of the former chosen people.

Of course, He said neither.

Still others like to merge the Rapture and the Second Coming into being the same event. This is done primarily because: a) people confuse the Church with Israel, and b) they apply the passages meant for Israel to the Church (i.e., the Olivet Discourse). They do this despite the obvious intended audiences each of the Gospels was meant to speak to—Matthew to the Jews, Mark to the Romans, Luke to the Greeks, and John to the Church. If this were not true, then the Gospel of John would also contain a version of the Olivet Discourse (it doesn't). Instead, John gives the Church the Upper Room Discourse, which makes no mention of the signs and warnings contained to in the Olivet Discourse.

Additionally, there are several passages in the Bible that refer to the Rapture as "that day" (2 Thessalonians 1:10, 2:3), the "day of redemption" (Ephesians 4:30), or the "day of Christ" (1 Corinthians 1:8; Philippians 1:6, 10; 2:16; 2 Thessalonians 2:9). While the phrase "that day" can speak to both the Rapture or the Second Coming (depending on the context of the surrounding passages), the last two are only found in the New Testament epistles, which were written exclusively to the churches the apostles were ministering to.

Thus, the "day of Christ" is beautifully juxtaposed against the "day of the Lord" passages (Isaiah 2:5, 12; 13:6, 9; 34:8; 2 Peter 3:9). The former points to a day when Christ Himself will descend out of Heaven with His angelic hosts and meet us (the Church) in the air. It marks a specific day to strive or aim for with regards to running our race. Contrastingly, the "day of the Lord" overwhelmingly speaks of a *cruel day* and a time of *God's vengeance* against an unrepentant world. As much as the Rapture critics would like it to be, these cannot be the same day.

Let us remember a simple, yet powerful, principle that we picked up a long time ago from a fellow watchman, the late Jack Kinsella. *Things that are different are not the same.* Although they have some similarities, they have A LOT of major differences. Thus, the Rapture and the Second Coming are not the same event. Here are a few examples:

THE SIMILARITIES

1. Both the Rapture and the Second Coming are scheduled to be future, last-days events. This means they have not yet been fulfilled.
2. Both events mention Christ arriving to our physical, corporeal reality.
3. Both events mention trumpets (Matthew 24:31; 1 Thessalonians 4:16; 1 Corinthians 15:52).

THE DIFFERENCES

1. At the Rapture, we believers leave the earth to meet the Lord in the air (1 Thessalonians 4:17). At the Second Coming, we believers return with Christ from Heaven to the earth where He physically touches down at the Mount of Olives, splitting the mountain in two (Revelation 19:14; Zechariah 14:4) The Apostle Paul makes no mention of Christ ever coming to the earth.
2. The Rapture has no required signs or events to precede it; it will catch the world off-guard (Matthew 24:44; 1 Corinthians 15:50–54; 1 Thessalonians 5:1–4). The Second Coming, however, is preceded by seven years full of signs, wonders, and events occurring in chronological/sequential order (Revelation 1:7; Matthew 24:29–30).
3. The Rapture will happen in blink of an eye (1 Corinthians 15:52) and will catch everyone off guard. The Second Coming will be a slow, processional-type event that tears the sky open with the whole world watching and mourning at His official arrival (Matthew 26:64; Revelation 1:7).
4. The Rapture removes the believers before the time of wrath as an act of deliverance (1 Thessalonians 1:10, 5:9; Revelation 3:10). The Second Coming destroys the unbelievers on the earth as an act of war (Revelation 19:17–21). For consistency's sake, there are

no "wrath of God" events described in the Bible in which believers were delivered from said wrath either during or after the event. They are always delivered *before* the event.

5. The Church (the Body of Christ) is "sealed" by the Holy Spirit for the day of redemption (Ephesians 4:30), meaning anyone who is "sealed" is removed by Christ Himself. The Second Coming speaks of a gathering conducted by angels (Matthew 24:31)

6. At the Rapture, Satan is not bound in chains and cast into the abyss for a thousand years. After the Second Coming, he is bound and cast into the abyss for a thousand years (Revelation 20:1–3).

The Charles Stanley quote at the beginning of this chapter mentioned adversity as being a necessary ingredient to God's supernatural outworking. God does not need adversity to display His supernatural abilities (e.g., the six-day Creation event). However, in our sin-stained world, His works displayed against adversity (our disbelief and skepticism) add the "wow" factor to the equation. Did God need Joshua to march around Jericho for seven days blowing trumpets on the seventh in order for the walls to "come tumbling down" (Joshua 6)? No. God could have just delivered the city to Joshua in a moment, but there are always deeper and finer points to why God does what He does.

So, who is the main antagonist against the Rapture? Obviously, Satan would be at the top of the list. Not only does he not want the Rapture to happen, but also, since he can't stop it from happening and doesn't know when it will occur, he has two strategies he can use: kill enthusiasm for it and/or confuse people about it. Additional adversaries include time (Satan uses this against believers), false doctrines and teachings (again, Satan uses these to add confusion about the Rapture), and the lust of the flesh and eyes (to keep people from knowing and watching for it) by being preoccupied with the world.

In terms of generating a crisis, the Rapture will make everything before it pale in comparison. For those who are saved, it will be the most joyous, amazing, and incomparable day mankind has ever known. It will be when believers of all walks of life, of all ethnicities, of all cultural backgrounds, of all shapes, ages, and sizes, are immediately transformed from frail, mortal creatures into immortal, immensely powerful beings (1 John 3:1–3).

However, for those who are left behind after the Rapture, the world will be turned on its head. If we were to look back over the past one hundred years, we could certainly point out some painful and tragic moments in our nation's history: Hurricane Katrina, the Category 5 storm that struck the Gulf Coast in 2005; the terrorist attacks on September 11, 2001; the Columbine High School shooting in 1999; the Space Shuttle Challenger explosion in 1986; the John F. Kennedy and Martin Luther King assassinations in 1963 and 1968, respectively; and the Japanese bombing of the US naval base at Pearl Harbor, Hawaii, in 1941. All of these certainly had a massive impact on our national psyche. These were events we grieved over as a nation with those affected.

Yet, unless we were directly impacted by those tragedies, we went back to work or school. We moved on, because life moved on. However, life will not move on after the Rapture. Its effects will be so profound that everything before it will be considered the "old order of things."

While we address in more detail the global effects of the Rapture later in this book, we intend to put the spotlight solely on the United States as being in the category of the "old order of things." This is primarily because what happens to the US will trigger a cascading series of devastating geopolitical and economic tragedies the world will not be able to recover from.

This is also not to say that the US has more Christians than any other nation; however, we do have more Christians in prominent positions of authority and leadership than any other nation. That is why, in our minds, Satan is working so tirelessly to purge the government, corporate America, and the public arena of anything remotely Christian. He is simply trying to lessen the impact of the Rapture before it occurs.

Although the Rapture will be a joyous event for tens, perhaps even hundreds, of millions of believers around the world, it will become a real-life horror show for the billions who remain. Not only will the Rapture remove the restraint of evil that has been held at bay now for nearly two thousand years, but the disappearance of all children and of the mentally impaired will also wreak havoc upon every parent in the world (more on this later). That is, those who cannot make cognitive decisions under their own natural abilities, as well as those under the age of accountability, will be removed instantly from the earth. The weeping and mourning in ancient Egypt (because of the angel of death) and in Bethlehem (because of Herod) over the deaths of their children will be magnified a hundredfold at the disappearance of all children at the Rapture. Those under the age of accountability will immediately be brought to Heaven and given their glorified bodies along with the rest of the believers, because God is both perfectly merciful and perfectly just.

THAT DAY (D-DAY)

For the Lord Himself will descend from heaven with a shout, with the voice of an archangel, and with the trumpet of God. And the dead in Christ will rise first. Then *we* who are alive and remain shall be caught up together with them in the clouds to meet the Lord in the air. And thus *we* shall always be with the Lord. Therefore comfort one another with these words.… For when *they* say, "Peace and safety!" then sudden destruction comes upon *them*, as labor pains upon a pregnant woman. And *they* shall not escape. (1 Thessalonians 4:16–18; 5:3, emphasis added)

The Apostle Paul spoke frequently about last-days events, particularly about the Rapture of the Church, which was first given to him to explain. Even to a fairly young church in Thessalonica, Paul did not hesitate to incorporate the great "blessed hope" we have in the promise of the Rapture. Furthermore, he went to great pains to differentiate the very different outcomes we as believers should expect when we face this momentous event. In the execution of the *harpazo* ("catching up"), "we" receive deliverance; "they" receive sudden destruction—two very different outcomes, indeed.

Therefore, it is of great interest to us how one of the most significant events in world history (aside from Christ's victorious death, burial, and resurrection) is treated with as much derision as it is, even within Christian circles. To a certain degree, we expect the Rapture to be ridiculed by the world, because it is presently blinded by the "god of this age" (2 Corinthians 4:4) and unable to grasp it. Nevertheless, how did it get to the point that pastors, priests, teachers, and preachers no longer believe, teach, or even care about the Rapture? Although they may not physically line through the Bible verses that address the Rapture, their unwillingness to teach it serves the same purpose.

We put the Rapture in the same category of those historic biblical, fantastical events like a six-day Creation, Noah's Flood, the parting of the Red Sea, Jonah's incarceration inside a giant fish, and Elijah's chariots of fire. These biblical accounts truly stretch the boundaries of our understanding of reality and physics. Yet, either they all really happened, or none of them happened. Either they are all fanciful myths passed down through history, or they were real, historical events. Either God can stretch and tweak reality as He deems fit, or He can't. This is to say that either God is all-powerful, or He is not.

Because Jesus spoke of these miraculous events as being real, His own claims of divine sonship and oneness with the God the Father (His credibility) are at stake. If they were not real, then Jesus cannot claim to be God in the flesh. Therefore, the preachers and teachers who dismiss the miraculous and only focus on Jesus being a good, moral man do not worship the Jesus of the Bible. As the late British writer and theologian C. S. Lewis wrote in his book, *Mere Christianity*:

> "I'm ready to accept Jesus as a great moral teacher, but I don't accept His claim to be God." That is the one thing we must not say. A man who was merely a man and said the sort of things Jesus said would not be a great moral teacher.... You must make

your choice. Either this man was, and is, the Son of God: or else a madman or something worse. You can shut Him up for a fool… or you can fall at His feet and call Him Lord and God. But let us not come with any patronizing nonsense about His being a great human teacher. He has not left that open to us.[5]

Thus, the outlandish claims made throughout the Bible are very much an either/neither situation when regarding the miraculous outworking of an infinitely powerful God. Jesus believed them, and we (Christendom) call Him Lord; why do so many now discount the Rapture as being too unbelievable? Has God not demonstrated throughout human history His ability to accomplish the impossible? Then, the Rapture is no different.

Rapture, like the aforementioned miraculous events, will happen—because God said it will happen. So how do so-called purveyors of the Word dismiss it out of hand? This has been one of Satan's greatest successes over the past two millennia: He has managed to get the Church to the point that believers are almost entirely irreverent about their own deliverance.

It is not as if the Rapture is a mystery any longer, since Jesus alluded to it in His Upper Room Discourse (John 14–16). The Apostle Paul explained it in detail in two of his epistles. The Church, and to a large degree, the world, knows what it is, or is at least familiar with the premise. So why will it catch the world off-guard? Because familiarity does not constitute belief.

This is why so many Christians (and pretend Christians) are going to be shocked when the great event actually does occur. Again, Satan's masterstroke of evil genius has been in confusing and conflagrating the issue to the point that Christians today are either too afraid to talk about it for fear being labeled a "prophecy nut" or too frustrated by the constant infighting surrounding it to bother. The truth is the truth. The Rapture will happen because God said it would.

Imagine if the Rapture got as much positive press as the Mayan calendar or Y2K did several years back. How many more would be saved?

Instead, the only time the Rapture is mentioned in the news these days is when someone publicly claims to know exactly when it is going to happen. "Nut jobs," worldly mockers, and irreverent clergy aside, the Rapture will happen, not because we believe it, but because Jesus guaranteed it.

> Let not your heart be troubled; you believe in God, believe also in Me. In My Father's house are many mansions; if it were not so, I would have told you. I go to prepare a place for you. And if I go and prepare a place for you, I will come again and receive you to Myself; that where I am, there you may be also. (John 14:1–3, emphasis added)

After Jesus ascended, where did He go? Heaven, of course. If He is coming again to take us where He is, then by sheer common sense, we know we will go to Heaven with Him. We go there (rather than the earth), because that is where He resides.

Yes, the Rapture will happen just as sure as the sun rises in the east and sets in the west. How and when it happens is, at present, largely left to speculation, because no one knows the day or hour (Matthew 24:36–44). Nevertheless, all the mocking and conjecture will be a moot point once it actually occurs. It will one day become a reality that humanity has to deal with in a very painful fashion.

Although the Rapture has no prerequisite events tied to its timing, it is the *de facto* (primal cause) necessary for the Tribulation (Daniel's Seventieth Week of seven years) to occur. It will be the perfect crisis for the Man of Sin to come and take advantage of. It is for this reason that we believe the world has long been in the shadow of two major events, the cross and the Seventieth Week, all these many years.

Moreover, just as terrifying and horrific as life will become on planet earth after the Rapture, there will be those who seek to profit from all the chaos and confusion. Even now, these individuals and organizations are preparing for the crisis they know is coming, but don't know when, how, or even what it is.

Thankfully, this is where Satan is in a real bind. He needs his human minions to prepare for what is coming—the perfect crisis. However, he cannot tell them why, exactly, they are preparing without losing them to the enemy camp (God's side). This is why he has spent the last hundred years conducting an extensive and relentless psychological operation upon the earth, springing ideas like UFOs, Gaia, aliens, superheroes, super villains, global warming, the multiverse, and so forth through books, television, and movies. He needs everybody believing the Rapture is something other than what it really is—divine deliverance. He needs the world to be distracted from what is coming. Satan does all this while knowing the truth that the Rapture will trigger the events necessary for the arrival of his final kingdom. After the Rapture, he knows he has very little time before his own judgment...

...which brings us to our day.

First, we know that Satan is the temporary ruler of this earth in our present dispensation (Luke 4:5–6). Second, we know that Satan has successfully infiltrated and taken over Hollywood—and basically the entire film and entertainment industries. We can think of the mainstream media, the film and entertainment industry, Silicon Valley, and most other places of power, as Satan's mouthpieces. Influencers in these realms do what he wants them to do, and they echo what he wants them to say.

Therefore, the fact that we have seen in recent years an increasing number of movies, television shows, video games, comics, and books aimed at mass abductions, mass disappearances, die-offs, plagues, aliens, zombies, meteors/comets striking the earth, superheroes, monsters, and magic occurring on an increasingly greater and greater scale must mean we are close. We are close, since these movies relegate our day to the end of the age, yet deny the true, biblical reasons for how and why the world really ends (the Rapture of the Church, the Tribulation, Armageddon, etc.).

It would behoove us to watch what our adversary is doing and take note of his frantic maneuverings. As evil and deluded as Satan might be, he is no dummy. We'd venture to say that he knows the Bible better than most, and you better believe he knows there is a pre-Tribulation Rapture. Why else would he expend the enormous amount of capital (time, people, money, and resources) to convey this message as greatly as he has if we were nowhere near the season of the actual Rapture?

Like sharks circling, the increase in the frenzied satanic activity is a warning sign that our time on this earth is drawing near. Satan knows his time is short, and he's pulling out all the stops to minimize the damage to the final Beast system by the Rapture. He is busily steamrolling globalism into every corner of our world. He's maximizing his efforts to minimize and corrupt Christianity or persecute it mercilessly if the first two avenues don't work. He has put immorality, debauchery, and wholesale wickedness on steroids, and now has most of the governments of the world doing his bidding in political and legislative efforts. Lastly, he is saturating our entertainment with things that appear to be like the Rapture, but are caused by other issues so as to muddy the waters before the real event happens.

In our estimation, there will be a small window of time after the Rapture (a gap in time of a few months to perhaps two to three years), but it will be filled with geopolitical, economic, and social tumult and chaos. It will make what we saw in the summer of 2020 look tame in comparison. The world will immediately reel to and fro as if teetering on the edge of an abyss. Yet, we believe many will see and recognize what just happened. Many will go online and search these things out until the Internet is shut down. This gap will not be a picnic, and no one reading this now should think, *perhaps I'll wait until after so I can really believe it.*

Be warned. One second after the Rapture of the Church, the world will, once again, be thrust into a time of magic and monsters as the gates of Hell finally burst open unimpeded. The supernatural will, once again, become the natural, and the wickedness will be amplified so much that people will wish they had to deal with zombie hordes instead of what they get.

But one second after will be too late for many. Those who recognize it for what it truly was will weep and mourn the opportunities they squandered in our present age. For then, if they want to receive Christ, it will cost them everything. Not just in Iran or North Korea, but in Kansas, Texas, and Florida. In England, and Australia. In Europe and Asia. In Africa and the island nations. True biblical Christianity will no longer be tolerated, and this Beast will usher in a new holocaust with extreme prejudice to stamp out these Tribulation believers, wherever he/they find them. Pray you are found worthy to escape these things ahead of time (Luke 21:34–36).

> And the beast was given a mouth uttering haughty and blasphemous words, and it was allowed to exercise authority for forty-two months. It opened its mouth to utter blasphemies against God, blaspheming his name and his dwelling, that is, those who dwell in heaven. Also, it was allowed to make war on the saints and to conquer them. And authority was given it over every tribe and people and language and nation, and all who dwell on earth will worship it, everyone whose name has not been written before the foundation of the world in the book of life of the Lamb who was slain. If anyone has an ear, let him hear:
>
> If anyone is to be taken captive, to captivity he goes; if anyone is to be slain with the sword, with the sword must he be slain.
>
> Here is a call for the endurance and faith of the saints. (Revelation 13:5–10)

TASK AND PURPOSE

The Tribulation serves to accomplish two overarching goals: discipline Israel and destroy the current geopolitical thrones and powers of this world (Jeremiah 30:7–11). The purpose of the Seventy Weeks of Daniel (Daniel 9:24–27) regarding Israel's disciplining are six things.

> Seventy weeks are determined for your people and for your holy city,
> To finish the transgression,
> To make an end of sins,

To make reconciliation for iniquity,
To bring in everlasting righteousness,
To seal up vision and prophecy,
And to anoint the Most Holy.

Nowhere in the Bible do we see cause or justification for the Church (the New Testament Body of believers) being in the Seventieth Week. The Church was not in the previous sixty-nine weeks (because Christ had not yet come), nor will we be in the seventieth. The Church is the Bride of Christ. It is also the Body of Christ, whom Jesus said He would build (Matthew 16:18). Jesus is also the Head of the Body who is the Church. Piecing together the metaphors and symbolisms we see spelled out in various passages brings us back to the institution of marriage. In marriage, the husband and wife become one flesh, which is what our marriage (hence our combining) then symbolizes.

For we are members of His body, of His flesh and of His bones. "For this reason a man shall leave his father and mother and be joined to his wife, and the two shall become one flesh." This is a great mystery, but I speak concerning Christ and the church. (Ephesians 5:30–32)

Our marriage is what the Church is doing in Heaven while the Tribulation is being poured out upon the earth. Various errant eschatological views have the Church being raptured either during or after the Seventieth Week. That is only possible by confusing who and what the Church is.

The Church (*ekklesia*) is a called-out assembly of believers that only exists between the resurrection of Christ and the Rapture. We couldn't exist before Christ died on the cross, because it takes the death of the testator in order for that New Testament (covenant) to take effect.

For where there is a testament, there must also of necessity be the death of the testator. For a testament is in force after men are dead, since it has no power at all while the testator lives. (Hebrews 9:16–17)

Now, there have been believers since the days of Genesis. Being a believer in and of itself does not mean that one is in the Church. Just as God divided people up by sex, ethnicity, and other distinctive traits, and just as there are separate classes of the animal kingdom as well as angelic hosts, so too will believers fall into different categories. There were Old Testament (OT) believers (believing in the One who would come), and there are New Testament believers (who were redeemed because of the death, burial, and resurrection of the One).

The OT saints were not saved at their point of death by the redeeming power of the cross, because Christ had not yet come. It is very likely Christ showed them who He was and what He did when He descended into Sheol to "lead captivity captive" (Ephesians 4:8). But they were justified as we are—by grace through faith in God at their point of death. In other words, the object of our faith is different, but the result is the same, in that we are ultimately redeemed by God. The idea that Christ had to die on a cross and be raised again was unknown to those who lived before that time.

However, we speak wisdom among those who are mature, yet not the wisdom of this age, nor of the rulers of this age, who are coming to nothing. But we speak the wisdom of God in a mystery, the hidden wisdom which God ordained before the ages for our glory, which none of the rulers of this age knew; for had they known, they would not have crucified the Lord of glory. (1 Corinthians 2:6–8)

When OT believers died, they went to a holding place known as Abraham's Bosom, or Paradise (Luke 16:22–23; 23:43). Unlike the Church who is resurrected/translated into our immortal bodies *before* the

Seventieth Week, they (OT saints) will be resurrected into their immortal, glorified bodies *after* that time along with those believers who are martyred during the Seventieth Week (Daniel 12:1–3; Matthew 24:31; Luke 11:24; Revelation 6:9–11; 20:4). So this resurrection is divided only by seven years (or so). This depends on whether or not a gap of time exists between the Rapture and the start of the Seventieth Week of Daniel.

We know currently that those believers (since Pentecost) who have physically died are spiritually alive and in the presence of God (2 Corinthians 5:6–8). These are those who come *with* Christ at the Rapture to meet those still alive, in the air, which may be a triumphal procession through the midst of enemy territory (Ephesians 2:2). This is where Christ parades His trophy (the Church; see 1 Peter 2:9) before His defeated enemies on our way to the Bema Judgment and marriage ceremony in Heaven.

Some argue that God's judgment doesn't begin with the seal judgments, but with the trumpets. This seems unlikely, since Christ is the only One found worthy to take and open the sealed scroll, thus *initiating* the subsequent chain of events (Revelation 5:1–7). If Christ's judgment only begins at the trumpet judgments, then shouldn't He blow the first trumpet? Since He was the *only* one worthy to open the sealed scroll, if the judgments aren't from Him, then to whom do they belong? It likewise seems counterintuitive for Him to pour out His judgments upon Himself (since His Body is the Church; Ephesians 5:23).

CONCLUSION

In God's providential wisdom, He chose the Rapture as the manner of delivery of His Church because it serves the purpose of removing His Body from the earth prior to His judgment and provides the necessary timing required for the Bema and Marriage Supper of the Lamb to occur. It also reinforces the "strong delusion" that will come upon the earth after the Rapture (2 Thessalonians 2:9–11). Lastly, because the world mocks at the very notion of a Rapture, God will use it to destroy the "wise."

For the message of the cross is foolishness to those who are perishing, but to us who are being saved it is the power of God. For it is written:

"I will destroy the wisdom of the wise, And bring to nothing the understanding of the prudent."

Where is the wise? Where is the scribe? Where is the disputer of this age? Has not God made foolish the wisdom of this world? (1 Corinthians 1:18–20)

We live in a world that is continually trying to reinvent and redefine truth. The problem the world keeps running into is that when it promotes one anti-biblical teaching as truth (i.e., Darwinian evolution, the Big Bang theory, manmade global warming, gender dysphoria, atheism, communism, etc., *ad nauseam*), it continually runs into the brick wall of another opposing humanistic ideology that contradicts it. The same can be said for liberal or progressive "Christian" pastors who deny some, most, or all of the Bible, to include the teaching of the Rapture.

Since the late 1700s, the topic of the Rapture has come back into our collective biblical understanding, primarily due to our nearness to it. An old argument by skeptics against the Rapture has been, if it were true, then why have fifteen centuries passed with hardly any teachings on it? Perhaps, from God's perspective, it wasn't as pertinent for those, for example, in the twelfth century to know the particular differences between the Rapture and the Second Coming as it was for those in the nineteenth century. Regardless of the lateness of our understanding of Rapture teachings, the fact that it has been in the Bible since the first century trumps any failures on our (humanity's) part to understand it.

Furthermore, it is relevant now in the twenty-first century. If we believe that God reveals things progressively to man, then He does so when it is appropriate for that particular generation. That's why we don't hear any cautionary sermons today warning people about a coming worldwide flood. That's why we don't hear sermons today speaking of an imminent Assyrian invasion. It was relative to Noah and Isaiah's audience, but not to us today. Today we warn of the coming Rapture of the Church and of the subsequent hellish vacuum that will follow.

This is why books like *The Late, Great Planet Earth* by Hal Lindsey and the *Left Behind* series by Tim LaHaye and Jerry Jenkins exploded when they did: timing. God's perfect timing. There is just enough going on in the world to make even the unbeliever wonder what is actually happening. It is in times like these that God the Holy Spirit works through humans (opens their eyes) to see how events are unfolding and fulfilling biblical prophecy. We don't have to read the newspaper into the Bible, because we can see events from the news heading down the same predicted path towards the Day of the Lord (the Tribulation or Daniel's Seventieth Week). Nevertheless, the end will come, and quickly. For some, the joy of eternity awaits. For many more, Hell on earth will be the best it ever gets.

Now Enoch, the seventh from Adam, prophesied about these men also, saying, "Behold, the Lord comes with ten thousands of His saints, to execute judgment on all, to convict all who are ungodly among them of all their ungodly deeds which they have committed in an ungodly way, and of all the harsh things which ungodly sinners have spoken against Him." (Jude 1:14–15)

4

THE DECLINE OF
WESTERN CIVILIZATION

Evil is ancient, unchanging, and with us always. The more postmodern the West becomes—affluent, leisured, nursed on moral equivalence, utopian pacifism, and multicultural relativism—the more premodern the evil among us seems to arise in nihilistic response.[6]
—Victor Davis Hanson

With all this talk of the New World Order, the "new normal," the Fourth Industrial Revolution, the Age of Aquarius, and all the other such futuristic phases we are seemingly meant to enter, we have become somewhat nostalgic for the old ones. Now, we know that, as Christians, this world is not our home and we are destined for glory upon glory in the eternal realm, but still, looking back, there were good moments in our lives that made us who we are.

Interestingly, we live in an age when we have a number of generations all living at the same time. From Centennials to Millennials and Generation X to Baby Boomers (even a few Silent Generation folks are still kicking around), the twentieth and twenty-first centuries have become a Petri dish of cross-generational experiences. Like many of you, we consider ourselves fortunate enough not only to have been born in the last century, but also in the last millennium as well.

This idea of cross-generational pollination got us thinking about dispensationalism and our current predicament as a nation. While it is easy to blame everything on Centennials (Gen Z, iGen [1996–present]) and their supposed laziness and discontent for America, can we blame them entirely? Most grew up either right before or right after 9/11. They went from witnessing the fallout from that terrible event to living in a nation engaged in decades-long wars (Iraq and Afghanistan). Right around the time they could get jobs and start making money, the market crashed (2008). They then got eight years of the Obama administration. They then lived through H1N1, Ebola, and now COVID-19, as well as every natural disaster under the sun. Adding insult to injury, they know our nation is so far gone into debt, they will likely never reap the benefits they're forced to pay into.

All this could make anyone jaded.

However, they weren't the first generation to suffer. The Silent Generation (1945 and earlier) saw two World Wars, the Spanish Flu, and the Great Depression. Baby Boomers saw the Korean and Vietnam wars, as well as the dreadful hippy movement. Still, Centennials have one greater disadvantage than all those previous generations, in that they live in a largely postmodern, post-American, and post-Christian world. Moreover, their entire lives have largely been ones of perpetual change—i.e., evolving into one technological upgrade after another.

Our thoughts on this rapid decline in light of late dispensationalism have bordered more on the ambiguous transitions between the ages rather than the dispensations themselves. At least the first two (innocence and conscience) had vastly different and physical ramifications in their before-and-after realities. For those who lived between them (Adam and Eve, Noah and his family), the differences must have been shocking. For the rest of the dispensations, if one was not spiritually attuned to God's changing economies, things were changing shades of gray.

Within traditional dispensationalism, there is a four-part organization regarding each particular age or epoch. The first part is the act, which separates it from the previous era. The second part is the challenge God gives mankind within that particular period. The third is mankind's failure to live up to said challenge. The fourth part is the judgment regarding that specific failure. The late Dr. Charles Ryrie explains:

> The principal characteristic of a dispensation is the economic arrangement and responsibility that God reveals in each dispensation. Such responsibility is a test in itself. Most men fail the test, and then judgment follows. The dispensational scheme has two perspectives: a cross-sectional aspect (which is sometimes misconstrued as cycles but which is in reality a spiral) and a longitudinal aspect (which emphasizes the unfolding progress of revelation and continuing principles throughout the ages of the dispensations).[7]

For example:

- **The Age of Innocence** began with man's creation in Paradise and the testing of the forbidden tree, and it ended with the introduction of sin, death, and expulsion from the Garden of Eden (Genesis 1:26–27; 3:6–24; Romans 5:12).
- **The Age of Conscience** began with fallen man and God's introduction of sacrifice (for temporary atonement), and it ended with the original depopulation plan by the global Flood (Genesis 3:21; 6:11–13; 7:11–24; Romans 2:15).
- **The Age of Human Government** began with the Noahic Covenant and God's command to be fruitful, multiply, and fill the earth. Man's failure in this resulted in the judgment of global dispersion and confusion of tongues at Babel (Genesis 9:5; 11:5–9; Acts 17:26; Romans 13:1–7).
- **The Age of Promise** began with the Abrahamic covenant and ended with his descendants in Egyptian bondage. Their failure for not having faith in the God who delivered them out of said bondage resulted in most of that generation not being able to enter

the Promised Land (Genesis 12–15; 26; 28; Numbers 14:26–36, 23:19; Micah 7:20; Romans 11:29).

- **The Age of the Law** began with God giving the Law to Moses at Mt. Sinai and ended with the Jewish people crucifying their own promised Messiah. Their punishment was a nearly two thousand-year diaspora (Exodus 19:1–8; Deuteronomy 7–8; Daniel 9:4–16; Matthew 27:25; Romans 3:19–20).

- **The Age of the Church** began by the giving of the Holy Spirit after Jesus' resurrection and will end as chronicled by Jesus in His seven letters to the seven churches. The Church Age will culminate with the final church epoch sliding (minus the Philadelphian remnant) into apostasy and the Rapture removing believers from the earth (John 1:17; Acts 1:9–2:4; Titus 2:11–14; 1 Peter 1:10–12; Revelation 3:10; 15–16).

- **The Millennial Age** will begin the Second Coming of Christ at Armageddon and introduces a thousand-year reign of righteousness and peace upon the earth. It will end with the loosening of Satan at the end of that thousand-year reign and concludes with one final rebellion that God immediately crushes, thus ushering in the Great White Throne Judgment and the age eternal (Matthew 25:31–34; Revelation 20:4–6, 7–15).

Thus, dispensationalism is not just some theological "construct" teasing out academic particulars so that it can be different from other interpretations like Reformed theology or Roman Catholicism. The repeat failures found in the dispensations uniquely validate God's Word both by history and current events. Simply look around today at the strength of the denominational churches. See how watered down they have become.

The modern church has suffered death by a thousand compromises, splintering and crushing professing Christendom under the weight of political correctness, governmental overreach, and the deconstruction of civil society. The failures highlighted by dispensational theology have everything to do with the reality we're currently living in, the future of

America and the Church, and the end of our age. Furthermore, we have been in a two-thousand-year silent era, not all that dissimilar to the intertestamental period.

Although the four hundred silent years between the prophet Malachi and John the Baptist did not have God physically speaking through His prophets, prophetic events were still unfolding. In fact, sixty-nine of Daniel's Seventy Weeks would unfold between Nehemiah 2 and Jesus' crucifixion on Mt. Calvary. While God has used Israel—and, in particular, Jerusalem—as His prophetic timepiece, the Church was given one additional way to measure our location on God's prophetic calendar. From the Church's conception in Acts 2, Jesus set forth the order of events using the seven letters to churches to represent seven epochs, which would come to mark where we were in history. More on this in a moment.

THE LONG SHADOW

Shadows are interesting things. They communicate a reality, yet, they themselves are not really real. They indicate the thing that is coming, yet, they are not the things themselves.[8]
—Pastor Ken Ortize, Calvary Chapel Spokane

For two thousand years now, humanity has lived in what has been labeled the "long shadow." We're not only living in the shadow of what Christ did on the cross, but also in the shadow of things to come. Those events are looming ever closer, and we believe that we are the generation of people who will see these final acts of human history play out.

- True, every generation has faced that same potential prospect, but it is also a fact that one generation will learn the harsh realities of ignoring it. Many people (religious and nonreligious alike) often think about the last days as being applicable only to some distant, far-off, future generation. We heard a minister the other day claim that, generations from now, people will look back and wonder at the events surrounding the march on the US Capitol in January 2020. We are fairly sure he does not believe we are the last generation.

- However, just like every generation that's come before us, many are blinded to the lateness of the hour by something known as the "tyranny of the present." They are consumed with what is right in front of them and are almost entirely unable (or unwilling) to step back and get the big-picture view of where we are in time.

The reality is a day is coming that will be unlike any other. It will turn the world upside down. We know that day as the Day of Christ, or the Rapture of the Church. Why is it so different? Because one generation of believers will not see death, but will be instantaneously translated (transformed) from mortality to immortality. This divinely appointed event will then set in motion an intensifying and cascading set of actions that will bring human history to a close.

While it is true that many have claimed to know the day and have foolishly attempted to name it, the Bible assures us that "no man knows the day or hour." However, the Bible also states that we (those looking for it) will see *that day* approaching (Matthew 16:1–4; Thessalonians 5:1–9; Hebrews 10:25; Revelation 3:3). The only way that is possible to both know and not know is to see the *shadow* of the event before it arrives.

Thus, the Rapture, for both its attractors and detractors, remains a highly disputed event. Nonbelievers simply look at the event as a joke or something to mock and ridicule, if they think about it at all. To the believers, however, there is much divergence of opinion as to its nature and timing. Nevertheless, one would be hard-pressed to state that the Bible doesn't mention the Rapture as a certainty. Only true heretics would deny that the Bible actually teaches it, because it is mentioned both as historical occurrences (Enoch, Elijah, Ezekiel, Jesus, Philip, and Paul) as well as a certain, future event. To deny that would be to reject what is clearly taught in Holy Scripture.

However, difference of opinion is to be expected when throwing people's interpretations into the mix as to when the Rapture will occur. If God had wanted us to know exactly when a thing was to occur, He would have had the writers state as much. Instead, God uses type (foreshadow) and doctrinal congruity to strongly suggest the nature of the Rapture and its timing. To summarize, the Rapture is a divinely appointed happening highlighting God's supernatural ability to rescue His own, prior to unleashing His wrath and judgment upon a Christ-rejecting earth.

Consequently, we've lived in this long shadow ever since that first Pentecost (circa AD 32), when the Holy Spirit was given to mankind as "cloven tongues of fire" by descending upon the disciples in an astonishing show of force (Acts 2:1–4). However, just prior to that, Christ ascended from the earth in front of His disciples in an equally glorious fashion. As they stood gazing intently into the sky, presumably wondering if He would return in short order, two angels appeared and communicated with those who had gathered there.

> Now when He had spoken these things, while they watched, He was taken up, and a cloud received Him out of their sight. And while they looked steadfastly toward heaven as He went up, behold, two men stood by them in white apparel, who also said, "Men of Galilee, why do you stand gazing up into heaven? This same Jesus, who was taken up from you into heaven, *will so come in like manner* as you saw Him go into heaven." (Acts 1:9–11, emphasis added)

This literal foreshadowing would indicate the manner of Christ's return. This serves two purposes: 1) to demonstrate the mechanism of the Rapture's validity (i.e., God can do this and has done it in the past); and 2) to help believers discern when false Christs appear claiming to be Him in the future. Jesus warned no less than three times in His Olivet Discourse that deception would be the key sign of the last days. Many would come claiming to be Him. If they don't or can't return in "like" manner (descending from Heaven), they couldn't possibly be the true Messiah.

As for the timing of the last days, the writer of Hebrews states:

God, who at various times and in various ways spoke in time past to the fathers by the prophets, has *in these last days* spoken to us by His Son, whom He has appointed heir of all things, through whom also He made the worlds. (Hebrews 1:1–2, emphasis added)

If the world was in the last days when Jesus walked the earth, how much closer are we today? Given that nearly two thousand years have since transpired, it would appear that every day we proceed forward, we are pressing that much closer to the edge of eternity.

Before He left, Christ's mandate to the disciples indicated that, while His return was absolutely certain (John 14:1–3), it might have some time built into it. They were to go into all the world, making disciples of all nations, baptizing them in the name of the Father, the Son, and the Holy Spirit:

And Jesus came and spoke to them, saying, "*All authority* has been given to Me in *heaven and on earth*. Go therefore and make disciples of *all the nations*, baptizing them in the name of the Father and of the Son and of the Holy Spirit, teaching them to observe all things that I have commanded you; and lo, I am with you always, *even to the end of the age*." Amen. (Matthew 28:18–20, emphasis added)

In the twenty centuries that followed, the inevitable ebb and flow of kingdoms rising and falling took place. While this book is not intended to chronicle every geopolitical deviation man has pursued, we will primarily look at history through the lenses of the epochs God set up through Israel and the Church. These are those important signposts, were one so inclined to watch, that would point to where the Church was in relation to the end of the age.

Naturally, as time progressed from that first Pentecost, believers' expectancy in His imminent return began to wane. Time itself began to form a wedge between believers' eager anticipation of Christ's return and the certainty of the event itself. During high times of persecution (AD 60–312), the Church fervently held to the belief that Christ would return. This served as a powerful preservative to those early Christians. Satan, having been defeated at the cross, discovered that the more he persecuted the Church, the faster it grew. Thus, he had to change his strategy. He needed a subtler approach, much as he did with Eve in the garden. Instead of violent persecution, he whispered subtly, "Hath God indeed said…?"

As time passed, the whisper changed to, "Will He return?"

Satan knows he cannot defeat the Church as a unified body of believers (Matthew 16:13–19). However, he knows humans, in and of themselves, are easily corruptible. He must have realized early on that he could not destroy the Church through persecution, therefore, he would need to neutralize the church through manipulation. He understood (knowing human nature) that if he could get the Church focused on this life and not the next, he could distract them with all manner of earthly things. Thus, after two centuries of intense persecution, Satan began the long game of hermeneutical (interpretational) corruption of Bible doctrines, beginning with the conversion of Emperor Constantine in AD 312. His conversion (real or not) allowed Christians to come out of the shadows and begin living openly in a still largely pagan empire.

THE CHURCH

During the fourth century, a popular yet heretical form of eschatology began to emerge as the dominant view within Christendom courtesy of an Ante-Nicene church father named Augustine. Since it wouldn't have been kosher for newly integrated Christians to champion their Messiah returning and destroying all the earthly kingdoms (including Rome), ambitious and ecumenically minded clergy began toning down Bible prophecy to minimize its apocalyptic nature.

This view (amillennialism) posited that the Church was now both Israel (which had by then been in Diaspora since AD 70) and the promised Kingdom to come, and thus, the Church had become inheritors of all the Old Testament blessings and promises. They then dumped all of Revelation into the events surrounding the sacking of Jerusalem by General Titus and his Roman legions. As for Christ returning, that event was relegated to some distant and unknowable future. In fact, amillennialism taught that Christ wouldn't even physically return, but would rule *the Kingdom* through the Church. This certainly helped feed the idea that the Roman Catholic popes (*pontifex maximus*) were the Vicars of Christ, with "Vicar" meaning "ruling vicariously."

Once Satan could corrupt the Church's understanding of what is coming, he then focused on what was in front of them. This new variation of state-sanctioned Christianity began absorbing many of the Romans' pagan rituals, temples, and even clergy as their own to make it more palatable to an empire increasingly in decline. This was a form of ecumenicalism, which sought to appease everyone by not offending anyone. Sound familiar?

And the shadow grew.

However, this hijacking was not unforeseen by God. Christ had predicted as much in His seven Kingdom parables (Matthew 13), by which He spoke cryptically about the entirety of the Church Age. As for the satanic corruption of the Church, Christ foretold what would begin to happen some three hundred years after His death, burial, and resurrection with the parable of the mustard seed.

> Another parable He put forth to them, saying: "The kingdom of heaven is like a mustard seed, which a man took and sowed in his field, which indeed is the least of all the seeds; but when it is grown it is greater than the herbs and becomes a tree, so that the *birds of the air* come and *nest in its branches*." (Matthew 13:31–32, emphasis added)

In the context of all these parables, the birds are viewed as unclean and evil. In the first parable (sower of the seeds), the birds devour all the seed (the new converts) that fell to the wayside. Here, these birds are now nesting inside the Kingdom of Heaven (Christendom). Later, the Apostle Paul would call Satan "the prince of the power of the air" (Ephesians 2:2), where birds also claim domain, indicating where Satan's domain really lay.

However, if we stay in context with the symbolism given here, the birds (unclean) take shelter in the mustard tree (the Church) that grows unnaturally larger than it should (mustard trees are not large at all). Thus, instead of the Church taking the gospel into the world, Jesus said the world would come into the Church and began trying to corrupt it. This theme was also presented in the parable of the wheat and tares, in which Jesus said:

> The kingdom of heaven is like a man who sowed good seed in his field; but while men slept, his enemy came and sowed tares among the wheat and went his way. (Matthew 13:24–25)

Tares are weeds that look like wheat, but are not wheat. You can't eat them, and they are only good for burning. According to one source:

> [A tare is] the bearded darnel, mentioned only in Matthew 13:25– 30. It is the *Lolium temulentum*, a species of rye-grass, the seeds of which are a strong soporific poison. It bears the closest resemblance to wheat till the ear appears, and only then the difference is discovered.[9]

Tares are commonly known as false wheat, then, for obvious reasons. However, there are two main distinctions between tares and wheat. First, when grown to maturity, the ears on the real wheat cause it to droop (or bend down), while the tare remains upright. In addition, wheat ripens to brown, whereas the tare turns black when fully ripened. Even more intriguing, then, is the contrast between Jesus' parable and Satan's intentions.

And the Lord said, "Simon, Simon! Indeed, Satan has asked for you, that he may sift you as wheat." (Luke 22:31)

Again, the night mentioned here when the enemy sowed the tares indicates a passage of time, the same as the maturing of the mustard tree. An interesting side note indicating the direction where the gospel would take root is in the ordering of numbers given in Matthew 13:8 (100, 60, and 30) and Mark 4:20 (30, 60, and 100). As the Gospel of Matthew was written with a Jewish audience in mind, it would indicate a decline in Jewish converts. The Gospel of Mark, however, was written for a Gentile audience. He prophetically reverses the numbers, indicating that the Gentiles would now become the harvest.

And the shadow grew.

Remember Jesus' parting statement in Matthew 28. He still *has all authority in Heaven and on earth* (v. 18). This worldly form of Christendom quickly assumed (and consumed) what had been the extent of the Romans' empire. However, this was to be short-lived. Since Jesus knew Christianity would be hijacked into this whorish variation of paganism and Christianity, He allowed a new force to arise that would quickly put an end to the worldly minded Holy Roman Empire.

The Muslims began to conquer and take hold of the lands that were once "Christian" (nations cannot be Christian—only individuals can). However, as Islam began to dominate, it too began to splinter into a million tiny factions, all vying for control. As the persecution intensified, Christendom began to split up into two major divisions: those who wanted to remain in the largely pagan Holy Roman Empire and those who did not. While the Holy Roman Empire (now the Roman Catholic Church [RCC]) maintained its foothold firmly in Europe, true Christianity continued to spread throughout the world.

The RCC, satanically covetous of the power and spread of true Christianity, began to declare through papal bulls and edicts that those who did not follow the RCC were heretics. These heretics were to be excommunicated, imprisoned, have their wealth confiscated, be tortured, and ultimately be killed (usually by burning) during a seven-hundred-year period known as the Inquisition. Examples of the persecuted groups in Europe centered on both Jews and Christian believers (e.g., Waldensians, Anabaptists, Lollards, etc.).

And the shadow grew.

Christ Himself gave more foreshadowing as to the time built into the Church Age in His seven letters to the seven churches (Revelation 1–3). These letters were to real churches in existence in John's day. However, by the time John was imprisoned on the island of Patmos (AD 95), thousands of churches were in existence throughout the world.

The Lord could have used, literally, any number of churches as examples to convey His messages. However, because He only used *seven* (as opposed to thirteen or eighty-two), there was a specific reason for why He did so. Here are the seven churches looked at in a cross-sectional manner.

(**Author's note:** These dates are estimates, not approximates. In addition, the boldened churches began to overlap each other like layers. See chart next page.)

Furthermore, though there were larger congregations at that time in places like Corinth, Galatia, Rome, Antioch, Jerusalem, and so forth, Jesus selected the seven churches—their quantity, type, and location—for very specific reasons. He then gave them to John in a particular order, because God does not do things arbitrarily or accidentally. These seven were not selected because they had issues unique to themselves, but because the concerns were applicable to all churches ("he who has an ear").

Even within each type of church, we can see the different kinds of believers represented. For example, within the Sardis era (the era in which one type of church dominates Christendom), we can see Philadelphian or Laodicean types of believers. We also note that Jesus had seven Kingdom parables (Matthew 13), which overlap with His seven letters, which can also be overlaid with Paul's epistles to seven churches (Galatians, Thessalonians, Corinthians, Colossians, Ephesians, Romans, and the Philippians). This is excluding duplicates, personal letters, and Hebrews (which remained unsigned).

	Church-Meaning	Pauline Epistle	Matthew 13 Parable	Era/Century	Letter Structure	Positive/Negative Message
1	Ephesus- "desired one"	Ephesians	"Sower"	1st	Title	+/-
2	Smyrna- "Myrrh"	Philippians	"Wheat & Tares"	2nd-3rd	Commendation	+
3	Pergamos- "Married"	Corinthians	"Mustard Seed"	4th-5th	Criticism	+/-
4	Thyatira- "Sacrifice"	Galatians	"Leaven"	5th - Present	Admonition	+/-
5	Sardis- "Escaping"	Romans	"Treasure of the Field"	15th - Present	Call	+/-
6	Philadelphia- "Brotherly Love"	Thessalonians	"Pearl of Great Price"	17th - Present	Promise to overcomer	+
7	Laodicea- "People ruling"	Colossians	"Dragnet"	19th - Present	Challenge	-

Ephesus (AD 30–100): Paul had previously taught and written to the church of Ephesus (Acts 18–20, Ephesians) and devoted a significant amount of time and energy to teaching the Ephesians the deeper mysteries of Christ and the Church. However, by AD 95, something had begun to happen. Christ reprimands them for having left their first love. What that is exactly, we do not know; however, Paul had warned them (Acts 20:28–31) that, after his departure, "savage wolves" would come in, not sparing the flock. Paul instructed the young pastor Timothy to remain in Ephesus to prevent the believers there from being divided over spurious and pointless issues (1 Timothy 2:3–4).

Ephesus is considered representative of the apostolic churches, which largely disappeared after the first century, since the apostles were tasked with spreading the gospel. Once the apostles died out, their disciples and the rest of the early church fathers were attempting to keep these churches intact. However, by AD 95, only John remained alive. There is no promise to return for this church to remove these believers from earth. There was only the threat to remove their "candlestick," which is to say remove them from being a church.

Smyrna (AD 100–312): Although the periods of intense persecution began prior to AD 100 (e.g., Nero and Domitian), the subsequent two centuries would provide the next eight periods of severe pagan persecution and poverty for the fledgling Church. According to *Foxes Book of Martyrs*, the following emperors either encouraged or tolerated the persecution of Christians during their reigns: Trajan (AD 108), Marcus Aurelius (AD 162), Severus (AD 192), Maximus (AD 235), Decius (AD 249), Valerian (AD 257), Aurelian (AD 274), and lastly Diocletian (AD 303). Emperor Constantine would go on to convert and legalize Christianity across the empire. This letter from the Lord contains no criticism, only a message that they endure, and their reward will be the crown of life.

Pergamos (AD 312–600): The Great Commission (Matthew 28:18–20) was the command Christ gave His disciples to go out into the world and "make disciples of all nations." Unfortunately, after the legalization of Christianity, instead of the church going out into the world, the world came into the church. Here, the merging of Roman paganism crosses the threshold of Christian churches. The Lord's promise of return here is not a good promise, but a threat; He said that if they did not repent, the Lord Himself would come and fight against them. What had been the deeds of the Nicolaitans in Ephesus became doctrine in Pergamos.

Pergamos is the last of the seven letters to have the two subsections (task and promise) placed in that order. Henceforth, these two (task and promise) are reversed. It is our belief (as with many others) that these churches no longer exist in shape, type, or form. However, we will see the remaining four churches come out of what was left of Pergamos.

Thyatira (600–present): To the church of Thyatira, Jesus offered commendation for their last works being more than their first. However, they tolerated a prophetess named Jezebel teaching sexual immorality in their church. Jesus spent much of this letter condemning those in Thyatira for many misdeeds, and His promise to return is limited to *only those* within this church who do not hold to the Jezebel doctrine or have sought out the depths of Satan.

Sardis (1517–present): If Thyatira represents the Roman Catholic Church, then Sardis represents the Protestant Reformers who came out of her. What began as a blazing torch leading millions out of the Dark Ages of Catholic subjugation and domination quickly became an extinguished candle. While Christ praised some within this church, He referred to the majority as a "dead church." In other words, they had a dead orthodoxy ("correct teaching") and orthopraxy ("correct practice") bogged down with legalism and works. The promise to return to the church at Sardis was a warning. Since they no longer watched for Jesus' return (i.e., studied Bible prophecy), it would be like that of a thief.

Philadelphia (1730–present): Out of the smoldering coals of the dying Reformation fires came a Spirit-driven spiritual revival in Europe and America called the First Great Awakening. Here, we see the great missionary movements begin to set out into all the world, sharing the light of the gospel to every nation.

This was followed by the Second Great Awakening beginning in the

1790s, and the Third in the 1850s. At this time, the United States and Europe were essentially Acts 2 populations (having basic Judeo-Christian principals as a societal foundation). As time moved on, the Awakenings would get smaller and smaller while the West became increasingly an Acts 19 culture (becoming more pagan). Out of all the letters, only this church has a promise that it will be altogether removed from this world. The rest of the letters, when taken in context, offer no such statement. While there may have been "Philadelphia-type believers" in each era, there is only one era when the Rapture will happen.

Laodicea (1900–present): Unsurprisingly, as the Great Awakenings began to spring up across the nation, pseudo-Christian groups (tares) also began to leech on and lead many astray. It is hard to pinpoint when these apostate movements began to make serious headway, but by 1900, they were firmly entrenched in Western society through the Mormons, Jehovah Witnesses, Christian Scientists, and so forth.

We also see the charismatic movement begin around 1906 with the Azusa Street Revival. While not condemning the charismatic movement at large, many of the false teachers today (think health and wealth, prosperity, dominionist gospel, Hebrew Roots, and emerging church movements) all seemingly have their roots connected back to someone in the charismatic movement.

This church believed they lacked nothing, but were, in fact, poor, blind, and naked in Christ's view. No promise was made by Christ to come; it received only a severe rebuke and chastening to repent. Even Christ stands outside this church knocking on the door.

However, why did the last church become lukewarm and apostate?

We believe the answer is something we see at the beginning of the Church Age and finds its culmination at the end of the Church Age.

In the letter to the church at Ephesus, Jesus said:

> Nevertheless, I have this against you, *that you have left your first love*. Remember therefore from where you have fallen; repent and do the first works, or else I will come to you quickly and remove

your lampstand from its place—unless you repent. But this you have, that you hate the deeds of the Nicolaitans, which I also hate. (Revelation 2:4–6, emphasis added)

The church at Ephesus had left their first love. What was that first love? The purity of the early church centered on their brotherly love, a sense of oneness in Christian community, charity, and love for one another. Then came rivalries and doctrinal disputes, leading to schisms that began to divide the early church into factions (see also 1 Corinthians 1:12; 3:5, 22). We also note that what had been the *deeds* of the Nicolaitans (which Christ hated) became their *doctrine* by the time we get to the church at Pergamos. If we allow the churches to represent ages, Pergamos became the dominant Church between the third and sixth centuries—right at the same time a heretical form of eschatology took root: amillennialism.

Amillennialism (and its ugly brother, preterism) denies the literal return of Christ to the earth to rule and reign for a thousand years. Instead, it proffers that the state-established church must conquer and become the kingdom on earth. A human kingdom also demands that a human leader such as the pope (the Vicar of Christ) rule on earth in His (Christ's) stead, thus ruling vicariously, as it were.

The rise of amillennialism in the third and fourth centuries was largely due to the unpopularity of preaching a "Kingdom message" with Christ returning to physically reign on the earth, thus disrupting the status quo of *Pax Romana*. This is what we are seeing today in similar fashion with the watering-down of the Bible. As the culture slides into wickedness, there is a greater desire by many so-called clergy to accommodate this effort to remain relevant in our culture. This is why we see the last church, the Laodiceans, become lukewarm and revolting to Christ.

Preaching that the United States, along with every other nation except Israel, will be destroyed is unpopular. This is why so many churches today have a been avoiding teaching prophecy altogether, as they're put under increasing pressure to water down not just the gospel, but any eschatological teaching that changes or upsets the status quo for the times in which we live. No, it is not necessarily obvious, but you can bet that on a spiritual level, this warfare is being waged as a form of negative persuasion to not give the pre-Trib Rapture (the "blessed hope") any type of footing in the public arena of ideas.

Now here is the rub. At the end of the age, not only is this prophetic shadow present, but its darkness has now almost completely covered the world. Things appear dark, because we are now in the shadow of the Seventieth Week of Daniel (Daniel 9:27). It is a foreboding time, pregnant with great horror, abominations, and wickedness, and is only recognizable to those who have been filled with the Holy Spirit and who have eyes to see and ears to hear.

The Bible states emphatically that the world at large will not see that day coming, just as those Pharisees could not see their Messiah right in front of them (Matthew 16:1–4). This blindness was also present thousands of years earlier. Before the Flood, the antediluvian peoples assumed things would continue as they always had since Creation. Jesus and His apostles allude to this condition of spiritual blindness in an even more descriptive fashion:

> For as in the days before the flood, they were eating and drinking, marrying and giving in marriage, until the day that Noah entered the ark, and did not know until the flood came and took them all away, so also will the coming of the Son of Man be. Then two men will be in the field: one will be taken and the other left. Two women will be grinding at the mill: one will be taken and the other left. Watch therefore, for you do not know what hour your Lord is coming. (Matthew 24:38–42)

From Paul:

> But concerning the times and the seasons, brethren, you have no need that I should write to you. For you yourselves know perfectly that the day of the Lord so comes as a thief in the night. For when

they say, "Peace and safety!" then sudden destruction comes upon **them**, as labor pains upon a pregnant woman. And **they** shall not escape. *But you, brethren, are not in darkness, so that this Day should overtake you as a thief.* (1 Thessalonians 5:1–4, emphasis added)

From Peter:

Knowing this first: *that scoffers will come in the last days*, walking according to their own lusts, and saying, "Where is the promise of His coming? For since the fathers fell asleep, all things continue as they were from the beginning of creation." For this they willfully forget: that by the word of God the heavens were of old, and the earth standing out of water and in the water, by which the world that then existed perished, being flooded with water. But the heavens and the earth which are now preserved by the same word, are reserved for fire until the day of judgment and perdition of ungodly men. (2 Peter 3:4–7, emphasis added)

From Jesus, to the church of Sardis:

Remember therefore how you have received and heard; hold fast and repent. Therefore, if you will not watch, I will come upon you as a thief, and you will not know what hour I will come upon you. (Revelation 3:3)

This warning was reserved for the third-to-last church, which, if in chronological order, represents the Protestant Reformation-era church onward. This signaled that mankind was entering the final period before His return. Here, the church was to be on the lookout for Christ's soon coming…yet, they would not look. Interestingly, when the Protestants broke away from the stranglehold of the Roman Catholic Church, they brought with them the Roman Catholic eschatology of amillennialism. Fast forward to the 2000s, and we see most of the mainline denominations capitulating to moral depravity, even going so far as to ordain homosexuals and transgendered clergy.

And the shadow grew.

Speaking of the depraved condition we're seeing a growing majority of churches descend into, Mark Steyn states the following (somewhat satirically) about the sad state of affairs we now find in our broken nation. In years past, we might have scoffed at words like this. Today, we sort of expect it.

> Most mainline Protestant churches are, to one degree or another, post-Christian. If they no longer seem disposed to converting the unbelieving to Christ, they can at least convert them to the boggiest of soft-left clichés, on the grounds that if Jesus were alive today he'd most likely be a gay Anglican bishop in a committed relationship driving around in an environmentally friendly car with an "Arms are for Hugging" sticker on the way to an interfaith dialogue with a Wiccan and a couple of Wahhabi imams.[10]

LAST-DAYS LAODICEAN

The gospel's most dangerous earthly adversaries are not raving atheists who stand outside the door shouting threats and insults. They are church leaders who cultivate a gentle, friendly, pious demeanor but hack away at the foundations of faith under the guise of keeping in step with a changing world.[11]
—Phil Johnson

Scripture foretold of the inevitable decline of Western Christendom and the intense ramping-up of persecution against Eastern Christendom. The spoils of World War II brought Western civilization affluence and decades of peace. In the leisure, modernity, and newfound wealth came the slippery, slimy corruption through the soft underbelly of the Western churches. The attacks not only on the churches, but also on the society, were well funded and multifaceted. They were demonically synchronized to break down the United States (who leads the Western civilization) so that it would be unable to support a global gospel mission field, as well as Israel.

The local and national denominations began crumbling under the weight of societal, Roman Catholic, and governmental pressure to compromise on key issues (such as homosexuality, abortion, gender identity, critical race theory, etc.) that were corrosive to the church and the family unit. Churches quickly found themselves having to be on the defensive so much, and for so long, that many could no longer bear the strain. All that many of these churches (particularly mega churches) wanted to do was remain relevant; thus began a cascading effect of the seeker-sensitive avalanche that rippled across Protestantism.

By the year 2020, a majority of churches and denominations no longer wanted to be associated with taking firm stands on hot-button issues. They didn't want the media spotlight or the doxing and personal attacks that came along with that spotlight; they acquiesced or remained silent. Thus, the Western churches (at large) became lukewarm and noxious to Jesus.

Whereas corruption seems to be Satan's weapon of choice against the Western churches, this tactic would not work against Eastern Christendom. Eastern Christendom (Africa, the Middle East, and the Far East) on the other hand, largely remain underserved and immune to this satanic strategy *vis-a-vis* modernity (i.e., Orwellian propagandists [the mainstream media], liberal universities, the Hollywood elite, social-media shaming, and other such Western trappings). Consequently, they found themselves on the receiving end of destruction through physical persecution. So prolific has been the terror and murders by groups like ISIS (Islamic State in Islam and Syria), Boko Haram, al-Qaeda, North Korea, China, Indonesia, and others, that more Christians have been killed in the twentieth and twenty-first centuries than in all the previous centuries combined. This trend will continue to escalate, even after the Rapture of the Church.

None of this was by accident, nor has it been a surprise to God. We with eyes to see and ears to hear should take some comfort in living through these dark days, because they are only darkened by the shadow of what's coming—our deliverance. While those who remain faithful in both the east and the west of Christendom watch faithfully, we find that our hope is not in this present world, nor are our solutions found in modern technology or political change, but in Jesus Christ Himself. He does not conform to our culture to be relevant; He is the Creator of reality. His relevance is supreme over everything. His *positions* on "hot-button" issues are not up for debate or interpretation, but are law. So while faithful churches might seem antiquated and uncivilized, here is what the Creator of the Universe has to say to that faithful Philadelphian church:

> *WORD*
> Because you have kept My command to persevere, I also will keep you from the hour of trial which shall come upon the whole world, to test those who dwell on the earth. (Revelation 3:10)

ISRAEL

While the ages of the church are markers for Christians pointing toward the last days, Israel has always been God's prophetic timepiece for everything. Its supernatural rebirth as a nation after the 1,878-year Diaspora is the super sign of the end times. The Bible plainly teaches that Israel MUST be back in the land before Christ Himself concludes human history (Amos 9:14–15, Isaiah 11:11, etc.). This is because Antichrist has to desecrate the Third Jewish Temple at the midpoint of the Seventieth Week of Daniel. Seeing that Jesus (Matthew 24:15, circa year AD 32), Paul (2 Thessalonians 2, circa AD 60], and John (Revelation 13, AD 95) all point to this as a future event, it can't have already been fulfilled, as many preterists erroneously presume. The Romans under General Titus destroyed both Jerusalem and the Temple in AD 70, thus could not desecrate it in the manner in which is described (Daniel 9:27, Matthew 24:15, 2 Thessalonians 2:4).

Bottom line: The Antichrist can't desecrate the Jewish Temple without a Jewish Temple. We can't have a Third Jewish Temple without Israel being back in the land. For nearly two thousand years, the land of Israel lay under the domination of foreign Gentile powers (Romans, Byzantines, Muslims, Crusaders, Turks, and Brits). None of them ever built a Jewish Temple, nor would they. Even the Jewish people themselves since 1948 have yet to rebuild their Temple for obvious political reasons.

This is why the Rapture will happen before (or pre) Daniel's Seventieth Week (again, aka the Tribulation or the Time of Jacob's Trouble). There are two primary purposes for the Tribulation: 1) to discipline Israel and bring her back into relationship with God; and 2) to destroy all the Christ-rejecting nations of the world in their current state (Jeremiah 30:7–11). Since the church did not exist in the first sixty-nine of Daniel's weeks (which ended with Christ's death on the cross), we can conclude with reasonable confidence that neither will it be in the Seventieth Week of Daniel. The focus must shift back to national Israel.

Furthermore, the Seventy Weeks of Daniel were exclusively determined for the Jews and Jerusalem. As members of the Church (the multi-membered, corporate Body of Christ), we are only beneficiaries (through Christ) of the six things listed in Daniel 9:24, which MUST find their fulfillment at the conclusion of the Seventieth Week:

- Finish the transgression.
- Make an end of sins.
- Make reconciliation for iniquity.
- Bring in everlasting righteousness.
- Seal up vision and prophecy.
- Anoint the Most Holy.

Since national Israel still largely rejects the Messiahship of Jesus to this day, we know that this last week of years must be yet future. Besides, if we are already seeing signs for events that happen after the Rapture, naturally, the Rapture must then be that much sooner. Therefore, since we cannot look for signs of the Rapture itself, we must look for signs of Daniel's Seventieth Week.

1. Israel. As mentioned earlier, the super-sign of the end times is the rebirth of the nation of Israel. The reason we can be certain of this is that there is no other explanation for the supernatural hatred for its existence amongst the nations. Not even the most tyrannical nation on the planet, North Korea, evokes as much vitriol from the leftists, godless, socialists, and Islamists as does Israel.

The world has not seen this level of anti-Semitism since the pre-World War II days in Europe. Unfortunately, this demonic hatred is not only at the geopolitical level, but it's also even within Christendom. Movements like Reformed and Covenant theology, as well as eschatological positions of amillennialism, preterism, and postmillennialism, were all designed to discredit Israel's legitimacy as both a nation and as the rightful heir of the Genesis 15 endowment (Deuteronomy 30:1–10, Ezekiel 37).

2. Jerusalem. The fact that Jerusalem is back under Israeli control, especially in light of how the nation reacquired that city, is simply miraculous. Moreover, since 1967, the world has furiously tried to wrest control of Jerusalem back out of Israeli hands. However, as of December 6, 2017, President Donald Trump became the first Gentile world leader (in over 2,500 years) to officially recognize Jerusalem as the sovereign capital of the nation of Israel, further enraging anti-Semites around the world (Zechariah 12:3, Luke 21:24).

Of interest is the shift in attitudes amongst the Arab nations during the Trump presidency and his Abraham Accords. Surprisingly, a number of Arab nations have already agreed to normalization policies with Israel. Saudi Arabia has even gone so far as to put sunlight between themselves (à la Mecca and Medina) and the so-called third holiest site in Islam, the Temple Mount. Essentially, the Saudis are stating that the Temple Mount isn't really all that important to them after all.

With Israel back in the land and in control of both Jerusalem and the Temple Mount, the shadow was taking shape. Juxtaposed to that fulfillment, the world since 1948 has greedily embraced the spirit of Antichrist. Lawlessness has become our new zeitgeist. Licentiousness and depravity have become normalized, and the remnant of true believers has, once again, little power. What had been the shadow of the cross was now taking on a new form: the shadow of a man. However, it was not the Man Christ Jesus, but another who would come in His name, one who will deceive the world into thinking he is the Messiah.

CHARLOTTE, NORTH CAROLINA

5:00 P.M. (EST)

MARCIE TUGGED ON THE NEW REEBOK RUNNING SHOES; she had worn them for two days to help break them in. Now the moment of truth had come. She would wear them on her two-mile run through the neighborhood, along the side streets, and, finally, onto the high school track before lapping several times, then returning to her apartment.

Her toes, on the outside of the little ones, were sore from the breaking-in walks. There was no telling what a jog of two miles would do to them...

She tightened the laces on the right shoe and began to make the loops for the final tie-down when her phone sounded. It was a text message from Clarissa. She picked up the device from the bed and read from the screen.

"Meet you at corner of Lamb and Montclair in 10"

Marcie typed: "Ten it is!"

She smiled slightly, thinking how the evening ritual—running and sweating—was never drudgery when her best friend jogged alongside. They were both in good shape and could carry on at least a cursory conversation while putting in their minutes of what was otherwise—running by herself—akin to torture.

Both women had graduated recently from the university and landed jobs as junior high teachers, although at different schools. She taught seventh-grade English and Clarissa eighth-grade pre-algebra.

She waved a hand with raised eyebrows and an expansive grin when she saw the tall, African-American woman waving back. They met and hugged, their usual greeting.

They called themselves the "Spectrum Sisters"—Marcie, with light-blonde hair and blue eyes, and Clarissa, with brown eyes, black hair, and beautiful, ebony features that landed her modeling jobs from time to time—because they claimed to encompass the entire spectrum of the rainbow.

"Jesus made this day just for you and me," Clarissa said brightly.

"Well, I don't know about that, Clare," Marcie responded. "But, however it was made, I'll take it."

TYPICAL

Anyone else who kept bringing up Jesus and religious talk would be off her friends list in a heartbeat. Marcie was a product of the progressive world of facts, not faith. She believed in change through activism and politics, not through the teachings in some dusty old book. However, she had made exceptions for her beloved friend since they were thirteen. Clarissa's incessant talk of Jesus, salvation, and God's love for her was just something to put up with, and she gladly did. This was her sister in every way possible but biologically, politically…and religiously.

"I want you to go to Heaven, Marcie," Clarissa would often say to her, sometimes with a big smile on her face and other times with a tear trickling from a corner of an eye.

"If there is a Heaven," she would sometimes respond, "I'll make it. I'm a good girl, ain't I?" The faulty English answers from the English teacher made Clarissa laugh. However, Marcie could see the concern deeply pooled in her friend's soulful eyes.

"Shall we race today?" Clarissa said, pumping her long, model's legs up and down as if to challenge her.

"No. I don't feel like beating you again today," Marcie said. "Let's just jog-talk 'til we're all jog-talked out."

"Okay with me, girlfriend," Clarissa said with a laugh. "You know I've got lots to say!"

They both turned to begin their run. Marcie turned her head slightly to speak in Clarissa's direction after striding forward a few steps. What she saw horrified her. Her friend instantaneously disappeared into nothingness. The face disappeared as if her beloved Clarissa had never been there.

Marcie's eyes widened, while in the next instant she looked at her surroundings. She still couldn't comprehend what had happened. No Clarissa!

She tripped while shuffling to turn to look around the area. Her feet were caught up in something. She looked, and then bent down to grasp the cloth her shoes were tangled in. She examined the material at eye level. It looked to be—it was!—Clarissa's running shirt. She looked around the street. Her mouth agape in shock, she retrieved the athletic shorts Clarissa had been wearing. The shoes…they were strewn in the direction they had begun their run. The socks were still streaming out of each shoe.

She picked up every piece of her friend's remaining apparel from the pavement. Lastly, she reached to pinch between her thumb and index finger the tiny gold necklace with the cross pendant Clarissa never took off.

A thought thundered through her remembrance. Clarissa always said the necklace and cross were to remind her of what Jesus did for her…He had died on the cross to save her soul. She also said it was to remind her to tell others about Christ's saving power and His love for all.

The cross, still held together by its clasp, glistened between her fingers while she was remembering. Jesus was coming back one day, Clarissa had always told her. Something about a "Disappearing" of some sort that would happen.

Tears of confusion began to stream down her cheeks. Fear gripped her as she began hearing the sounds of car-honking in the distance. It wasn't just one car, but, by the sound of it, dozens…as if everyone had suddenly run into trees or other immovable objects at the same time. Shock moving through her emotions, she couldn't shake those haunting words echoing in her mind…*Jesus was coming back one day.*

What was the word? she thought. *The vanishing prophesied by the Bible that would one day happen?* Clarissa had been, as she put it, "saved," after reading a series of books. What were they? *Left Behind*. That was the books, a series of stories about people disappearing or something. Clarissa said she had been saved while reading those stories.

Marcie had laughed at her friend for believing that fiction could somehow come to life. Clarissa had said that she didn't believe in the fiction, but in the facts in the Bible.

Clarissa's words were rolling through her mind as she stumbled back toward her apartment.

The tranquility of the early evening was now shattered, she suddenly noticed. Sirens pierced the air while she moved up the steps of her building. She looked at the darkening sky and saw that night would come early this day.

Just then, her neighbor, not much older than herself, burst out of her front door, crying...screaming the words while she ran up to Marcie. "My baby! Somebody has taken my baby!"

One moment, Clarissa had started running with Marcie, and the next, she heard what she thought was a trumpet and a shout. She hadn't even had time to mentally process it before she was flying up through the air as if she had stepped on the head of a rocket taking off.

"Oh, my! This is it!" she shouted. She knew what it was, and felt her body changing instantly, effortlessly, and painlessly. She couldn't explain it, but power surged through her, from her fingertips to her hair. It felt like she was being forged out of a bolt of lightning.

She glanced down the moment she began moving upwards and saw her friend frozen in a midstride jogging step as if time had stopped for her. She glanced in both directions and saw countless others rising upwards as she was. They all looked like lightning bolts shooting up in the direction opposite their normal course. She no longer had time to register that thought, though, before she saw Him. Jesus.

High above her, completely encapsulated in pulsating waves of energy and what she thought resembled a kaleidoscope of unfathomable light, was Jesus, surrounded by thousands of angels. Not only were there lights and colors she didn't even know existed, but she heard a chorus of angelic singing, beautiful music, beyond words. It wasn't like the sound of a church choir, but it was like legions of singers whose voices swam perfectly in harmony, yet, offered different songs simultaneously. Their words were interweaving into a continuous crescendo of praise.

As they were moving towards Him, He was moving towards them. Millions upon millions were ahead of her, already meeting our Lord in the stratosphere, high above the earth's atmosphere. Clarissa held her breath, thinking she may not get oxygen at this height, but then she realized that she didn't need to breathe. Neither did she feel cold, or pressure, or any of the manifestations of the old laws of nature, which would have killed a normal person who wasn't wearing any protective gear.

She glanced back one last time to earth and could, amazingly, still see her friend below. She offered one last prayer for her Marcie, in the hope that she might still be redeemed in the days, weeks, months, and years that followed.

5

THE DISAPPEARING

And therefore, when in the end the Church shall be suddenly caught up from this, it is said, there shall be tribulation such as has not been since the beginning, neither shall be.
—Irenaeus, *Against Heresies*, 5.29, AD 170

The Lord does not come to the world at the time of the Rapture, but only reveals himself to the members of His Body. At the time of his resurrection He was only seen by those who believed on Him. Pilate and the High Priest, and those who crucified Him, did not know that He was risen. So it will be at the time of the Rapture. The world will not know that He has been here, and will have no knowledge of Him until He comes with the members of His Body, at the close of the Tribulation.
—Billy Sunday, The Second Coming of Christ, AD 1913

Within moments of the Rapture of the Church, the world will realize that something has gone terribly wrong. Setting aside the obvious issues at hand like the massive spike in vehicular accidents (automobiles, boats, trains, aircraft, etc.) as drivers and operators disappear, the spiritual void left in the world will have been altered to such a degree that even the spiritually dead will notice it, just as one would notice a sudden change in the weather. For a brief moment in human history (the first, actually), there will be no redeemed people living on the earth.

The world then will be thrust out of the age of men and science into an age of monsters and the supernatural. For nearly two millennia, God the Holy Spirit, acting through the Body of Christ (the Church), was a restraint against evil on the earth. At the Rapture of the Church, He (the Holy Spirit) will set aside this role and return to the one He had during the Old Testament times—empowering select individuals rather than restraining evil at large.

Even the average, unsaved person sitting alone at home in the country far away from the hustle and bustle of the city will know something has changed, like goose bumps that streak across your body when you're walking into a darkened room and you get a feeling that something is there with you. Something in you would sense a change in the nature of reality, as if some great, terrible, evil has been unleashed from the heavens.

Although the specific change will be unknown to the unredeemed, the change is God the Holy Spirit removing His hand of restraint to stop, slow down, or redirect the hordes of demonic legions waiting to move in. Those same demons, who will be shaking their fists as the redeemed go up, will then look down upon the earth with a savage hatred.

It's likely that the immediate, tangible effects of the Rapture will be traffic accidents. Some planes may crash, but the primary mode of travel in the United States is by car, and in an instant, thousands of cars will suddenly be abandoned. Second in the sequence of effects will be that the vehicles not only crash all at the same time, but the pile-ups will also tie up every major highway and freeway in every urban center simultaneously. This will put an immediate strain on all emergency services across the nation.

The next thing people will start to notice is that many of their family members, friends, and coworkers are nowhere to be found. Most "normal" unredeemed people will be trying to figure out what just happened; however, the wicked will sense a moment of great opportunity. Between car crashes and missing-person reports, whoever is left in law enforcement will be overwhelmed to the point that the entire system will fail, giving the wicked the perfect opportunity to commit crimes. Murders, rioting, looting, thefts, and robberies will immediately skyrocket because of all the unattended businesses, unlocked and unoccupied cars, dropped purses and wallets, open and vacated houses, etc. The season of wickedness will have finally arrived.

It won't just be the 100 percent spike in criminal activity that shakes the world; the global disappearances will demolish what people believed to be reality. Religious, academic, media, and pop-cultural skeptics and scoffers, who for years have mocked the Rapture, will now have their *II Pet,* worlds turned upside down. Although Scripture records at least eight *3:* people in the Bible who experienced or will experience this supernatural "catching up" or "catching away" we call the Rapture, the world has never seen an entire generation "disappear." It will challenge the very fabric of reality people thought they understood. This event will be so troubling for those left behind, they will seek any answer, any explanation, and believe anything that helps put their minds at ease. Many will turn to drugs and alcohol for comfort as the bereaved intoxicate themselves to deal with this new reality.

The left-behind leaders will desperately seek answers, as well as military solutions, for the disappearances and for the unrest left in their wake. Presumably, the day will begin as usual, but it will end in various forms of lockdowns and the administration of martial law across the planet. The average person will turn to the media and local elected officials for answers about why so many of their family members, friends, and neighbors are suddenly gone.

The media will play a key role in propagating the numerous myths and wild speculations that will circulate in the aftermath of the Rapture. In fact, the media will be significant in perpetuating the anxiety that prompts the public to act with the herd mentality, causing widespread panic and producing much greater damage to an already-fragile society.

The bankers, politicians, technocrats, and power brokers—who will have for decades been planning for globalized government with initiatives like UN Agenda 2020 and 2030, the Green New Deal, etc.—will be handed their perfect crisis, if they can get ahead of it. This is why the 2020 COVID-19 pandemic has been such a gift to them—a trial run, so to speak. Not only that, but many experts believe the process of digitalization was sped up by nearly six years because of the global lockdowns. In other words, it might have taken the world another six years to get to where we are today being online if COVID-19 had not happened. However, with as much globalization preparation as these one-world-order types have already done, the suddenness of the Rapture itself will still catch them off-guard.

The economic markets, for instance, will feel the crash almost instantly as scared investors began a frenzied selling to cash out of the market as quickly as possible. Some of the first ones to exit will make it; however, the majority of investors will be caught unawares and will suffer significant losses. The losses will then eclipse the Wall Street crash of 1929, the 1970s energy crisis, 1987's Black Monday, and the subprime mortgage crisis of 2007–08. This is why the push to ditch the US dollar as of late has been put into high gear through the COVID-19 restrictions and the repeated economic stimulus packages.

In summary, the Rapture will go down in the annals of history as just a day of global confusion. Not only will the world be suffering from countless crashes, collisions, abandoned vehicles, unpiloted planes, and unmanned boats, but the ensuing financial crisis will be the death knell for all fiat currencies and national autonomy. Like nothing else has, this will force the world into creating regional digital currencies or into establishing a single global, digital currency. Those who have money will seek to pull out of the markets or convert early, while many others will go underground and disengage from a world in chaos. Aside from the numerous physical calamities simultaneously facing the world, the greatest economic impact will come from the loss of human capital (wage earners, spenders, sellers, and professionals of every stripe).

However, the most catastrophic overall loss from this day will be the disappearance of the children, a subject we'll look at closely in the next chapter.

This day of chaos will also trigger a mass exodus from urban areas. Those who don't have money (or means) will look at the pandemonium as an opportunity to riot and loot, burn and pillage, and exact revenge (e.g., anarchists) on modern society. Any restraint people had before in the old order of things will be stripped away. The government will not have answers, nor will the apostate church (the church left behind). The religious who are left behind will not be able to admit it was the Rapture, because that would invalidate everything they will have taught and believed in the years leading up to it. Yet, even without answers, they will offer conjecture as to what happened, concocting explanations based on anything and everything except what actually happened.

That day will be a lost cause to the world. We would also venture to say that the Rapture (at least for the United States) will happen during the daytime. The reason for this is if Bible prophecy centers its direction (nautical direction of events) based on Jerusalem, we think that this would apply to time as well. New York City is seven hours behind Jerusalem, thus, if this were to happen at midnight in Jerusalem (Matthew 25:1–6), it would be 5:00 p.m. in New York City…right in the middle of evening rush-hour traffic.

6 AM ISRAEL (DAYBREAK JEWISH)
1 PM NYC (EST)
~9 AM CAL (PRIOR DAY)

NATALIE RICHARDSON, NEWS ANCHOR

CHANNEL 12 NEWS, NEW YORK CITY

LIVE BROADCAST A FEW MINUTES AFTER THE RAPTURE (Eastern Standard Time):

We are getting numerous reports of vehicular crashes all around the city. Paul, can you confirm the… (puts her finger to her earpiece) …we are getting breaking news that LaGuardia has just had an airliner crash shortly after takeoff. We aren't… (finger back to her earpiece) …more breaking news, this isn't just happening in New York City, but it appears to be some kind of national phenomenon, occurring across numerous cities in the US. Standby— we're getting incoming reports by the second of what appears to be a massive breakdown in both air and ground transportation. Let's go to Jenna Johnson, who is reporting live at LaGuardia. Jenna, what are you seeing on the ground there?

The camera switches to the live feed from LaGuardia, with Jenna Johnson narrating the carnage behind her.

"Paul, what is going on?" Natalie Richardson asked her afternoon co-anchor as she sank back into her chair at the anchor desk. "Is this another terrorist attack? I can't handle another 9/11."

"I don't know, but this might be the story that puts us at the top of the ratings," Paul said from his seat beside her, rubbing his hands callously.

"I get that. But first, I'd like to wrap my mind around what's actually happening so I don't look like an idiot on live television," she replied, then sat up a little taller in her chair and positioned her gaze toward the camera. "Game face! Jenna is wrapping up her segment."

An in-station news courier ran up and handed her some papers just as the broadcast was switching back to Natalie and Paul again.

"It looks like," Natalie said, speed-reading the note, "it looks like this is happening everywhere. Massive spike in traffic accidents, both air and ground, and it appears to be happening around the globe simultaneously. Paul, what are you hearing?"

"My sources from LA, Miami, and London are all reporting the same thing," Paul said. "London is experiencing crashes, but not to the same extent we are here. No one really knows for sure. Maybe some kind of virus or terrorist attack."

"Viewers out there, we aren't quite sure what's happening, but the minute we find out, we will report it to you here first, on channel 12."

"Cut!"

As the channel turned away to its regularly scheduled commercial broadcasting, the newsroom was buzzing with activity. Not a single person was sitting down. The media manager came in and began barking directions and assigning whole sections of rooms to particular subjects.

"You guys will be Team A," he said, pointing to one section of the media office. "You're no longer covering weather; this is your top priority. Dig up everything you can from whatever source you can NOW! Whatever you get, bring it to me and let's get it on the news. We can fact-check it later."

He turned to another area of the room. "You all will be Team B. I want you to hit this from the religious and extraterrestrial angle. Is this an alien attack? Is this the Second Coming? I don't know. You find out and get it back to me ASAP."

He turned to the remaining section of people at desks. "You all are Team C, and I want leadership reaction to this—everyone from the governor, the president, and other world leaders. Make it happen, people!"

Natalie was at the broadcast desk texting her husband back home: "Are you there? Is Mika all right? What is going on?"

Before she knew it, the in-studio lights indicated they had thirty seconds left before going back live.

She glanced back at her phone's screen. Nothing.

What's going on? she thought anxiously. She glanced over to the media manager, who was furiously sorting through stacks of papers.

"What do we have folks?" she shouted over to them. The manager had his back to her, but waved in the air as if to say, "Hold on."

"Okay, we are live in 10, 9, 8, 7, 6, 5, 4..." then he silently signaled the 3, 2, 1.

"Welcome back to Channel 12 news at the top of the hour; we are getting breaking news of a mass shooting on Main Street near Riverside. Preliminary reports say that a person, or persons, has opened fire inside a grocery store. Early reports put the death toll at twenty-six dead, and twice as many wounded. However, due to the numerous accidents already in progress, local law enforcement and emergency services are not able to respond at this time. Please, if you are listening to this broadcast, please avoid this area.

"More breaking news. We are getting reports of at least a half-dozen fires in downtown due to rioting. Again, fire and rescue units are having a difficult time responding due to the congested roadways. The mayor is urging citizens to assist in putting these out if possible. To repeat: fire and rescue may be delayed up to twelve hours before being able to respond.

"We are being inundated with calls from viewers that their children and babies are missing. We cannot confirm this, but in just the last ten minutes, we have received over ninety calls asking us to publish pictures of their missing children. We will get these on the air as soon as possible, but please direct your calls to local law enforcement as we are being overwhelmed with information at present.

"This just in, the president is set to make a national announcement in thirty minutes. He is urging Americans to stay calm and stay home. It appears as if he is about to announce a nationwide state of martial law. Stay tuned for more breaking news after this."

6

CHILDREN AND THE RAPTURE

That stunning split second when the disappearance of millions takes place will have ramifications beyond all we can anticipate. However, one aspect of that vanishing will doubtless stagger the world as perhaps no calamity that has struck planet earth since the Flood of Noah's day. No small children will remain on earth. This will produce fear and agony the likes of which will make other disasters seem like non-events. *CHILDREN DIED IN NOAH'S FLOOD, EVEN INFANTS*

We believe that all children will be raptured—that is, all children who have not come to the age of accountability. We will look at that more in-depth in this chapter a bit later. Most always the confutation over the issue of children and the Rapture of the church is wrapped around the following Scripture:

> For the unbelieving husband is sanctified by the wife, and the unbelieving wife is sanctified by the husband: else were your children unclean; but now are they holy. (1 Corinthians 7:14)

THE CHARACTER OF GOD

The very character of God, Himself, is at the heart of the issues involved in the often-raised question about children and the Rapture: whether they will stay on earth or go to be with Christ.

And, there is nothing of more profound eternal significance than the individual human being's consideration of God's character. The importance of that consideration is cocooned within the words of Jesus Christ, Himself, at the center of whom God's great character is made manifest for fallen mankind.

> When Jesus came into the coasts of Caesarea Philippi, he asked his disciples, saying, whom do men say that I the Son of man am? And they said, some say that thou art John the Baptist: some, Elias; and others, Jeremias, or one of the prophets. (Matthew 16:13–14)

Jesus' question was straight from the heart of God. He was God who came to the earth in the flesh. Therefore, He, of course, knew what the people were saying about Him. He wanted His disciples to consider the question through spiritual eyes and ears, regarding themselves, individually. His follow-up question was plain and direct: "Whom say ye that I am?" (Matthew 16:15).

The totality of Scripture before and after Jesus asked that question encapsulates—attests to—the holy, loving, merciful character of mankind's Creator. His inquiry is directed not to corporate mankind, but to everyone who has lived upon earth since He asked it. The answer each of us gives will determine our position in Jesus Christ and where we will spend eternity. And, make no mistake, each person who ever lives—and that means from conception onward—will spend eternity in one of two places: Hell or Heaven.

The creation of mankind and the fall from innocence is a matter for another study. Suffice it to say that a quick perusal of any news story will attest to our fallen state. We human beings do not walk a perfect walk. We sin and come short of the glory of God (Romans 3:23). The fact is

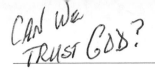

that we need redemption—we must have reconciliation with God or we remain lost forever. And, keep in mind that the matter isn't based on a corporate or collective relationship, but on an *individual* relationship with God. This is where the awesome, loving grace—the very character of the Lord—comes into view. God's Word says:

> The Lord is not slack concerning His promise, as some men count slackness; but is longsuffering to us-ward, not willing that any should perish, but that all should come to repentance. (2 Peter 3:9).

We need God's grace gift of salvation. Each of us must repent for the sin into which we were born. God's holiness requires blood sacrifice for remission of sin (Hebrews 9:22; 10:18). This is why God, Himself, in the form of His Son Jesus Christ—the Lamb slain from the foundation of the world—came to die on the cross at Calvary:

> For God so loved the world, that he gave his only begotten Son, that whosoever believeth in him should not perish, but have everlasting life. (John 3:16)

About each of us, God's Word says further:

> He that believeth on him is not condemned: but he that believeth not is condemned already, because he hath not believed in the name of the only begotten Son of God. (John. 3:18)

Remember this verse; it is profoundly important when looking at the matter of children and the Rapture of the Church.

BELIEF ESSENTIAL

We are born into sin because the first man (Adam) disobeyed, or rebelled, against his Creator. The human bloodline has been, since that time,

NOAH'S DAY BY FALLEN ANGELS

polluted—contaminated. Because of the fall, disease, deterioration, decay, and death entered the world. God has provided a way for humans to reconcile with Himself—redemption, through the blood sacrifice of His Holy, Perfect, Sacrificial Lamb, Jesus Christ, on the cross at Calvary (read John 14:6). Now, all can be saved through belief in Jesus as the only Way back to God the Creator.

This belief is the sort of faith Jesus spoke to Thomas about, when the disciple doubted that Jesus had been raised to life after the crucifixion. When Thomas saw Jesus stand among the disciples, the Lord, having passed through solid matter to be with them, bid Thomas to touch His wounds. Thomas believed, and could but only mutter, "My Lord, and My God!"

Jesus then said:

> Thomas, because thou hast seen me, thou hast believed: blessed are they that have not seen, and yet have believed. (John 20:29)

With that statement, Jesus was looking not only at the disciples who were in that room, but down through time to all who would believe in His death, burial, and resurrection for salvation. So, again, belief is absolutely essential—the kind of belief that saves in order to be "born again" (John 3:3) into God's eternal family.

The Apostle Paul gave the precise formula required by God for the salvation of the individual soul:

> That if thou shalt confess with thy mouth the Lord Jesus, and shalt believe in thine heart that God hath raised him from the dead, thou shalt be saved. For with the heart man believeth unto righteousness; and with the mouth confession is made unto salvation. (Romans 10:9–10)

When we are saved, God no longer looks at us as fallen, as rebellious, or as a sinner, but He looks at each of us through the prism of the shed blood of His Precious Son. About that, God's Word says:

There is therefore now no condemnation to them which are in Christ
Jesus, who walk not after the flesh, but after the Spirit. (Romans 8:1)

He that believeth on him is not condemned: but he that believeth
not is condemned already, because he hath not believed in the
name of the only begotten Son of God. (John 3:18)

It is obvious beyond any rationale to the contrary that this sort of
belief—the kind that brings us into the very family of God for all of eternity—must require understanding that Jesus is ONLY way.

POSITION IN JESUS CHRIST

God's Word says without reservation that life begins at conception. We
will not argue the point. That truth becomes more than obvious when
studying records of children in the womb. Two examples are Jacob and his
twin brother, Esau, struggling within the womb of their mother. Another
is the account of John, who would become the baptizer, who recognized
the Messiah, Jesus, who was in His mother's womb when the two women
were in the same proximity. Children in the womb are living beings with
God-given souls.

These babies have certain abilities to think, and, in John's case, he had
a supernatural understanding about the fact he and his mother were in the
presence of God, Himself, who had come to earth in the flesh. However,
it is a fact understood by anyone with common sense that children in the
womb or in the first, formative years of life are incapable of understanding
anything like deciding where their souls will spend eternity. These little
ones are sinners every bit as much as any adult human being. The difference is that adults—presuming they don't have severe mental incapaci-
tation—can understand and make decisions about things like whether
to accept Christ for salvation. They are therefore "accountable" for their
belief or lack thereof. Children, whose reasoning powers haven't devel-
oped, are not yet "accountable" for that decision.

NOAH's FLOOD KIDS

Adults whom the Holy Spirit has called to salvation through Jesus Christ are accountable for their own soul at the point at which they accept or reject His invitation to follow Him. Children are not called to salvation because they haven't, at that point, achieved through growth the cognitive ability to make such decisions. They are not accountable. Children who haven't reached the age of accountability have a position in Jesus Christ, the same as adults who have believed for salvation. If children die before becoming responsible for their own decision to accept or reject Christ, they go directly into the presence of God, for all eternity.

God Knows His

Remember King David. He took off his robes of mourning for his baby when the son died, because David said that the baby couldn't come to him, but that he, David, would go to the child. The baby was in Heaven with God, for all of eternity, where the king would surely go upon his death. We know this is where David would go, because God called him "a man after my own heart."

So, the position we as individuals (not collectively) have in Jesus Christ is the all-important matter in considering where we will spend eternity. All children before they reach the age of accountability are positioned securely in the Lord Jesus Christ, whose shed blood is the only remission for the soul-destroying thing called sin.

RAPTURE: A SALVATION ISSUE

The Rapture of the Church is a salvation issue. These realities—the Rapture and salvation—are inexorably linked in God's great economy. This truth is based upon a vast body of scriptural proof text, but is wrapped up by the Apostle Paul in one particular passage of Scripture:

> For God hath not appointed us to wrath, but to obtain salvation by our Lord Jesus Christ. (1 Thessalonians 5:9)

Paul had just gone through the facts surrounding the Rapture of believers. He used the personal pronouns "we," "us," "our," etc., as opposed to the third-person words such as "they" and "them" to separate believers from unbelievers. Believers (Christians of the Church Age) were not, Paul said, appointed to wrath, because they were children of the day (the light found in Christ). The unbelievers were children of the night—the sin-blackened darkness of the fallen realm. Paul prophesied that the Day of the Lord will begin like a thief-in-the-night experience. The children of the night would be taken by surprise, but the children of the day (believers) would escape the coming wrath of God, which the Day of the Lord will bring upon a rebellious world of earth-dwellers.

This escape from God's wrath will come, Paul said, through salvation, which is in Christ Jesus. The individual's position in Christ will provide the escape. This is the same escape foretold by Jesus—through John—in Revelation 3:10:

> Because thou hast kept the word of my patience, I also will keep thee from the hour of temptation, which shall come upon all the world, to try them that dwell upon the earth. (Revelation 3:10)

Children below the age of accountability are within Christ's salvation ark of soul-safety—the salvation that keeps believers out of Hell—out of the time of God's wrath, which will come upon the whole world of unbelievers.

Again, children, like all of lost mankind, are sinners, but those who haven't reached the age of being able to understand God's grace gift are not unbelievers. The blood of Jesus Christ covers them. Their names are, individually, written in the Lamb's Book of Life.

LAMB'S BOOK OF LIFE

Let's look for a moment at this all-important volume called the Lamb's Book of Life. Here are two relevant Scripture passages about it.

He that overcometh, the same shall be clothed in white raiment; and I will not blot out his name out of the book of life, but I will confess his name before my Father, and before his angels. (Revelation 3:5)

And there shall in no wise enter into it anything that defileth, neither [whatsoever] worketh abomination, or [maketh] a lie: but they which are written in the Lamb's book of life. (Revelation 21:27)

God's Word is telling us here that there is a volume in which every human being's name is written at some point. No one whose name isn't written in this book can enter God's holy presence for eternity. The word "Life" in the book's title refers to eternal life. Everyone who has been conceived in the procreation process has his or her name written in the Lamb's Book of Life, but, there is obviously the chance that one's name can be blotted out of, according to Revelation 3:5. Since it isn't possible to lose one's salvation once a person has believed in the only begotten Son of God, the term "blot out" in Revelation 3:5 needs to be explained. The meaning becomes clear, when thinking on the fact that each and every individual's name is written in the Lamb's Book of Life.

The name remains there until the person is shown that he or she is a sinner, and is convicted or called by the Holy Spirit to repent of sin and believe in the Lord Jesus Christ. When the person fully realizes that call, but refuses or rejects God's grace gift offer, that name is "blotted out" of the Lamb's Book of Life. The individual who rejects that offer of salvation until his or her death will die in sin and spend eternity apart from the Creator. That person who has reached the age of accountability for his or her soul will also be left behind when the Rapture occurs.

The name will be written back in that book when the person subsequently accepts the Lord Jesus as the Savior. Jesus Christ's shed blood is the only payment God the Father accepts. But, once a person accepts that free gift from the Lord Jesus, he or she is a member of God's family forever.

So, our position in Christ is the all-important thing, whether considering going to Heaven when we die or at the Rapture, when Jesus comes to take us to our home that He, personally, has prepared (read John 14:1–4). This is the only family gathering that counts in God's economy, in consideration of the matter of the Rapture and salvation. Here on earth, our relationship with our parents is tremendously important, of course. But, it is our place in our heavenly family and in our heavenly home that is absolutely crucial. This is an eternal matter. And, it all relies upon our position in Jesus Christ, not upon our position in our earthly home, or upon the spiritual condition of our parents.

YES, BUT WHAT ABOUT THIS?

A number of questions about the Rapture and children crop up consistently. We thought it good to look at a couple of them.

Q. Why do you believe children will be taken in the Rapture, when God hasn't intervened for them in wars and in other horrible events and circumstances that have happened to the children throughout the centuries? Why do you think God will keep them out of the Tribulation, when millions have already died, and continue to die?

A. These are two different matters entirely. This question involves physical death versus spiritual death (the "second death," as the Scripture puts it.) It is the death of the flesh versus the death of the soul. Sin brought death to the flesh and to the soul (physical and spiritual death), but Christ brings eternal life. That's what we've spent the bulk of this chapter addressing. Wars and other terrible happenings on earth indeed take physical life—especially, it seems, the lives of innocent children.

Unrepented-of sin takes the soul in death (resulting in, of course, eternal separation from God). It is comforting to know that all children who have perished over the millennia have gone directly to be with the Lord. Not one single child has died in the eternal sense. Again, these are two separate issues: physical death versus spiritual death. The Rapture is in the realm of the spiritual or the eternal sphere.

Q. But, won't there be children in the Tribulation? Jesus says so in His Olivet Discourse.

A. Yes, the Lord does prophesy that there will be children during the time of Tribulation. He foretells the following: "And woe unto them that are with child, and to them that give suck in those days!" (Matthew 24:19). Notice carefully: Jesus issues a special "woe" for the parents of children in the time of Tribulation. But, He specifically gives two ages of children here: 1) children who are nursing, and 2) children still in the womb. There is absolutely no mention of older children.

These children will be those born AFTER the Rapture. And, there will doubtless be millions upon millions born. Sexual debauchery will explode as the Holy Spirit withdraws from governing the consciences of men and women (read 2 Thessalonians 2). No doubt, most of these little ones will perish in the horrors of that time. As many as two-thirds of all mankind will die during that period.

Not fair of God, you say? Consider this: Every single child who is born after the Rapture will spend eternity with God the Father. None will have reached the age of accountability by the time Jesus Christ brings this decaying, dying world to an end as recorded in Revelation 19:11. For those who are thinking ahead of us, we realize that children who go into the Millennium under the age of accountability will have to make the decision to accept Christ for salvation at some point.

As stated in the beginning of the chapter, God's very character is at stake in the matter of whether ALL children (below the age of accountability) will go to be with Jesus at the electrifying moment of Rapture. What, exactly, is wrapped up in 1 Corinthians 7:14 is a matter for another study. But, this much the overall context of God's Word—when speaking to salvation matters—plainly and loudly proclaims. The Bible teaches that the individual's position in Christ, not his or her position in the physical family here on earth, determines the final disposition of the eternal soul. The Rapture is an eternal matter wrapped up in God's salvation guarantee. And, it is a guarantee to the individual, not to the corporate, even though the collective will go as the Bride of Christ, the Church.

Every child below the age of accountability—including those in the womb—will go to be with Jesus when He steps out on the clouds of glory and shouts: "Come up here!"

CLARISSA WAS STANDING WITH COUNTLESS OTHERS ON WHAT appeared to be a sea of glass mingled with fire. She couldn't explain it any other way. Since being caught up, she was being exposed to a level of reality that she had previously believed existed—but to see it now in all its spectacular glory was another matter altogether.

Even though she felt like she was miles back, she could see the throne just as clearly as if she were sitting on the front row. Seeing Christ in His glorified state was breathtaking. Wearing a brilliant white garment that cascaded down to His feet, He wore a finely woven golden band around His chest. He sat on His throne projecting a sense of majesty. His head and hair were white as snow. His piercing eyes were like flames. Although His overall countenance was like the sun, He still bore the marks of His crucifixion clearly on His hands and feet. In this state, He appeared both like the slain Lamb of God, but also like the Lion of the Tribe of Judah.

Clarissa knew that if she were in her natural, mortal body, she would not have been able to gaze upon Him. She was in her glorified state, and thus, could stand to be in His presence without keeling over.

Then He spoke. His voice echoed through the heavens like the sound of many waters.

At that sound, every knee bowed. Ten million upon ten million shouted in perfect unison, "Jesus Christ is Lord!"

The Bema Judgment was about to begin.

Clarissa thought back to that morning many years ago to the article she had read her parents about this very moment. She knew she wasn't being judged for all the wrong things she did in her life, because she had already traded all her sin for Christ's righteousness—even the sins she committed after she became a Christian.

Rather, she, like all other born-again believers, was going to be judged on what she did with her salvation, what she did with all the gifts God gave her. Her works (what she did for Christ or in the name of Christ) would be tested by fire. She used to struggle with that "testing by fire" meant, exactly.

But, after becoming an adult and watching certain ministers and ministries who either just focused on money, or worldly riches, or began leading people astray with faulty teachings, she began to understand why God does this. God's judgment was to begin with His church. These kinds of ministries, like wood, hay, and stubble, would be burnt up.

Others, whose works were done with the right intentions, would go through the fire as would gold, silver, and precious stones. The fire would not burn up their work, but rather, would refine it.

As Clarissa saw each person kneeling before Christ, she saw that their life's work for the Lord was shown instantaneously. The sum of each act, thought, deed, and word, was balanced against what the Lord required in that instance, to what was carried out. The fire was the ultimate purge/purifier of each event.

Many, walked away empty handed—still saved, yet without rewards, crowns, to cast at the feet of the Lord. Many others, however, received rewards, and they eagerly and gladly cast these crowns back to the Lord of lords as tribute.

The event, while it would have taken decades on the earth to carry out, was done efficiently and effortlessly in the eternal realm. Jesus, took the time to address each individual, both in love and in earnestness, regarding what they could have had, had they followed His plan for their lives. It was a somber and yet joyous event, certainly, one Clarissa had long feared—not for fear of Jesus, but out of concern that she had not done enough for the Lord.

Then she heard her name.

Therefore we make it our aim, whether present or absent, to be well pleasing to Him. For we must all appear before the judgment seat of Christ, that each one may receive the things done in the body, according to what he has done, whether good or bad. Knowing, therefore, the terror of the Lord, we persuade men; but we are well known to God, and I also trust are well known in your consciences. (2 Corinthians 5:9–11)

Meanwhile, back on the earth…

Marcie rolled over on her side in the makeshift bed. She could make out a pinprick of light coming through a vent, which was proof enough she had made it through the night.

She lay there a few more minutes to let the fog clear from her sleepy mind. She thought back to the day it happened—jogging with Clarissa, and then, her just vanishing right before her eyes.

Even though it had only been a couple of days, it felt like ancient history, way back in time when everything sort of made sense.

Now everything was chaos.

After the Disappearing (that is what they were calling it now), the rest of the day was a blur. Sirens, car alarms, fires, smoke, people running around acting crazy. Missing babies and children. The news was all over the place on what they thought had happened, which didn't help calm anyone's nerves. At first, they were trying to tell people that it was aliens, but no one reported any UFOs or spaceships, so that rather fell flat. Next, they were trying to say it was Mother Nature cleansing the planet, but again, if that were true, why leave all the maniacs, murderers, criminals, etc.?

She did not need the media to tell her what happened; Clarissa already had. It was the Rapture. The very thing she had laughed at her friend for all those years had just so happened right before her very eyes.

Now she was sleeping in the attic of her parents' house in the country. She didn't know where to go to after the disappearance, but she knew her apartment in the city was just too dangerous. There had been three shootings and two stabbings on her street, despite that she lived in what she thought was the "good" part of town. She shuddered to think of what the rest of the city was going through. She had tried calling her parents ahead of time, but cell service was intermittent, and when her call did go through, they weren't answering. So she came out here to check on them. Maybe that was just the excuse she needed to go home after all these years.

Her parents had divorced in her junior high years. Then, in her first year of college, they had gotten back together and became all religious, like Clarissa. Supposedly they had "found Jesus" and tried to make their marriage work once again.

Marcie supposed they were wherever Clarissa had gone. If that was true, then she truly was alone in a world that had decided to dive headfirst into the deep end.

She lifted up from the mass of blankets and pillows, and wondered how many mice and spiders were up here with her. She did not trust sleeping alone in her parent's big house, not after what she had seen. Thankfully, Rocky, her parent's dog, was still here and curled up near her feet. He cast a concerned eye her way.

She didn't know if dogs knew what was going on, but he had seemed pretty shaken up by the time she arrived. She supposed they did; animals can usually sense things like earthquakes and storms long before humans can.

But even she knew a storm was coming, and they were just about to enter it.

7

MIND THE GAP

For you know perfectly that the day of the Lord so comes as a thief in the night. For when they say, "Peace and safety!" then sudden destruction comes upon them, as labor pains upon a pregnant woman. And they shall not escape. (1 Thessalonians 5:2–3)

Although Scripture has foretold of the times we live in, you could say that the time from the Rapture until the start of the Seventieth Week is intentionally unscripted. In other words, the outline is there, but the details are still somewhat mysterious. Keep in mind, however, that though they might be a mystery to us, they're not to God. Nevertheless, we thought we should ask why are they a mystery at all.

> **After these things** I looked, and behold, a door standing open in heaven. And the first voice which I heard was like a trumpet speaking with me, saying, "Come up here, and I will show you things which must take place after this."
>
> Immediately I was in the Spirit; and behold, a throne set in heaven, and One sat on the throne. (Revelation 4:1–2, emphasis added)

"After these things" is a three-word phrase that is jam-packed with underlying meaning. Comparatively, it's just as pregnant with context as the passage in Galatians 4:4, which states "But when the **fullness of the time** had come" (emphasis added). The passage Paul wrote to the Galatians is referring to all the geopolitical and prophetic events that had to have taken place for Christ to come to the earth the first time as a man through the virgin Mary.

The "fullness of time" meant that all of what was given to the prophet Daniel had to have taken place. This included but was not limited to: the rise and fall of three kingdoms (Babylon, Persia, and Greece), the rise of the fourth (Rome), the regathering of the Jews back in their homeland, and the rebuilding of the Second Jewish Temple since the Babylonians destroyed Solomon's Temple. However, to have a rebuilt Jewish Temple meant the Jews would have had to be securely back in their land. Thus we see the first repatriation under the Medo-Persian King Cyrus, and later, under the Persian King Artaxerxes II. From a military, economic, and political standpoint, that was a considerable list of things to occur in just five short centuries.

However, back to the passage at hand. So what is this "after these things" referring to? Revelation chapters 1–3 are all about John's vision—i.e., the glorified Christ's revelation to him, and Jesus' seven letters to the seven churches. Jesus tells John that he was chosen to be the messenger to all he was about to witness and that he would be tasked with ensuring its distribution to all the churches (the chain of custody).

Now we get back to the crux of the issue. The last letter of the seven churches Jesus spoke to was to the church at Laodicea. Jesus stated they were lukewarm and offensive to Him, even though they believed they were wealthy and in need of nothing. Jesus offers nothing positive to say to this church, only condemnation. He concludes with His cursory remarks about "he that hath an ear let him hear what the Spirit says to the churches."

Then, immediately (remember, there weren't chapter or verse breaks in the original text), we jump to the scene where John sees a door standing open in Heaven, and then hears a voice like a trumpet, saying, "Come up here, and I will show you things which must take place after this."

Since there were hundreds to thousands of churches existing in AD 95 as well as larger and more predominant congregations, the seven churches were chosen to convey the totality of churches for all time. The number seven represents the concept of completeness throughout Scripture. Furthermore, the order in which these seven churches are arranged also speaks to the sequential nature of how the church would progress through time.

Paul also wrote to seven churches (Thessalonians, Corinthians, Galatians, Philippians, Ephesians, Colossians, and Romans), and Jesus had the seven Kingdom parables in Matthew 13. Interestingly, all three (the seven letters in Revelation, Paul's letters, and the Kingdom parables) perfectly overlay each other in a complementary fashion. Thus, let us conclude with confidence that the "after these things" is referring to what John saw (resurrected and glorified Christ) and to the totality of the Church Age.

The Rapture always reminded us of the *Tortoise and the Hare* parable in *Aesop's Fables,* in which the swift rabbit loses the race to the sluggish tortoise. He loses because he thinks he has lost track of time.

A Hare was making fun of the Tortoise one day for being so slow.

"Do you ever get anywhere?" he asked with a mocking laugh.

"Yes," replied the Tortoise, "and I get there sooner than you think. I'll run you a race and prove it."

The Hare was much amused at the idea of running a race with the Tortoise, but for the fun of the thing he agreed. So the Fox, who had consented to act as judge, marked the distance and started the runners off.

The Hare was soon far out of sight, and to make the Tortoise feel very deeply how ridiculous it was for him to try a race with a Hare, he lay down beside the course to take a nap until the Tortoise should catch up.

The Tortoise meanwhile kept going slowly but steadily, and, after a time, passed the place where the Hare was sleeping. But the Hare slept on very peacefully; and when at last he did wake up, the Tortoise was near the goal. The Hare now ran his swiftest, but he could not overtake the Tortoise in time.[12]

The vast expanse of twenty centuries has lulled the world to sleep, thinking the end of all things is never going to arrive. But as men have slept, time has kept ticking away, goose-stepping the world ever closer to its divine date with destiny. Nevertheless, by the beginning of the nineteenth century, many within the church were beginning to recognize the lateness of the hour. From the embers of the First Great Awakening came the dispensationalist movement, which would begin to wake the church from its millennia-long slumber.

Although the principles of dispensationalism were not new (even in the early nineteenth century), what was new were men like John N. Darby and Cyrus I. Scofield beginning to return to teaching from a literal, grammatical, and historical understanding of God's Word. When they did this (often to the dismay of their local, established Protestant churches), they realized how close humanity really was to the end. It led to the inescapable conclusion that Israel must return to its ancient homeland. Even non-dispensationalists such as Charles Spurgeon recognized that Israel must return to its homeland before the Lord will return.

On September 18, 1876, Spurgeon presented to the Metropolitan Tabernacle congregation this overview of eschatological events:

I am no prophet, nor the son of a prophet; neither do I profess to be able to explain all the prophecies in this blessed Book. I believe that many of them will only be explained as the events occur which they foretell. Yet there are some things which are plain even to the most superficial reader.

It is plain, for instance, that it is certainly foretold that the power of Antichrist shall be utterly and eternally destroyed, and

that Babylon, that is to say, the Papal system, with all its abominations, shall be cast like a millstone into the flood, to rise no more
forever. It is also certain that the Jews, as a people, will yet own
Jesus of Nazareth, the Son of David, as their King, and that they
will return to their own land, "and they shall build the old wastes,
they shall raise up the former desolations, and they shall repair the
old cities, the desolations of many generations."

It is certain also that our Lord Jesus Christ will come again to
this earth, and that he will reign amongst his ancients gloriously,
and that there will be a thousand years of joy and peace such as were
never known on this earth before. It is also certain that there will
be a great and general judgment, when all nations shall be gathered
before the Son of man sitting upon the throne of his glory; and his
final award concerning those upon his left hand will be, "These
shall go away into everlasting punishment;" and concerning those
upon his right hand, "but the righteous into eternal life." How all
these great events are to be chronologically arranged, I cannot tell.[13]

Thus, many dispensational and evangelical theologians began declar-
ing, decades before it happened, that Israel would return as a nation—and
they were right. As impossible as that seemed, in the nineteenth and early
twentieth centuries, they argued that Israel's return to the international
stage would be the super sign of the end. And it is.

The twentieth century arrived, and it did not disappoint. The First
World War (1914–1918) wrenched the rest of the land of Israel out of the
hands of a dying Ottoman Empire. Even by 1916, the British and French
had begun drawing up plans for how to divide the expansive Ottoman
Empire with legal documents like the Balfour Declaration. While later
backtracking on the original size of the deed this future Jewish state would
receive, the Jews began making their way back to their homeland between
1918 and 1939.

The British betrayal began incrementally though the San Remo Conference (1920), which offered up some of the original land given by the

Balfour Declaration to create the new nation of Trans-Jordan. Although Winston Churchill was pro-Zionist, he was caught in a bind trying to keep the peace between England, France, and the Arabs by arranging a deal that made everyone happy. Nevertheless, Jewish repatriation back to the Holy Land (Aliyah) after nearly eighteen centuries began fulfilling the old prophecies as described in Deuteronomy 30, Isaiah 11, Ezekiel 36–37, and Amos 9.

Year	Jewish Population	Arab Population
1922	84,000	590,000
1931	174,000	760,000
1933	450,000	900,000[14]

In 1929, there was a change in the British Administration, which had no ties to Balfour nor any sympathies to the Zionist movement. In fact, they began allying themselves with the Arabs for the precious oil that lay beneath the nation's desert sands. At that time, oil was just becoming a valuable commodity due to the rapid development in automobiles, planes, and military equipment.

By 1939, the infamous "British White Paper" appeared. To avoid upsetting the Arabs and partitioning Palestine, the British government, now led by new Prime Minister Neville Chamberlain (1937–39), compromised the Balfour Declaration once again. The White Paper of 1939 became the official British policy for the Holy Land. Its provisions included denial of the partition plan, denial of a Jewish state, prohibition on the sale of land to Jews, and a limitation on Jewish immigration to fifteen thousand people each year for five years. After that, it would cease altogether!

With such a blatant reversal of the Balfour Declaration, it was no wonder that the Jews felt betrayed. David Ben-Gurion aptly declared that *asking the Jews to stop their immigration into Palestine would be like asking a woman in labor to stop giving birth.* The Arabs demanded that Jewish immigration cease, and the British caved. For the new Chamberlain administration, the Balfour Declaration had served its time. However,

Chamberlain's consistent and disastrous policy of "appeasement" soon led to his own resignation. Within six months of the White Paper's release, Britain was involved in World War II. Churchill's criticism expressed his own country's betrayal:

> This pledge of a home of refugees, of an asylum, was not made to the Jews of Palestine, but to the Jews outside Palestine, to that vast, unhappy mass of scattered, persecuted, wandering Jews whose intense, unchanging, unconquerable desire has been for a National Home... That is the pledge which was given, and that is the pledge which we are now asked to break.... This is the abandonment of the Balfour Declaration; this is the end of the vision, of the hope, of the dream. [15]
>
> But he was wrong. It was not the end of the dream. That dream survived, but for the coming years, it would be interrupted by the nightmare of the Third Reich.

What World War I did for the physical, geographical restoration of the land of Israel, World War II did for its people. So vile and vicious was the German Nazi hatred for the Jewish people that it resulted in what they deemed the "Final Solution." The Final Solution was the official, legal, plan the Nazis (under Adolf Hitler) dreamed up to finally rid all of Europe from what they called the "Jewish problem."

They first began ostracizing, targeting, boycotting, and attacking Jews (primarily in Germany). They then began to arrest and confiscate their wealth. The Jews they arrested were either killed or deported to these prison camps. However, their efforts were not "efficient" enough, and Hitler's appetite for domination could not be abated; thus, the Final Solution was crafted in 1942 at the Wannasee Conference, which gave "legal" cover to what the Nazis had already been doing for years. By the end of World War II (1945), the official death toll for European Jews was over six million dead.

So horrendous was the loss of human life that the newly formed

United Nations approved (narrowly) UN Resolution 181 to provide a homeland for the Jewish people. President Harry Truman (who replaced President Franklin Roosevelt after his sudden death) was the first to officially recognize Israel on May 14, 1948. Thus, nearly a century of dispensational and evangelical Christians' prophetic recognition that Israel must be reborn as a nation, solely because of the certainty of God's Word, was finally validated.

Satan had lulled the churches into a long slumber through legalism and dead orthodoxy. However, the dynamism of the twentieth century (prophetically speaking) was forcing his hand. God's will was being executed no matter what Satan threw at it (the German Third Reich, for example).

Despite Israel's supernatural return, Satan's plan for destroying the churches through complacency was still in effect. Much of Christendom still lay in the dark regarding God's timeline for the last days. Thus, a schism between mainline Protestantism, Roman Catholicism, and biblical Christianity began to grow. The formers refused to accept the Bible at its word regarding Bible prophecy. The latter began to splinter into its differing views regarding how and when the end would come.

Although Satan is already a defeated foe, he is supremely intent on dragging everyone else down with him. His four chief objectives are the destruction of Israel, the corruption of the doctrine of the blessed hope, the advancement of his Beast kingdom, and the destruction of humanity.

Given that somewhat lengthy historical backdrop, now we understand a little better as to why God's Rapture of the Church is played so close to the vest. That is why "no man knows the day or hour," because when God chooses to execute this strategic deliverance, it will not just be to maximize the redeemed retrieved, but also will maximize the chaos and confusion Satan will have to undo to hobble back the nations to move his plans forward. Think Tower of Babel-level confusion.

However, we should preface this chapter with the knowledge that although a lot has been written about the events mentioned here, not much has been written prescribing when they take place. For example, we know the war of Gog and Magog (Ezekiel 38–39) is still a future event; however, we are not 100 percent certain about when it takes place. The ordering we put in place is a reasonable assumption, but we are in no way dogmatic about what happens first, middle, and last.

Revelation 1:19, on the other hand, does provide an outline for the entirety of the book. In it, John is told to write the "things which you have seen" (chapter 1, John's vision), "the things which are" (chapters 2–3, the seven letters to the seven churches), and "the things which will take place after this" (chapters 4–22). Most reputable theologians acknowledge the change in both tone and scenery between Revelation 3:22 (the letter to Laodicea) and Revelation 4:1–2 (the heavenly throne room).

Although there is not a perceived gap of time in the text between Jesus' scathing letter to the Laodiceans and the time John is "caught up" into Heaven, there are two matters to consider. First, when John was raptured into Heaven, he went from existing in the temporal, physical realm bound by time to the eternal realm (not bound by time). Second, the next two chapters (Revelation 4–5) are devoted entirely to the throne room scene in Heaven. Given the precious literary real estate these two chapters take up, we could refer the reader back to passages like Galatians 4:4–5 (i.e., the fullness of time), where a passage of time is not explicitly laid out, and is neither a denial nor a negation that one has occurred. Rather, the passing of time could then either be implied or at least assumed, given the surrounding context. Thus, it is very likely that a gap of time does exist between Revelation 3:22 and Revelation 6:1; however, its length is uncertain. It might be anywhere from a few months to a few years at the most.

Therefore, let's categorize this as the things that must take place between the Rapture (the end of the Church Age) and the start of the Seventieth Week (he opening of the first seal judgment).

According to Daniel 9:27, the Seventieth Week begins with a treaty enforced by none other than the Antichrist. The Apostle Paul writes in 2 Thessalonians 2:7–8 that we (Christians) won't know who he is, because we will be raptured prior to his unveiling. Consequently, we must either conclude that this man is already in a position of authority and will use a global crisis (such as the Rapture) to assume his authority, or he will use the crisis to get to said position of authority. Regarding the Antichrist, the late W. A. Criswell explains quite succinctly the kind of leader this man will become.

> This man accepts the gifts that Jesus spurned when Satan offered him all the glories of the kingdoms of this world; and the whole earth acclaims the man as the very incarnation of glory and wisdom and might and power and honor…This final anti-Christ will be received in gladness and the kings of the earth will peaceably yield their authority to him, "for there is none like him." How will that come to pass? Here is another instance of how, if we interpret the Revelation correctly, every little detail will fit precisely.
>
> John says he stood upon the sand of a raging sea. That raging sea, pictured also in Daniel, is a symbol of the violent, chaotic masses of humanity in a day of crisis and revolution. Out of these horrible, chaotic, revolutions, arise these tyrannical leaders. Out of the chaos of the blood and mass of the French Revolution, Napoleon was born. Out of the chaotic revolution of the labor movement, Lenin was born. Out of the chaos and mass of revolution, Hitler was born. Always out of the raging turmoil of social chaos, these anti-Christs come.[16]

As mentioned previously, the Rapture will, if nothing else, cause a global reordering to occur. Millions of Americans cannot be removed without affecting our fragile economy in a profoundly negative way. If even one million Americans were suddenly taken from all social strata, we would definitely see our economy crash. The Rapture is likely to take ten times that number of people or more. Furthermore, if the American economy crashes, the global economy will as well, since so much hinges on our strong currency or our reliability for transnational goods and services.

There is a reason there is no nation like the United States in history.

Our great wealth and abundance and our rapid departure from our Judeo-Christian roots will serve as the calamitous forerunner to the economic Babylon, which also meets its ruinous fate in one hour.

The kings of the earth who committed fornication and lived luxuriously with her will weep and lament for her, when they see the smoke of her burning, standing at a distance for fear of her torment, saying, "Alas, alas, that great city Babylon, that mighty city! For in one hour your judgment has come." (Revelation 18:9–10)

This is why there is no singular nation like the United States anywhere in the last book of the Bible, even though many other nations are mentioned. Since there is an all-powerful global government, and the United States is not mentioned, it can only mean that this final global government (the Beast) replaces us. Thus, as nature abhors a vacuum, another, final, last kingdom must arise to fill our sudden departure as the world's chief nation.

FOREKNOWLEDGE

But we speak the wisdom of God in a mystery, the hidden wisdom which God ordained before the ages for our glory, which none of the rulers of this age knew; for had they known, they would not have crucified the Lord of glory. (1 Corinthians 2:7–8)

In the fifth century BC, God had given a prophetic outline to Daniel who was still living in Babylon. The outline (the Seventy-Weeks prophecy) foretold the successive Gentile kingdoms, which would come to be the predominant world powers of their day. In Daniel's time, the Babylonians were the head of nations. Next, came the Persians, followed by the Greeks, and lastly, the Romans in three parts. Two of the parts of Rome would be the division between the iron legs, indicating the split between eastern (would become the Holy Roman Empire) and western Rome (would become the Byzantine Empire). The last subdivision of Rome was between the legs and the feet, which was made of iron mixed with miry clay.

So, although Daniel was able to interpret King Nebuchadnezzar's dream of this multi-metal statue, as well as being given the corresponding hybrid beasts (Daniel 7–8) that represent the same thing (successive Gentile kingdoms), he was not shown if there were gaps in time. For all he knew, they would all run consecutively. After all, he lived through one transition (Babylonian to Persian kingdoms). However, we know historically that this was not the case. Since God's Word must come true (always has and always will), this final version of the Roman Empire must still be yet future.

The last kingdom Daniel sees is one in the form of a giant rock that destroys the metallic statue. He was told that the rock was cut without human hands, thus, this last kingdom would not be from man. As for the timing, the bulk of what plays out in Daniel's Seventy-Weeks prophecy takes place in the period between the Old Testament and the New Testament. The Seventy Weeks of Daniel are weeks of years (see also Genesis 29:26–30) specifically designed for the Jewish people and Jerusalem. This prophecy will accomplish six things, as follows (emphasis and elaboration added in brackets):

Seventy weeks are determined
For your people and for your holy city,
(1) To finish the transgression,
(2) To make an end of sins,
(3) To make reconciliation for iniquity,
(4) To bring in everlasting righteousness,
(5) To seal up vision and prophecy,
(6) And to anoint the Most Holy.
Know therefore and understand,
That from the going forth of the command [Nehemiah 2, 444 BC]
To restore and build Jerusalem

Until Messiah the Prince,

There shall be seven weeks and sixty-two weeks [483 years];

The street shall be built again, and the wall,

Even in troublesome times.

[(7 x 7 = 49 years) + (62 x 7 = 434 years) = 483 years]

And after the sixty-two weeks

Messiah shall be cut off, but not for Himself [Christ crucified; Isaiah 53];

And the people of the prince who is to come [the Romans]

Shall destroy the city and the sanctuary [this happened in AD 70].

The end of it *shall be* with a flood,

And till the end of the war desolations are determined.

[So far, there has been nearly a two-thousand-year gap between the sixty-ninth and seventieth weeks.]

Then he shall confirm a covenant with many for one week [this is what begins the Tribulation];

But in the middle of the week

He shall bring an end to sacrifice and offering [a future Temple would need to exist].

And on the wing of abominations shall be one who makes desolate [see Matthew 24:15],

Even until the consummation, which is determined [Isaiah 46:9–10],

Is poured out on the desolate" [(1 x 7 = 7 years) + (483 years) = 490 years]

That is the divine outline in Daniel 9:24–27. The New Testament prophetic companion, Revelation, has a much more condensed outline, but covers the gap in time from Christ's death until the Rapture of the Church, and it is found in Revelation 1:19. It states:

Write the things **which you have seen**, and the things which are, and the things **which will take place after this**. (Emphasis added)

Because the Revelation deals with everything after Christ's death, burial, and resurrection, understanding the basic outline of that book will prevent a lot of confusion before it even begins. The "things" that John saw pertained to the vision of the glorified Christ (chapter 1). The "things which are" are the seven letters to the seven churches (chapters 2–3). Revelation was written around AD 95, so the Church Age would have already been around for at least sixty years by then. The "things which take place after this" (after the Church Age) include everything that follows Revelation 3. Chapter 4 begins with John being caught up to Heaven. Thus, if John's catching-up is a foreshadowing of the Rapture, which divides man's time on earth before the Church Age from what comes after (the Tribulation, the Millennial Kingdom, and eternity future), what has to happen between the two?

A reasonable theory is that chapters 4–5 (the heavenly throne-room scene) are given precious and exclusive real estate in this final book of the Bible to show (without showing) a gap in time between the Rapture and the official start of the Seventieth Week. Remember, the Rapture does not begin the Tribulation, but it does lay the necessary foundation for it to begin. Chaos. Considering that the events laid out in Daniel 9:24–27 (four verses) cover a four-hundred-year period known as the "silent years," it's reasonable to assume that two chapters (with 51.4 verses) can encompass a period of nearly two thousand years (or the Church Age). In addition, there are not really any *silent years*, because God has already filled out the details. He is simply letting events catch up to their fulfillment.

The Rapture does not cause the Tribulation to begin; the two events are not connected. If they were connected (with a cause-and-effect relationship), the Bible would have indicated so, and there would be a correlation. However, the reason they aren't connected is because many things need to take place before the Tribulation can begin. Again, the Rapture is imminent; it does not depend on anything other than God the Father to give permission for it to happen.

The Tribulation however, requires a covenant to be confirmed. For there to be a covenant between this prince who is to come (out of the

Roman Empire) and the many, and for him to desecrate the Holy of Holies (see Matthew 24:14; 2 Thessalonians 2:4), several things need to happen first.

1. Israel needs to be in control of its ancestral homeland again.
2. Israel needs to be in control of Jerusalem again.
3. The Jews need to rebuild their Third Temple.

At least two of the three things did not happen in a vacuum.

First, increasing anti-Semitism would play a major cause in driving the Jews out of Europe. In 1897, Theodore Herzl formed the First Zionist Congress, which began buying back deserted land from absentee Turkish landlords. They also created a constitution that would cement the Jews' plans for returning to their ancient homeland. Second, World War I would need to wrench the lands from the hands of the Ottoman Turks (who had been in control of most of the Middle East for the previous four centuries). Third, World War II would need to prepare the people for the land (hence their motto, "Never Again," regarding the Holocaust). Fourth, the Jews would need to declare their statehood (1948). Fifth, the Jews would need to regain control of Jerusalem (the 1967 Six Day War).

So far, all of these things have been done.

Here is where we are today:

Sixth, the Jews need to have the political and national will to build their Third Temple, presumably removing or destroying the Dome of the Rock and the al-Aqsa Mosque. They have had at least two major organizations since 1987 begin to seriously gather funds, resources, and ritual necessities (priestly tools and garments, people identified to be from the tribe of Levi, the red heifer, etc.) Likely events that will cause them to act upon this idea for a new Temple are the collapse of the world's former superpower, the United States; the divinely spectacular defeat of Gog and Magog; the arrival of the Two Witnesses of Revelation, the rebuilding of the Third Jewish Temple, and the exponential rise of wickedness. We are already witnessing (as of 2020–2021) a change in attitudes by Saudi Arabia regarding the supposed importance and "holiness" of the Temple Mount to the religion of Islam. From their standpoint, it's not all that important.

Since we know those events are still future, and Revelation doesn't spell out exactly where they fit on a timeline (with the exception being the Two Witnesses), all we know is that a Third Temple is already standing by the middle of the seven-year Tribulation, primarily because the Antichrist desecrates it.

Now, given what we know about the world today (roughly 192 countries), they are highly segregated into sovereign nations. Each nation (more or less) always acts on its own behalf. Also true is that if the Rapture were to occur today, some nations would be affected more dramatically than others. For example, the Rapture will have a far greater impact on the United States than it would, say, on Uzbekistan or Saudi Arabia. However, for the sake of global reorganization, let's focus on the United States. As stated previously, the collapse of this nation will throw the entire world's economic system into chaos.

The collapse of the United States (for any reason) would seriously upend the global pecking order. Aside from the obvious disturbances (vehicular crashes; looting; riots; major vacancies of corporate, medical, and political positions; and general lawlessness), the US economy will implode, taking down the US dollar along with it. Every nation that has major holdings of US debt (i.e., we owe them money) will also have their reserve currencies fold. Not only that, but the manufacturing, shipping, service industries, and energy markets will also fail. If that happens, it will take time to strip the United States of its resources (as back payment) and reallocate them back to the Old World.

While Satan is not omnipotent, he has (presumably) read the book of Revelation (Matthew 4:5–6). He understands that a third of the earth will be burnt up, as well as a third of the oceans and freshwaters in the trumpet judgments alone. The Americas (North, Central, and South) make up a third of the world's trees, fresh waters, and oceans (those territorial to our coastlines). It doesn't take a rocket scientist or brain surgeon to see that Satan's footprint is going to be reduced and channelized so that he (and his forces) are being increasingly confined to the lands near Israel.

This may also speak to why Satan is so intent on destroying the United States. It's not simply to corrupt us just for the sake of it; he has a much more pragmatic need to do so (he needs our military aircraft, weapons, technology, gold, soldiers, etc., back over to Europe to outfit and finance his final world empire). He also needs to destroy our currency so that it forces the global economy to collapse, and he can then introduce (through his human agents) the digital currency necessary for the implementation of the mark of the Beast system. *ALREADY IN THE WORKS WORLD(?)*

Therefore, while things appear to be "unscripted" and "unknowable," we should take comfort in the reality that God has this all under control. What we're witnessing today is not merely random acts of violence and chaos, but an orchestrated, strategic maneuvering by Satan to ready the world to accept his Beast government with an imminent Rapture hanging overhead. Satan (like us) knows it is going to happen; he just (like us) doesn't know when.

So what else needs to happen?

THE REMOVAL OF THE RESTRAINER

For the mystery of lawlessness is already at work; only He who now restrains *will do so* **until He is taken out of the way. And then** the **lawless one will be revealed**, whom the Lord will consume with the breath of His mouth and destroy with the brightness of His coming. (2 Thessalonians 2:7–8, emphasis added)

Paul also confirms and provides a different perspective to this "coming of the lawless one" by adding that he cannot come UNTIL the Restrainer is removed. Who is the Restrainer? Who has restrained evil across the world for the past two thousand years? Well, we know who it cannot be: the archangel Michael, because Michael is a singular being (not omnipresent), thus, he is not physically capable of restraining evil all over the world at the same time. Neither is it Satan, because he would not do anything to suppress evil, being the very embodiment of it. The Restrainer is not the government. Although governments are designed to curb man's lawless intentions, there are plenty of examples of evil governments. The only *Being* it could be, who is both omnipresent and capable of restraining evil simultaneously, is the Holy Spirit.

During the Last Supper, Jesus told His disciples that it was beneficial that He leave because another would come and be with them. He referred to God the Holy Spirit as both a helper and comforter—descriptive names as to the nature of the role of the Holy Spirit. Furthermore, He stated:

> Nevertheless I tell you the truth. It is to your advantage that I go away; for if I do not go away, the Helper will not come to you; but if I depart, I will send Him to you. And when He has come, **He will convict the world of sin, and of righteousness, and of judgment: of sin, because they do not believe in Me.** (John 16:7–9, emphasis added)

Jesus, while in His physical, corporeal body, was not omnipresent. He was confined (as a man) to the geographical location of where He was at any given moment. The Holy Spirit, on the other hand, can be everywhere at the same time, with the same omnipotence as the other two members of the Triune Godhead. Since the Holy Spirit is omnipresent, it's not as if the Holy Spirit can be taken out of the way. Rather, it's a matter of in whom the Holy Spirit seals and indwells (i.e., the Church). Paul reveals later that the Holy Spirit seals the believer at the very moment of salvation, and that we are sealed *for* the day of redemption. Well, that day is the Rapture (see 2 Corinthians 1:21–22, Ephesians 1:13–14).

> And do not grieve the Holy Spirit of God, by whom you were sealed **for** the day of redemption. (Ephesians 4:30, emphasis added)

If the believer is sealed by God the Holy Spirit *for* the day of redemption, then "for" means something. An event such as spiritual rebirth (being born again) must have some payoff at the end. That payoff is the Rapture of the Church, when the Church (the unified, singular, multi-membered Body of Christ) is transformed in an instant from mortal to immortal and from corruption into incorruption. Once the believers are translated from life into eternal life, they no longer need to be sealed *for* the day of redemption, because that day will have already come to pass. The Apostle Paul, in his letter to the Romans, stated this as well:

> For whom He foreknew, He also predestined to be conformed to the image of His Son, that He might be the firstborn among many brethren. Moreover whom He predestined, these He also called; whom He called, these He also justified; and whom He justified, **these He also glorified.** (Romans 8:29–30, emphasis added)

So, what is that glorification?

We know that after His resurrection, Jesus did many miraculous things that normal humans cannot do (see Luke 24). He appeared and disappeared at will. He could alter His appearance so as not to be noticed until He chose to be noticed. He could pass through solid objects. Of interest to the believer is what the Apostle John wrote about in his first epistle:

> Beloved, now we are children of God; and it has not yet been revealed what we shall be, but we know that when He is revealed, **we shall be like Him,** for we shall see Him as He is. And everyone who has this hope in Him purifies himself, just as He is pure. (1 John 3:2–3, emphasis added)

Every believer will need to change physically in order to live where God lives. We cannot live in Heaven or receive our eternal inheritance in our earthly, physical bodies; we could not survive. Neither are we going to spend eternity as wispy, ethereal spirits floating and flittering about. We will have a new, perfect, imperishable body to house our souls. When and where we receive these bodies (for both the living and the dead) is at the Rapture.

What else must happen?

THE RISE OF THE KINGDOM OF THE BEAST

> Then I stood on the sand of the sea. And I saw a beast rising up out
> of the sea, having seven heads and ten horns, and on his horns ten
> crowns, and on his heads a blasphemous name. (Revelation 13:1)

WEF

At present, there is much discussion and debate regarding the major geopolitical directions the world could go. One direction is nationalism or the Old World Order. The other is globalism, more commonly referred to as the New World Order. There is yet another direction the world could go (and is likely to do so), and that is regionalism. This would mean that instead of every nation doing its own thing, or every nation fitting into a "one-size-fits-all" model, the world could (and already is) align regionally, financially, and culturally.

We know that, at the end of World War I, world leaders rushed into the ill-conceived League of Nations. They did this even though WWI largely only impacted Europe. At the end of World War II, the world rushed into a weak but better-planned United Nations. They did this even though the war did not reach every corner of the world. With the exception of Pearl Harbor, the Americas (North, Central, and South), and central to southern Africa, world leaders largely remained personally unaffected by the war. Yet, they still rushed into a global covenant.

At the Rapture, every nation will be impacted, simultaneously. What are the chances world leaders won't rush into some new form of reinforced global government?

Zero. Zilch. Nada.

Wu-Fu

Given our recent history of cause-effect reactions to global crises, world leaders will once again rush into another form of governmental control, this time, through regional and technocratic powers. This would be somewhat similar to how, at his death, Alexander the Great's kingdom was divided amongst his four generals—Ptolemy, Seleucus, Cassander, and Lysimachus.

The world will be parceled out amongst the remaining (but weakened) nations to form regional alliances. Given the likely objections to technological powerhouses remaining within just one region (i.e., Google, Amazon, and other powerful transnational organizations), there presumably has to be some "leveling of the playing field" by pairing each region with a strong nation like Russia, China, the United States (whatever remains of it), and the European Union. We imagine that is the only way this final world conglomeration will get full participation. The world then would break into ten regions, mutually assuring trade and resources. Nevertheless, it won't be long before certain regions begin to dominate others. *TEN TOES*

The ten regions will form the foundation of the Beast. These will (presumably) be united by some form of digital currency they all use as a common form of money after the demise of the American dollar. Likely, there will be a center region (the Mideast, perhaps?) that serves as the new economic hub for the ten. It is here where we believe this new Babylon will emerge. Furthermore, out of this new, regionalized global government will arise two leaders. The first will be a political, possibly military, leader (or both) who is able to wrest control of power from three leaders, then the rest.

The second is his chief propagandist, who serves the former. It is believed that he will begin a global, completely ecumenical religion that will accompany this final Gentile kingdom (as its official state-sponsored religion). He will do this until the midpoint of the Tribulation, when he will then begin demanding that all worship the Beast (the man) once he is deified. To be clear, two versions of Babylon are spoken of in Revelation: the economic/financial/governmental Babylon and the religious Babylon, which serves the former.

WAR OF GOG AND MAGOG

"And it will come to pass at the same time, when Gog comes against the land of Israel," says the Lord God, "that My fury will show in My face. For in My jealousy and in the fire of My wrath I have spoken: 'Surely in that day there shall be a great earthquake in the land of Israel, so that the fish of the sea, the birds of the heavens, the beasts of the field, all creeping things that creep on the earth, and all men who are on the face of the earth shall shake at My presence.

The mountains shall be thrown down, the steep places shall fall, and every wall shall fall to the ground.' I will call for a sword against Gog throughout all My mountains," says the Lord God. "Every man's sword will be against his brother. And I will bring him to judgment with pestilence and bloodshed; I will rain down on him, on his troops, and on the many peoples who are with him, flooding rain, great hailstones, fire, and brimstone. Thus I will magnify Myself and sanctify Myself, and I will be known in the eyes of many nations. Then they shall know that I am the Lord." (Ezekiel 38:18–23)

Because the Rapture will become such a tumultuous, global crisis, we stated that those who are left behind will likely see the "rise" of the Beast system begin to come together before, during, and after the Rapture. Furthermore, not every nation will be on board with handing over their sovereignty to another power. Nations like Turkey, Iran, Russia, and others will, presumably, be against this rush to a regional/global authority.

We believe this is part of why they (Gog-Magog) form a "counter" regional alliance, and then not only attack Israel for personal and economic plunder, but also as a power play to gain control over the Suez Canal. Seeing as they (Russia, Iran, Turkey, Libya, and other nations in this Gog coalition) lack the technological backing by organizations like Amazon and Google at their disposal, their play has to be for raw resources and geographical choke points. By controlling the Mediterranean Sea, the Suez Canal, and the Red Sea's Strait of Hormuz, they could effectively control a huge flow of oil and shipping for much of the world. Just remember one thing: the largely American/European, Western global elite will not be the only ones seeking to reshuffle the world's power structure when the perfect crisis (the Rapture) arrives.

The Gog-Magog invasion will meet its defeat in the mountains to the north of Israel. While their strength in numbers and their indomitable forces will seem to be insurmountable for the Israeli Defense Force (IDF), God will allow them to make it to their borders. There, He'll shake the ground under their feet, cause flooding rain, brimstone, and fire to descend upon them; this will confuse them to such a great degree that they'll begin fighting and killing each other.

Not only will this be a massive defeat for the Gog forces, but it will also likely neuter what is left of militant Islam. Since this demonically inspired task force is comprised of both Sunni (Libya, Sudan, and Turkey) and Shiite (Iran and her acolytes) loyalists, it seems their divine defeat will cause the rest of Islam to shuck off religious extremism and embrace the harlot of ecumenicalism. In other words, after this massive defeat, Israel's neighbors aren't going to be protesting too much when they clear the rubble off the Temple Mount and replace the Dome of the Rock and the mosque with their Third Jewish Temple.

THE ARRIVAL OF THE TWO WITNESSES

Then I was given a reed like a measuring rod. And the angel stood, saying, "Rise and measure the temple of God, the altar, and those who worship there. But leave out the court which is outside the temple, and do not measure it, for it has been given to the Gentiles. And they will tread the holy city underfoot for forty-two months. And I will give power to my two witnesses, and they will prophesy one thousand two hundred and sixty days, clothed in sackcloth."

These are the two olive trees and the two lampstands standing before the God of the earth. And if anyone wants to harm them, fire proceeds from their mouth and devours their enemies. And if anyone wants to harm them, he must be killed in this manner. These have power to shut heaven, so that no rain falls in the days of their prophecy; and they have power over waters to turn them to blood, and to strike the earth with all plagues, as often as they desire. (Revelation 11:1–6)

When the Great Disappearance happens, nations and leaders around the world will begin scrambling to position themselves to land on all fours when the Rapture dust settles. When things go bad and disaster strikes, the average person is usually in too much shock to react or understand what is happening. The globalist elite are not like that. When disaster strikes—and, presumably, even before—they begin scheming and maneuvering to see how they can come out on top. Thus, the Rapture presents them this opportunity. Gog-Magog will launch a preemptive and seemingly unstoppable, *blitzkrieg*-styled attack on Israel, only to be handily defeated by God.

Elitists not involved in the Gog-Magog invasion will be watching from afar. In their minds, God (whoever they presume that to be, whether fate, luck, aliens, etc.) will have just done them a huge favor. Not only will the Russians, Turks, and Iranian militaries be almost entirely annihilated, but this defeat effectively will neuter the remaining vestiges of militant Islam. Thus, the globalist-elite schemers will begin to tweak their machinations to not attack Israel themselves, but to lull them into a duplicitous treaty. But then God will throw another monkey wrench into their plans: Enter the Two Witnesses.

These two men, presumably Moses and Elijah, will arrive on the scene in Israel on the heel of that nation's greatest victory, albeit one it didn't actually earn. We can reasonably assume one of the identities as being Elijah, given their appearance together at the transfiguration (Mark 9:4–5) as well as their mention together in the verses at the end of the book of Malachi:

Remember the Law of **Moses, My servant**, Which I commanded
him in Horeb for all Israel, With the statutes and judgments.

Behold, I will send you Elijah the prophet Before the coming
of the great and dreadful day of the Lord.

And he will turn The hearts of the fathers to the children, And
the hearts of the children to their fathers, Lest (or else) I come and
strike the earth with a curse. (Malachi 4:4–6, emphasis added)

Initially welcomed as heralds of Israel's forthcoming Kingdom, these
two men will quickly wear out their warning in a twenty-first-century
world full of ecumenicalism, political correctness, and cancel culture.
However, they are probably (speculation here) going to be instrumental
in helping the Orthodox Jews figure out where the Temple should be
built, and presumably will give them the final official tools they need to
do the job correctly (which is why the Temple measurement information
is included in Revelation 11).

For three and a half years, these men will increasingly be the thorn in
the side of this New World Order. To make matters worse (for these elite)
is that the pair can't be stopped or silenced. When anyone tries to remove
them, they'll get scorched (literally). Not only that, but the men can cause
judgments to fall all over the earth, not just in Israel. Here's verse 6 again:

These have power to shut heaven, so that no rain falls in the days
of their prophecy; and they have power over waters to turn them to
blood, and to strike the earth with all plagues, as often as they desire.

YouTube, Twitter, and cable networks will not be able to censor these
men. World leaders will not be able to negotiate with them. These two
will be unrelenting in calling out evil and chastising the Jews for not rec-
ognizing the signs of the times. We believe they'll arrive on the scene after
the Rapture, but before the official start of the Seventieth Week. We know
at the midpoint of the Seventieth Week, they'll be killed, and their bodies
will be left in the streets of Jerusalem for three and a half days. The whole

world will see their bodies lying in the streets via satellite television, and at the end of the three and a half days, God will resurrect them and then rapture them up in front of a global audience.

THE REBUILDING OF THE THIRD JEWISH TEMPLE

"Therefore when you see the 'abomination of desolation,' spoken of by Daniel the prophet, standing in the holy place" (whoever reads, let him understand), "then let those who are in Judea flee to the mountains." (Matthew 24:15–16)

Jesus, in the Olivet Discourse, His epic treatise on the last days, only gives one time stamp for the Seventieth Week of Daniel: the midpoint (at exactly three and a half years). Here, Jesus states that the Antichrist commits the "abomination of desolation" in the holy place. The "holy place" referred to here is the Holy of Holies, which can only exist inside a Jewish Temple. Interestingly, Jesus began the Olivet Discourse by discussing how the Temple (the Second) would be so utterly destroyed that not one stone would be left atop another. Now Jesus is stating that, in the last days, a man will come who will commit the gravest of desecrations against the Temple.

So which is it?

The Romans, under General Titus, destroyed the Second Temple (Herod's Temple) in AD 70. There has not been a Jewish Temple standing in Jerusalem since that time. Thus, this Third Temple that Jesus, Paul, and John later reference must be a future structure, since the second was destroyed (and never rebuilt) nearly two thousand years ago.

This brings an interesting issue to bear, though: Will the Third Temple contain the Ark of the Covenant? To the Gentile world, that holy vessel has been lost to the annals of history despite Hollywood's best speculations. To the Jews and, more importantly, to the Orthodox Jewish Temple Mount Institute, the Ark is not lost, but well hidden. They claim to know exactly where it is, but until the current occupiers of the Temple Mount vacate their present location, they will keep the Ark safely where it is. Whether they truly know where it is, its reappearance, as well as the arrival of the Two Witnesses, will be powerful reasons to build the Third Temple.

Rev 11:19

As mentioned previously, given the spectacular defeat of the Gog-Magog invasion, there will likely be collateral damage of a divine nature. It is believed by many that the massive earthquake will subsequently destroy the Dome of the Rock and al-Aqsa Mosque during the Magog melee. Thus, this opens the opportunity for the first time in over seventy years for the Jewish people to rebuild their Temple.

8

THE SATANIC TRINITY/ANTICHRIST ZEITGEIST

The masses have never thirsted after truth. Whoever can supply them with illusions is easily their master; whoever attempts to destroy their illusion is always their victim.[17]

—Gustave Le Bon

It would be impossible to write a treatise on the final act of our human drama without mentioning the three main antagonists: the devil, the Antichrist, and the False Prophet. Because the devil cannot create anything (since he is a fallen angel himself) he is restricted to imitating God. The reason we have three main antagonists is that the devil (called, of course, Lucifer before his fall) is attempting to mimic the Triune Godhead (the Trinity). Due to his prideful nature, Lucifer has placed himself at the top of this satanic trinity in the role of *the Father*.

The two human individuals he brings along are the Antichrist and the False Prophet. He will endow these with supernatural power and hand over to them all the kingdoms of the world. Together, this evil trio will bring about so much catastrophic destruction that even being associated with or named as such has historically only been attributed to the very worst of humanity. However, they will not be presented as such at the beginning. They will be seen as the very best of humanity, saviors in their own right. They will be the epitome of reason, intelligence, wealth, status, wisdom, and power.

Similar things were said about past antichrists. On their ascendancy, men like Adolf Hitler and Joseph Stalin were heralded as great leaders and thinkers. Hindsight credits these odious men with being responsible for the death of tens of millions, and in fact they're generally who come to mind first when thinking of *antichrists*. However, these men, as bad as they were, did not accrue their destructive power and appetites overnight. They were shaped and molded by other antichrists (inspired by corrupted men) and even by the *spirit of antichrist* (inspired by doctrine of demons) in the years prior to their rise to power.

For example, we can reasonably assume, then, that there would be no Adolf Hitler (as history knows him today) were it not for those who, years earlier, had paved the foundation for his ideology—men like Friedrich Nietzsche and his existentialist belief in the "will to power" and the *Übermensch*; Charles Darwin and his evolutionary (and antibiblical) theories on the origin of life; Francis Galton, piggybacking off Darwin and promoting racial superiority through selective-breeding *vis-a-vis* eugenics; and the post-Civil War American Democrat policies for segregation (i.e., the Jim Crow laws). These were all concepts the Third Reich borrowed from when building their own Aryan ideological/political constructs. They were dangerous *doctrines of demons*, whose true aim was only to stir dissention and sow destruction. However, it's not just the poisonous philosophies of corrupted men who are antichrist. The Bible states that anything that denies the deity of Jesus Christ is antichrist.

Who is a liar but he who denies that Jesus is the Christ? He is antichrist who denies the Father and the Son. (1 John 2:22)

And every spirit that does not confess that Jesus Christ has come in the flesh is not of God. And this is the spirit of the Antichrist, which you have heard was coming, and is now already in the world. (1 John 4:3)

For many deceivers have gone out into the world who do not confess Jesus Christ as coming in the flesh. This is a deceiver and an antichrist. (2 John 1:7)

Even before Christ came, there was a similar antichrist spirit (spirit of rebellion) that has been present in mankind since the beginning. From the way of Cain to the error of Balaam and the rebellion of Korah, the seditiousness of the unrepentant human heart has been a mainstay in fallen mankind (Jude 1:11). We see more examples with people like Nimrod, Pharaoh, Haman, Jezebel, Herod, and Judas Iscariot. In truth, Satan doesn't have to do much to prompt men and women from jumping headfirst into wickedness (Jeremiah 17:9).

From a biblical standpoint, many antichrists have come throughout history, and even now are alive in our world today. Seemingly, when enough antichrists arise in a generation, they create a predominant spirit of the age (*zeitgeist*) by flooding the public arena of ideas with doctrines of devils. Still, even this *zeitgeist* has ebbed and flowed over the past two millennia, largely restrained by some "unseen" force guiding the affairs of humanity.

As believers, we know this unseen force can be none other than the work of the Holy Spirit (John 16:5–11). While many respected theologians believe the Restrainer, as mentioned in 2 Thessalonians 2:7, as the Holy Spirit-sealed and empowered Church (we would agree), history has also shown how God uses even the Gentile governments as tools to curb and thwart evil. Certainly, if the British and the Americans had not stood up against the rising tide of the German Third Reich, the Italian fascists, and the Empire-minded Japanese, the world would be a much darker place today. The Bible is also clear that there is one, final Antichrist who is coming. He will be the last world ruler who is both the culmination of all those former antichrists and the personification of the antichrist zeitgeist.

Little children, it is the last hour; and as you have heard that the Antichrist is coming, even now many antichrists have come, by which we know that it is the last hour. (1 John 4:3)

In a broader sense of the word (referencing both the Old and New Testament), an antichrist is one who opposes God, His agenda, or His people. Although there are only four New Testament passages using the term "antichrist" (*antichristos*; Greek-ἀντίχριστος), Scripture affords an abundance of clues as to the nature of the coming future Antichrist. He is called the "worthless shepherd," "little horn," "man of sin," "lawless one," "son of perdition," "beast," "dragon," and "rider on the white horse."

Interestingly, the same John who exclusively used the term "antichrist" in his epistles does not use that same term when given the Revelation. Instead, he used the term the "Beast" when speaking of both this final world ruler and his global government. Although we cannot be dogmatic regarding this point, it may have something to do with the "mystery of lawlessness [iniquity]" the Apostle Paul speaks of in his second letter to the Thessalonians.

> For the mystery of lawlessness is already at work; only He who now restrains will do so until He is taken out of the way. (2 Thessalonians 2:7)

The word "mystery" (Greek: *musterion*) is used in the New Testament to denote something that God chooses not to reveal until the time is right. Thus, this mystery is the shrouding of the identity of this final world ruler. In the context of this passage (and the chapter), the mystery is at work now *until* the Restrainer is taken out of the way. It is our belief that the only logical choice for the identity of "He who restrains" can be none other than the Holy Spirit.

Whether this restraint is solely through the Holy Spirit-sealed Church (Ephesians 11:13–14; 4:30) or simply by His stirring of nations to put down cataclysmic evil (Romans 13:1–3), it is the Holy Spirit's work to keep evil at bay until the fullness of time when the Church is physically removed at the Rapture (1 Thessalonians 4:16–17; 1 Corinthians 15:50–56; Revelation 3:10)—after which the world will cross the threshold from the mystery of lawlessness into the short-lived, but unbelievably brutal, *age of lawlessness.*

THE ANTICHRIST: "THE UNHOLY SON"

Many have long wondered and speculated on details regarding this final Antichrist. How does Satan go about selecting him? Is he alive today? Does he know he is the Antichrist? If he does know, when and how did he find out? What does he hope to achieve? Does he have a long-term plan, or is it more like playing out things as they unfold? Is he like Hitler with his unsustainable four-year economic plan, or is he like Hitler with his thousand-year Reich plan? Does he know his fate? Does he even care? Revelation 13 gives a full description of his rise and achievement of total, global domination.

> Then I stood on the sand of the sea. And I saw a beast rising up out of the sea, having seven heads and ten horns, and on his horns ten crowns, and on his heads a blasphemous name. Now the beast which I saw was like a leopard, his feet were like the feet of a bear, and his mouth like the mouth of a lion. The dragon gave him his power, his throne, and great authority. And I saw one of his heads as if it had been mortally wounded, and his deadly wound was healed. And all the world marveled and followed the beast. So they worshiped the dragon who gave authority to the beast; and they worshiped the beast, saying, "Who is like the beast? Who is able to make war with him?"
>
> And he was given a mouth speaking great things and blasphemies, and he was given authority to continue for forty-two months. Then he opened his mouth in blasphemy against God, to blaspheme His name, His tabernacle, and those who dwell in heaven. It was granted to him to make war with the saints and to overcome them. And authority was given him over every tribe, tongue, and nation. All who dwell on the earth will worship him, whose names have not been written in the Book of Life of the Lamb slain from the foundation of the world. (Revelation 13:1–8)

The crisis of the Rapture will present the devil with the perfect opportunity to reveal his final candidate to the world in an extraordinary display of lying signs and wonders. Just as there is a very real spirit of Antichrist that has existed since Nimrod, there will also be a culmination of this false spirit with this final world ruler. Even today, the world's increasing appetite, infatuation, and fascination with all things magic, the occult, and superheroes proves that it will not take much for the world to be wowed by the revelation of this coming "superman" (*Übermensch*).

> The coming of the lawless one is according to the working of Satan, with all power, signs, and lying wonders, and with all unrighteous deception among those who perish, because they did not receive the love of the truth, that they might be saved. And for this reason God will send them strong delusion, that they should believe the lie, that they all may be condemned who did not believe the truth but had pleasure in unrighteousness. (2 Thessalonians 2:9–12)

THE FALSE PROPHET: "THE UNHOLY SPIRIT"

At his side, and the third part of this satanic trinity, is the False Prophet. He will be the Antichrist's primary promoter and chief propagandist, championing him to all the people and nations, and ultimately, at the midpoint, deifying him above all else. He also can work great signs and wonders. Together, they deceive the world and are the "strong delusion" that God allows to happen.

Although much less is written about the False Prophet, we have seen the spirit of this second Beast of Revelation chapter 13 as far back as the Tower of Babel. His work will culminate after the great disappearance as the great harlot (Revelation 17), who represents the wholly anti-God and anti-Christ religion that arises to fill the spiritual vacuum after the true Church is removed at the Rapture. Even now, we are seeing his handiwork come to fruition in these last days through the promotion of paganism, the corruption of orthodox Christianity, and marriage of the two with the rise of technology (biometrics, implantable technology, artificial intelligence, etc.). Again, he is known as the second Beast, and he appears to come out of the earth.

> Then I saw another beast coming up out of the earth, and he had two horns like a lamb and spoke like a dragon. And he exercises all the authority of the first beast in his presence, and causes the earth and those who dwell in it to worship the first beast, whose deadly wound was healed. He performs great signs, so that he even makes fire come down from heaven on the earth in the sight of men.
>
> And he deceives those who dwell on the earth by those signs which he was granted to do in the sight of the beast, telling those who dwell on the earth to make an image to the beast who was wounded by the sword and lived. He was granted power to give breath to the image of the beast, that the image of the beast should both speak and cause as many as would not worship the image of the beast to be killed.
>
> He causes all, both small and great, rich and poor, free and slave, to receive a mark on their right hand or on their foreheads, and that no one may buy or sell except one who has the mark or the name of the beast, or the number of his name. Here is wisdom. Let him who has understanding calculate the number of the beast, for it is the number of a man: His number is 666. (Revelation 13:11–18)

Just as Jannes and Jambre were able to supernaturally mimic some of Moses' miracles in his dealings with Pharaoh (Exodus 7:11–13, 2 Timothy 3:8), the False Prophet will be able to counter the supernatural signs and wonders that the Two Witnesses will do, further hardening their hearts and of those who are being deceived (Revelation 11:5; 13:13).

While we cannot know exactly who these final two miscreants are exactly, there are hints as to the identity of both of them. Daniel 9:27 indicates the "prince who is to come" comes from somewhere within the boundaries of the old Roman Empire. Revelation 13 further points to the fact that this Beast rises up from the *sea* (the sea of Gentile nations), whereas the False Prophet rises up from the *land*. In the context of this symbolism, the "land" has always been attributed in Scripture to the geographical confines of national Israel. Therefore, it is likely that the False Prophet is of Jewish descent and uses his ethnicity to promote this Gentile leader (the Antichrist) as the long-awaited Messiah to the Jewish people.

Granted, every generation has had their favorite candidate for the Antichrist, and up until now, they've all been wrong. We can be certain they were wrong because all of those Roman Emperors, Catholic popes, and brutal tyrants have thankfully come and gone, yet the world has continued. Christ Himself will overthrow the last Antichrist at His Second Coming and before ushering in His own Millennial Kingdom. Since that is the case, we know this final world ruler has not yet been revealed.

THE DEVIL: "THE UNHOLY FATHER"

And another sign appeared in heaven: behold, a great, fiery red dragon having seven heads and ten horns, and seven diadems on his heads. His tail drew a third of the stars of heaven and threw them to the earth. And the dragon stood before the woman who was ready to give birth, to devour her Child as soon as it was born. She bore a male Child who was to rule all nations with a rod of iron. And her Child was caught up to God and His throne. Then the woman fled into the wilderness, where she has a place prepared by God, that they should feed her there one thousand two hundred and sixty days.

And war broke out in heaven: Michael and his angels fought with the dragon; and the dragon and his angels fought, but they did not prevail, nor was a place found for them in heaven any longer. So the great dragon was cast out, that serpent of old, called the Devil and Satan, who deceives the whole world; he was cast to the earth, and his angels were cast out with him. (Revelation 12:3–9)

Last, but certainly not least, we have the titular figurehead for this satanic trinity, the devil himself. The devil's personal name, of course, is "Lucifer," which means "light-bearer," while "Satan" is his title (meaning "accuser"). In half of one brief chapter, the Bible sums up the entirety of Lucifer's strategy to dethrone God. When he fell, a third of the angelic host chose to follow him. Since we know the angels are as innumerable as the stars in the sky, we can reasonably assume one-third is still quite a lot of adversaries (Hebrews 1:22, Revelation 5:11).

Before God created Adam, sin came into being by one creature—Lucifer. Before mankind was created, Lucifer was the pinnacle of God's creation (Ezekiel 28). He was the anointed cherub who led the musical orchestrations for the innumerable angelic hierarchy in the heavens. Even though he was the highest of the angels and commanded legions of them, even he was beneath the One in the form of a Man (Ezekiel 1:26–28) who was high above the throne of God. Lucifer resented this immensely and purposed in his heart to rise above.

How you are fallen from heaven, O Lucifer, son of the morning!
How you are cut down to the ground, You who weakened the nations!
For you have said in your heart:
"**I will** ascend into heaven,
I will exalt my throne above the stars of God;
I will also sit on the mount of the congregation on the farthest sides of the north;
I will ascend above the heights of the clouds,
I will be like the Most High."
Yet you shall be brought down to Sheol, To the lowest depths of the Pit. (Isaiah 14:12–15, emphasis added)

Unmatched in beauty, Lucifer became prideful and began plotting how he could be like the Most High. Isaiah the prophet records the five "I wills" for which sin came into being. So it was, at some point before Creation, that Satan led a third of the angels to commit open rebellion and warfare against God and His holy angels. A great war ensued, and Lucifer and his angels were cast out of Heaven (Revelation 12:7–9). Here is where Genesis 1 begins:

> In the beginning, God created the heavens and the earth. And the earth was without form and void. (Genesis 1:1–2a)

After the angelic rebellion, God created the universe and all therein. On the sixth day, He took some dirt and formed a man (Adam) in His own likeness, and then breathed life into him. Not only did God bring Adam to life, but He then gave the man dominion over the entire earth. This further infuriated Lucifer. Man was created in the image of God and consequently supplanted Lucifer as the highest created being in the universe.

At some point after the Creation, Lucifer assumed the body of a serpentine creature in the Garden of Eden. He approached Eve, then lied to her by implanting doubt against God's one commandment that they not eat from the tree of the knowledge of good and evil (Genesis 3:1–7). He inspired Cain to rise up against his brother Abel (Genesis 4:6–8). He persuaded some of his fallen angelic brethren to leave their domain, take up human wives, and rule as gods on the earth (Genesis 6:1–4, 2 Peter 2:4, Jude 1:6). He didn't do this to create a super race of hybrid humans, but to corrupt the super race (mankind) and prevent the One from coming who would ultimately destroy him (Genesis 3:15). In response to the almost total corruption of the human race (except for Noah and his family), God flooded the earth for forty days and forty nights (Genesis 6–9).

Since the Great Flood, Satan has been relentlessly attempting to reestablish a one-world system on the earth that would be decidedly anti-God. Beginning with the Tower of Babel (Nimrod), He raised up a nonstop series of pagan world powers who would attempt to suppress faith in God through the likes of the Egyptians, the Chaldeans, the Assyrians, the Babylonians, the Persians, the Greeks, and the Romans.

Nevertheless, in a lonely, forgotten, backwater province of the Roman Empire around the turn of the first millennium, Jesus the Messiah was born into this world. He was born without fanfare, except for a few shepherds and a host of angels announcing His arrival. He lived an unassuming life until it was time to take the stage as the most important Man who ever lived.

At the beginning of Jesus' ministry, Satan offered Him all the kingdoms of the world (Luke 4:5–6). Jesus didn't dispute the legitimacy of the offer; since Adam had forfeited his dominion over the earth when he disobeyed, the kingdoms were Satan's to give away. Yet, this Man, Jesus, could not be bought (Luke 4:5–6). Satan, either not understanding who He was, exactly, or not understanding what was happening, eagerly convinced the Jews and the Romans to execute this "troublemaker." It is clear here that Satan did not understand the grand strategy, but instead became a tool God used to carry out His divine agenda.

> However, we speak wisdom among those who are mature, yet not the wisdom of this age, nor of the rulers of this age, who are coming to nothing. But we speak the wisdom of God in a mystery, the hidden wisdom which God ordained before the ages for our glory, which none of the rulers of this age knew; for had they known, they would not have crucified the Lord of glory. (1 Corinthians 2:6–8)

Satan did not kill the Messiah; Jesus came into this world knowing what He had to do (Matthew 17:23; Luke 9:22–23). Furthermore, God already knew Satan would be true to his nature, as he was a "murderer from the beginning" and the "father of lies" (John 8:44). Satan would incite the Jews to crucify their Messiah through the Romans. God used Satan to accomplish not just the redemption of Israel, but of the entire world.

Thus, Satan's defeat, in a way, was his own doing. By inciting the Jews and Romans to kill the Messiah, in effect, Satan's actions triggered the events that would afford mankind the opportunity he (Satan) never had (redemption). Think about the biggest blunders of your own life, and then magnify that by infinity, and that is what Satan did to himself. He enabled God to redeem the creation he (Satan) hates with all his being by killing the perfect, sinless Sacrifice (on Passover, no less) and then watching Him arise from death three days later.

Since the first man, Adam, everyone who had ever lived had sinned. This is why Satan was so self-assured (presumably) that Jesus was still bound under the eternal laws regarding sin and death. As the Scripture states, "For the wages of sin is death" (Romans 6:23).

Yet Jesus had never sinned, ever. Instead, He willingly went to the cross to take the wrath of God the Father upon Himself for our sins. In fact, He was the only person in the entire universe who could serve as our "Kinsman Redeemer" (Leviticus 25:47–55; Revelation 5:9–10). Furthermore, the Scriptures state:

> Fathers shall not be put to death for their children, nor shall children be put to death for their fathers; a person shall be put to death for his own sin. (Deuteronomy 24:16)

Since Jesus Himself had never sinned, the sting of death (sin) could no longer hold Him in the grave (1 Corinthians 15:55–57). Death had to let Him go, but He did not come up from Sheol (the abode of the dead) empty-handed (Ephesians 4:8–9). He brought with Him to Heaven the Old Testament saints who had been in holding in Abraham's Bosom (the Paradise side of Sheol).

Satan's defeat was sealed the moment Christ rose from the grave, and he knew it. His plan had utterly and completely backfired. Therefore, he had no other choice than to try to destroy both the Jews and this newly founded Church. By AD 70, the Romans, under General Titus, besieged Jerusalem, destroyed the Temple, and killed and enslaved millions of Jews.

Again, in AD 135, the Roman Emperor Hadrian reconquered Jerusalem, exiled the remaining Jews, salted the ground, and renamed the Jerusalem *Aelia Capitolina* and Judea *Palaestina*.

After Jerusalem and its Temple were destroyed, and after the Jewish people were killed and scattered, Satan went after the church. But persecuting the church only made it spread faster. Satan's plan was again failing, and he needed to change tactics. He then began corrupting the church through the same lies and deceit he had successfully used in other endeavors. In AD 312, Emperor Constantine legalized Christianity across the empire, and something rather terrible happened. Instead of the church going into the world to share the gospel, the world came into the church to spread its paganism.

By the fifth century, the state-sanctioned Roman Catholic Church (RCC) became the Holy Roman Empire. Five hundred years after that, the RCC was so debased that Catholic leadership actually came to believe they were doing the Lord's good work by persecuting, torturing, and killing Christians and Jews courtesy of the Crusades and the Inquisition. To this day, the RCC has never apologized for the hundreds of thousands of Christians they tortured and murdered around the world. In fact, the RCC leadership will become the prime movers in the last days for the global, ecumenical push to combine all religions into one, *vis-a-vis* the False Prophet.

This goes back to the reality of how wrong things feel in the world today. It is not just that mankind is becoming more unrepentant and more wicked (it is), but the geophysical world itself has become so saturated with the blood of the innocent, it will no longer remain silent or stable. Nature is groaning and straining under the judgment (Romans 8:20–22). Our increasingly violent and unpredictable weather is not because of human-caused "global warming," but because of Satan-induced hardening of mankind's hearts.

In the meantime, the Bible depicts Lucifer as still having access to Heaven, but only to go there to accuse the brethren day and night (Revelation 12:10). Satan does not live in Hell now, nor does he even live underground. Paul calls him the "prince of the power of the air" (Ephesians 2:2). While many people use the names "Lucifer" and "Satan" interchangeably, we should never confuse the imagery of a red, pointy-tailed, pitchfork-carrying Satan with his true appearance.

The fact that the Bible describes Satan as a red, fiery dragon is a depiction of his nature rather than his appearance. Lucifer approaches those he chooses to deceive by appearing as a beautiful, enlightened, "angel of light" (2 Corinthians 11:14). He promises the world—and those who take the deal might get riches, power, and fame for a short season—but there will be hell to pay for it. An eternity in torment, darkness, and absolute misery is an impossibly high price to pay for a fleeting moment of pleasure.

Furthermore, Satan is obsessed with becoming like God. Since Satan cannot create anything, he is limited to copying God's triune nature. However, he still needs two others to round out his faux triune godhead. Satan is looking for the perfect man to assume the role of the son. As far back as Nimrod, Satan has continually attempted to enshrine his candidate at the top of the geopolitical power structure.

Since the Tower of Babel dispersion and scattering severely limited Satan's options, he has had to labor intensely to bring mankind up to speed to achieve his dream of a singular, global, anti-God government. He has come close several times (Alexander the Great, Adolf Hitler), but even they could not pull it off. It will take the Rapture of the Church and the removal of restraint to bring about the revelation of this final world leader, the Antichrist.

Halfway through the Tribulation (at the three-and-a-half-year mark), there is an apparent assassination attempt, which seemingly kills this man, Antichrist. At the same time, Satan is officially cast out of Heaven and confined to the earth. Satan has to indwell this man to keep this Beast government going, and this is the point where the "man of lawlessness" transitions into the "son of perdition." The only other person in the Bible described as the "son of perdition" is Judas Iscariot, and we all know what he did (see John 17:12, 2 Thessalonians 2:3).

(Authors' Note: Some have wondered why the Antichrist and the False

Prophet are thrown into the Lake of Fire alive without trial and formal judgment by God, yet Satan is only bound in the Abyss for a thousand years. We believe that it is because these two, as mentioned previously, represent the six-thousand-year culmination of the totality of man's wickedness. The Antichrist's wickedness is representative of the lust for power, violence, and treachery that culminated in the world's final dictator, while the False Prophet represents the culmination of all the false religions that have led millions to Hell and eternal separation from God.)

One final comment regarding the antagonists of Revelation. Only one other fallen angel in the entire Bible is mentioned by name, and that is Abaddon (Revelation 9:11):

And they had as king over them the angel of the bottomless pit, whose name in Hebrew is Abaddon, but in Greek he has the name Apollyon.

At the fifth trumpet judgment, an angel opens the bottomless pit, and out of it appears an army of demonic locusts led by this Apollyon character. They are sent out to torment all who do not bear the mark of God on their foreheads for five months. Since it seems counterproductive for Satan to release this demonic horde to torment his own followers, we must conclude this demon king is a judgment by God against the Antichrist.

CONCLUSION

History serves as a great teacher (for those who are willing to learn) about what is coming in the last days. All of these men were antichrists in their own right and served the purpose of being cautionary examples. Just as the aforementioned leaders came in promising things, appealing to people's emotions, using persuasive language, and even displaying signs and wonders to woo the masses, they hid their true, beastly natures.

Is the Antichrist alive today? It is very likely. However, we (the Church) will not be here to find out). The Antichrist will most likely be someone most people do not expect at all. He is called the "little horn" not because of his physical stature, but because he arises out of obscurity and dethrones three other rulers rather effortlessly (Daniel 7:8; 8:9). Moreover, because Satan is not omniscient and cannot see into the future, he doesn't know when the Lord will return at the Rapture. There are probably numerous Antichrist candidates alive today; depending on the circumstances, Satan can activate those whom he thinks will most likely achieve his ends most efficiently.

Thinking back to World War II, Hitler wasn't the first leader Satan began to bestow with access to the kingdoms; Satan also did this for Benito Mussolini, Emperor Hirohito, and Joseph Stalin. All of these leaders began to rise to power around the same time the Ottoman Empire was defeated and the Balfour Declaration was written, giving Jews the right to return to their ancestral homeland.

So what makes someone a good contender to be the Antichrist? Well, if Satan thought the World War II era was likely to be prophetically significant, and he exercised his options with four world leaders then, we don't think he will shoot for any less than ten world leaders in the future. In addition, considering he was limited in his options given the technology of the World War II era, he will have exponentially more opportunities in our day.

Satan saw the collapse of the Nazi Third Reich and the Axis powers. He saw the prophetic return of Israel to its ancestral homeland. He has seen how Israel has survived and even thrived in a sea of Islamic instability for the past seventy years. He knows he is running out of time and will not make the same mistakes again. He will shape events and technology to such an Orwellian extreme that it will make anything less than total, global domination inescapable for those who are left behind after the Rapture of the Church.

Satan has seen the explosion of the interest in the Rapture of the Church from within Christendom with the likes of Hal Lindsey's *Late Great Planet Earth* and the LaHaye/Jenkins' *Left Behind* series. Satan, if anything, is a master of observation and probably senses long before most when the prophetic winds are beginning to shift. It would seem that with the surprise 2016 election victory of the longshot Donald Trump, Satan might have been caught off-guard. More likely, he wasn't caught by surprise, but his human agents (the secular, Christ-rejecting world) were. We would be willing to bet that he is currently scrambling to line up his frontrunners for the upcoming position of Antichrist.

What is interesting is that throughout the last two and a half years of Trump's presidency, he was thwarted/obstructed/attacked at almost every turn, with the exception of his actions as they pertained to Israel. It's as if Trump were being channeled into almost singularly focusing on that tiny nation in the Middle East. He promised to recognize Jerusalem as Israel's capital, and he did. He promised to move the US embassy from Tel Aviv to Jerusalem, and he did. He stood with and supported Benjamin Netanyahu as a close ally during the Israeli elections. He officially recognized the Golan Heights as part of Israel. He was able to bring the "Deal of the Century"—the Abraham Accords—into reality. None of these would have happened had Hillary Clinton won the election.

We believe this has emboldened the Jews who want a Third Temple as nothing else could. President Trump turned the decades-old status quo on its head. What the Orthodox Jews lacked since 1948, they finally have in the form of hope—hope that now is the time to rebuild the Third Temple. This, in our opinion, is why Satan moved earth and hell to get Trump dethroned from the highest political office in the world. Satan is not ready just quite yet; the conditions are not perfect enough for him to play his grand strategic hand that he has been dealt. Perhaps after four years of a Biden presidency?

This is what we believe Satan is watching extremely closely, and we think he is now readying his man/men, to assume control. He will stir up the Gog-Magog coalition to try to preemptively thwart the rebuilding of the Third Temple. This will backfire on him gloriously, and will be the impetus for actually making the construction of that important structure a reality. Somewhere in this conflict, both the Dome of the Rock and the al-Aqsa Mosque will likely be destroyed, which will open the door for the rebuilding.

With this much prophetic activity going on, Satan understands that the Rapture is near; however, he doesn't know when it is exactly. Because he is familiar with Scripture, he realizes it has to happen before the Seventieth Week begins, and that Scripture shifts the focus from the Church back to the nation of Israel in the last days. Moreover, if Satan did not believe the Rapture happened before the Tribulation, he would not have wasted as much time and energy in trying to destroy/corrupt/malign the sound, biblical teaching of the pre-Tribulation Rapture.

We also know that there is no mention of a USA-type nation in the prophetic Word, so the next most likely options for his pool of candidates seem to come from either Europe or the Middle East. In the last days, Satan will also use the kings of the east (Revelation 16:12) to come against Israel, but will keep them in his reserve forces to use as a last resort. What was lacking in World War II (and before) was the technology to accomplish all of what Revelation 11 and 13 seem to indicate; technology has finally reached the point to achieve all that Scripture states must happen (such as the implementation of the mark of the Beast, worldwide communications and travel, weapons of mass destruction).

We believe that Christianity has entered the final stage of church history—the Laodicean Age. This is because the culture (primarily in the West) is rapidly deconstructing itself and is becoming increasingly barbaric, hedonistic, pluralistic, and pagan. Intense pressure has been put on the church to make it bend to the will of the culture, rather than standing firm on the gospel of Jesus Christ.

What this all means is that Satan's man/men of the hour are alive today. These men likely have access to great power, but will not have expended any of that political capital as of yet. They will not even be known by the public, but most probably are thought to be the "power behind the throne" for many in the geopolitical world. These (like the Antichrist prototypes before them) are likely great observers of the state of the world and know how to achieve their ends without appearing to want a one-world government.

They will perhaps be watching the current crop of world leaders fumble, stumble, and make a mess of things today, and are learning from their mistakes. They are probably tied heavily into both the banking and technology industries. They will have access to and knowledge of the breaking technologies that will change the landscape before anyone else does. These privileged men are like walking Manchurian Candidates who are waiting to be activated at the right moment to begin their conquests in their respective areas.

Then a third angel followed them, saying with a loud voice, "If anyone worships the beast and his image, and receives his mark on his forehead or on his hand, he himself shall also drink of the wine of the wrath of God, which is poured out full strength into the cup of His indignation. He shall be tormented with fire and brimstone in the presence of the holy angels and in the presence of the Lamb. And the smoke of their torment ascends forever and ever; and they have no rest day or night, who worship the beast and his image, and whoever receives the mark of his name." (Revelation 14:9–10)

After the Bema Judgment, the place was absolutely electrified with anticipation of what was coming next. Clarissa had been rewarded with the imperishable crown, the crown of righteousness, and the crown of life, which she gladly cast before the feet of Jesus. Many other believers, too many to count, barely made it, as all of their works had been burned up as quickly as wood, hay, and stubble.

Clarissa thought back to her life on earth, and, even though it paled in comparison, it was like being at a concert and the lights dimming right before the main act came on stage. An angel broke the silence when he cried out, "Who is worthy to open the scroll and loose its seals?"

The ensuing silence following these words was deafening.

She saw at a distance someone she immediately recognized—the Apostle John. He was weeping at the silence, and immediately, an elder came up, comforted him, and spoke to him.

Then Jesus reappeared, this time, looking like He had after the crucifixion, but before His resurrection. His garments, as well as His head, were now covered in blood. He walked over to the Father's throne and took the scroll out of His Father's right hand. Just then, the four living creatures and the twenty-four elders (all twelve apostles plus the twelve righteous saints from the Church Age) began to sing:

You are worthy to take the scroll,
And to open its seals;
For You were slain,

And have redeemed us to God by Your blood
Out of every tribe and tongue and people and nation,
And have made us kings and priests to our God;
And we shall reign on the earth."
Then the rest of us, and the angels, and every creature in heaven,
    under and upon the earth, as well as the sea began to sing
"Blessing and honor and glory and power
Be to Him who sits on the throne,
And to the Lamb, forever and ever!"

Then Jesus opened the first seal on the scroll.

Marcie had been wandering for who knows how long now through what was left of the small ghost towns that dotted central Ohio. Quite frankly, the days all blended together and she didn't know how long she had been on her terrifying journey. Most everyone in the United States, as far as she could tell, had abandoned the center part of the country for the coasts. She'd left North Carolina and gone in the opposite direction, trying to get away from all the crazies.

After the Great Disappearing and the collapse of the US dollar, the nation quickly broke apart as the federal government feebly tried to maintain control. But with cell and Internet service becoming unreliable, and with the breakdown of the whole supply-chain system of goods and services, businesses and markets quickly dried up and shuttered their stores.

Large parts of the US became completely ungovernable; the Constitution was shelved and replaced with a nationwide martial-law mandate. Because there weren't enough personnel who remained to maintain law and order at the state and local levels, law enforcement and the military joined forces and created a quasi-paramilitary law organization called "Judges." However, even they were withdrawn to the predesignated urban centers to reorganize and reassess their options.

Those who had the means moved to one of the major urban centers that the governments still had control of: Los Angeles and Seattle on the West Coast and Colorado Springs and Houston in the central South. Atlanta and New York City were all that remained in the East. Not even Washington, DC, survived the collapse. Rioters had burned the city to the ground within days after the Disappearing.

After the state and federal governments pulled out, large, roving bands of biker gangs would roll through the center part of the US, from as far east as Kentucky down to Florida, to as far west as California. The Mexican cartels moved north and reclaimed large portions of Texas, New Mexico, Arizona, and Southern California. Other cities like Detroit, Chicago, and St. Louis were handed over to the rest of the criminal underworld—various gangs, zealots, extremists, and the mafia.

Small- to medium-sized towns were fair game for the criminal world. At first they came in raping and plundering. After that, they began murdering and destroying everything they could get their hands on. Marcie and Rocky had only survived this long by moving at night and hiding during the day. It truly felt like she was living in some nightmarish world like what's depicted in the *Mad Max* films. Thankfully, water supplies were still intact in most places.

From time to time, Marcie met up with some other semi-normal people who were out scavenging. Sometimes they'd paired up for a week or two, but things never worked out. Either they would eventually try to take advantage of her or they would do stupid things to get themselves caught or killed. But during the times when she had company, they would trade information about what they knew was going on in the rest of the world.

From what she heard, things weren't going great elsewhere either; war, famine, and great plagues of locusts and viral diseases were sweeping through large parts of the world. It could have swept through here as well, except there were hardly any people left to talk about it. After the cities were turned over to the criminal elements, they basically fought and warred amongst themselves to the point that they eventually wiped each other out and had to abandon their temporary kingdoms back to nature.

One evening, Marcie had found a small gas station on the outskirts of town that looked like it had been deserted long ago. She found the rest-room and peeked in to see if it was clear. It was there she saw her image in the mirror for the first time in a long time. She could hardly even recog-nize herself. Her hair had gone from a pristine blonde to almost brown, due to all the dirt and grime. Her face looked gaunt and aged, as if these past few years had been a few decades. Her eyes were sunken and her skin was pale from becoming nocturnal.

The last good memory she had was of the day it happened. She thought about how happy and oblivious to everything she had been the evening she had gone running with Clarissa. Marcie had had a steady teaching job, men who were interested in her, good friends, a nice apart-ment, and a cozy life. Now, she was eking out a living by scavenging like a stray dog. To add insult to injury, she even looked like a stray dog. She wondered where Clarissa was, and missed her friend dearly.

For the first time in her adult life, Marcie dropped to her knees—on the filthy restroom floor—bowed her head, and prayed. She cried out to God and to His Son, Jesus, to save her. Tears began streaming down her cheeks and not only washed away the dirt from her face, but cleansed the blindness from her heart. As if sensing the change, Rocky nudged her with his nose to be petted.

After what seemed like hours spent on the floor, Marcie rose to her feet again and looked into the mirror. There was something different now that hadn't been there before. She was still dirty and unkempt, still with gaunt reflection and all—but her eyes were different.

There was hope in them now.

9

THE SEAL JUDGMENTS

The Seventieth Week of Daniel (the Tribulation) does not begin with the Rapture; the Rapture merely *sets the conditions* for the Tribulation to begin. The Tribulation begins with the confirming of the covenant (or treaty), as mentioned in Daniel 9:27.

Since Jesus is opening the seals from Heaven, and Heaven exists in the eternal realm, outside of our time-based reality, it's difficult to say which happens first. Presumably, the opening of the seal triggers the event of Daniel 9:27, but it could be the other way around. However, we do know that the seal judgments, as well as the rest, are opened sequentially.

Dr. Andy Woods, pastor of Sugar Land Bible Church in Texas, had an interesting perspective on the Revelation judgments in one of his teachings, in that he styled these judgments as both sequential and "telescoping" in nature. What he meant by that is when we see the percentages given (one-third, one-fourth, etc.), these judgments cannot be all concurrent, or else they would be nonsensical. They must be sequential. With that said, let us do a little backwards planning.

- We know that by the midpoint of the Tribulation, there is a rebuilt Jewish Temple that the Antichrist desecrates in what Jesus termed the "abomination that causes desolation" (Matthew 24:15).

- In order to have a standing Jewish Temple with an intact Holy of Holies (for the Antichrist to desecrate), there must be a sovereign Jewish nation, one that is politically able and willing to build said Temple *in the place of* its present occupants (the al-Aqsa Mosque and the Dome of the Rock).
- In order to replace these iconic Islamic landmarks, Islam itself must be either nonexistent or in a position of weakness so as not to oppose their destruction or dismantlement.
- Islam is presently not in that position, but the tides are turning, with many Sunni nations aligning themselves with Israel over their even more extreme Shia cousins.
- There is a presumed gap in time between the Rapture of the Church and the official start of the Seventieth Week. There must be some level geopolitical stage-setting that answers these issues.
- We also know these judgments (primarily the seal judgments) factor into the beginning of the Seventieth Week. What we aren't entirely sure of is exactly when, since the Antichrist is unleashed by the first seal. So does seal 1 proceed the Daniel 9:27 treaty? Or vice versa?

When considering all the seal, trumpet, and vial judgments we see played out in the pages of Revelation, we often only look at them one-dimensionally. What we mean by that is we read it, but we often fail to ask *why* something is, rather than *what* it is. Why do hundred-pound hailstones pummel the earth? Why do the seas turn to blood? Why does a third of the vegetation on earth burn up? Is it just for the shock factor? Or are there more pragmatic reasons these particular types of judgments happen? Let's apply a considered perspective to all twenty-one judgments.

The judgments found in Revelation are often only viewed in terms of their effects on a Christ-rejecting world. However, shouldn't these judgments also serve a more practical purpose by reducing Satan's arsenal and limiting his ability to fight and maneuver? In other words, through these specific judgments, God is canalizing the Beast and his forces into certain courses of action by reducing his options. Much in the same way the judgment at the Tower of Babel delayed mankind's ability to unite by millennia, so do these actions serve a more strategic purpose.

However, none of this will happen until the greatest crisis in earth's history occurs, the *Rapture of the Church*. Once the Church (the multimember, singular Body of Christ on the earth) is removed, the restraining influence it held (through the Holy Spirit) is also removed. For clarification, the Holy Spirit is not removed (He is omnipresent), but the Holy Spirit-*filled-and-sealed* Body of Christ (the Church) is removed off the earth. This introduces the greatest period of darkness and unrestraint mankind has ever known (Matthew 24:21–22).

And I saw in the right hand of Him who sat on the throne a scroll written inside and on the back, sealed with seven seals. Then I saw a strong angel proclaiming with a loud voice, "Who is worthy to open the scroll and to loose its seals?" **And no one in heaven or on the earth or under the earth was able to open the scroll, or to look at it.**

So I wept much, because no one was found worthy to open and read the scroll, or to look at it. But one of the elders said to me, "Do not weep. Behold, the Lion of the tribe of Judah, the Root of David, has prevailed to open the scroll and to loose its seven seals."

And I looked, and behold, in the midst of the throne and of the four living creatures, and in the midst of the elders, stood a Lamb as though it had been slain, having seven horns and seven eyes, which are the seven Spirits of God sent out into all the earth. Then He came and took the scroll out of the right hand of Him who sat on the throne.

Now when He had taken the scroll, the four living creatures and the twenty-four elders fell down before the Lamb, each having a harp, and golden bowls full of incense, which are the prayers of the saints. Now when He had taken the scroll, the four living creatures and the twenty-four elders fell down before the Lamb,

each having a harp, and golden bowls full of incense, which are
the prayers of the saints. And they sang a new song, saying:

"You are worthy to take the scroll,

And to open its seals;

For You were slain,

And have redeemed us to God by Your blood

Out of every tribe and tongue and people and nation,

And have made us kings and priests to our God;

And we shall reign on the earth...."

Now I saw when the Lamb opened one of the seals; and I
heard one of the four living creatures saying with a voice like thunder, "Come and see." (Revelation 5:1–10, 6:1, emphasis added)

THE SEAL JUDGMENTS

Jesus initiates the judgments by opening the first seal. In fact, He was the
only One in all the universe who could have opened the seals, which triggers the succeeding twenty-one judgments. Here is a brief overview of the
complete list.

1. Seal 1: The white horse arrives (arrival of final world tyrant—the
   Antichrist).
2. Seal 2: The red horse arrives (peace is taken from the earth).
3. Seal 3: The black horse arrives (bringing global famine and
   scarcity).
4. Seal 4: The pale horse arrives (one-fourth of the earth dies).
5. Seal 5: The cry of the martyrs is sounded.
6. Seal 6: Cosmic disturbances and a great earthquake take place; the
   wrath of the Lamb is recognized.
7. Seal 7: Heaven falls silent for about a half-hour (Heaven is never
   silent).
8. Trumpet 1: One-third of the vegetation is struck.
9. Trumpet 2: One-third of the seas are struck.

10. Trumpet 3: One-third of fresh waters are struck (Wormwood).
11. Trumpet 4: One-third of the heavens are struck.
12. Trumpet 5: Demonic locusts emerge from the bottomless pit.
13. Trumpet 6: Angels from the Euphrates are released, killing one-third of mankind.

Seven thunders are proclaimed, not written down.

14. Trumpet 7: Kingdoms are proclaimed.
15. Bowl 1: Loathsome sores erupt.
16. Bowl 2: The sea turns to blood.
17. Bowl 3: Waters turn to blood.
18. Bowl 4: Men are scorched (does the sun supernova?).
19. Bowl 5: Darkness and pain fall.
20. Bowl 6: The Euphrates dries up.
21. Bowl 7: The earth is utterly shaken.

The seal judgments then, mark the beginning of the Seventieth Week of Daniel, and are the opening salvo against a Christ-rejecting world. Again, these are opened by none other than Jesus Christ Himself. Since the subsequent trumpet and bowl judgments are tied into the seal judgments, it is Christ who triggers ALL of the wrath during the Tribulation, period. Thus, we should deduce conclusively that Jesus is the One initiating the wrath of God open the earth (Revelation 5:1–5).

First Seal Judgment

And I looked, and behold, a white horse. He who sat on it had a bow; and a crown was given to him, and he went out conquering and to conquer. (Revelation 6:2)

The rider on the white horse has long been commonly accepted as the physical, literal, arrival of the Antichrist on the world stage. Even before the Apostle John was given the Revelation in AD 95, he had previously written that although many antichrists had already come, one final Antichrist was coming (1 John 2:18). That is quite an accomplishment, considering the long list of tyrants like Artaxerxes, Augustus Caesar, Genghis Khan, and Adolf Hitler.

This final one is different, however. He doesn't come to power through military conquest, but by deceit. He conquers by means of either a false peace or a threat of violence, but not with the violence itself. The mention of him as having a bow (a shooting weapon), one theory indicates that he gains control of some nation's ability to project intercontinental ballistic missiles (ICBMs) against those who would oppose him.

His aide-de-camp is none other than the False Prophet. One very likely theory is that this individual is not initially a religious figure, but a political public-relations person. Through his relentless public relations campaigns in social and traditional media, he champions the rightful rule of the Antichrist against all the other leaders, creating a "cult of personality" movement for the Antichrist. Since, after the Rapture, the restraining influence of the Holy Spirit is removed from the earth, this quickly turns from hero worship into deification (similar to that of the Pharaohs and Caesars of old).

Since Satan is the temporary manager of the earth, he possesses limited dominion in whom he loans his favor to. Examples of this satanic favoring in history were to men like Alexander the Great, Genghis Khan, and even Hitler's meteoric rise to power in the late 1920s/early 1930s in post-World War I Germany. Nothing seemed to be able to stop these men until that favor was rescinded or God intervened. A recent and very obvious example of this satanic favoring was the faux victory by the Joe Biden campaign.

Everyone knew that the victory of a seventy-eight-year old candidate was a façade. Biden's extensive career was marked repeatedly by political gaffes and serious moments of confusion. Even still, he barely squeaked through the Democratic primaries. Given all that, the press propagandized his message so that somehow he received more votes than any president in US history? But such was the victory. It made no sense to the average person, but to the Deep State, the established political class, and the media, it was a risk worth taking in destroying the Constitution. The Democrats' political machine knew they didn't need to commit political fraud across all fifty states, but just enough in the swing states to throw the entire election. They did this through delayed vote counting, universal mail-in ballots, compromised voting machines, and complete political and legal top cover by a complicit mainstream media.

But why?

Because President Trump threatened and was in the process of dismantling the globalization they had worked so hard to achieve. There was zero willingness to aid Trump and his team in their legal recourse. There was zero willingness to stop it by the Department of Justice. The unwillingness by establishment Republicans and the media, and even by the Supreme Court of the United States, was not just political, but spiritual. The Apostle Paul warned us in Ephesians 6:12 that our battle is not against flesh and blood, but against principalities and forces of darkness that influence their human minions to do their bidding. The spirit of Antichrist is alive and well ahead of his physical arrival in the not-too-distant future.

The satanic forces realized that another four years of Trump would have created a serious logistical situation problem for their Beast kingdom. It would set back their century-long efforts to establish a one-world government. Thus they waged a relentless campaign of fear, blackmail, and intimidation against the established political classes to ensure that no effort by the Trump legal team or any other legal proceedings would succeed.

The arrival of the Antichrist will be similar in its inevitability. He will begin as an unknown military or political entity, but will quickly rise through the ranks. His rise will be just as meteoric as Barack Obama's was from being a no-named community organizer, to a state senator, then to US president in just a matter of eight years. It is without a doubt we believe this man, the Antichrist, is alive today, presumably being groomed for this position as we write this.

Probably a better term for this final Antichrist is not "Antichrist," but "Pseudo Christ." The rider on the white horse (seal 1) is the political arrival of the Antichrist.

Takeaways:

- The Antichrist and False Prophet's reign of terror is summarized in Revelation 13.
- He is a master politician and strategist. He will be unassuming in his initial rise to power in the final Gentile kingdom, which, through the turmoil caused by the Rapture, will become the revived Roman Empire.
- He'll capitalize on the crisis left by the Rapture by garnering the tools at hand: the Internet of Things, quantum technology, global Wi-Fi, global satellites and surveillance systems, artificial intelligence, holography, and digital currency, etc., to solidify his authority.

SECOND SEAL JUDGMENT

When He (Jesus) opened the second seal, I heard the second living creature saying, "Come and see." Another horse, fiery red, went out. And it was granted to the one who sat on it to take peace from the earth, and that people should kill one another; and there was given to him a great sword. (Revelation 6:3–4)

After the Rapture, the world will be thrown into chaos by the collapsing of the United States. Since the end of the Second World War, the United States has been the *center of gravity* by which the rest of the world moved economically, politically, and militarily. Once the US collapses due to the loss of its Christian population, the geopolitical status quo is thrown into disarray. Nations will scramble to make their claim as the head nation.[18]

The logical conclusion that will be drawn by the remaining global leaders is the formation of regionally aligned governments (aligned by economic cultural similarities and geographic proximity). It is then theorized that this will trigger a counter-alliance (the Gog-Magog coalition). This initial attempt to invade Israel will fail, and those forces will be utterly destroyed by God.

This creates a secondary vacuum, which the newly revised Roman Empire will begin to fill. They will need to solidify their claims of prominence, but this also touches off wars as smaller nations and/or civilian populations refuse to be dragged into it. The Antichrist will use war and crises to consolidate his control over nations and populations that refuse to yield to his authority economically or politically.

Takeaways:

- The rise of an all-powerful political leader will necessitate the need for a powerful military to match his ambitions, which is only possible after the Rapture of the Church decimates the United States.
- NATO will be converted into the European Defense Force and will use our collapse to assume the role of the new world superpower by harvesting our massive weapons stockpiles. They also will likely recruit forces from around the world to join their ranks.

THIRD SEAL JUDGMENT

When He opened the third seal, I heard the third living creature say, "Come and see." So I looked, and behold, a black horse, and he who sat on it had a pair of scales in his hand. And I heard a voice in the midst of the four living creatures saying, "A quart of wheat for a denarius, and three quarts of barley for a denarius; and do not harm the oil and the wine." (Revelation 6:5–6)

The Antichrist will use economic means initially to assume control. But how does he assume total economic control when there are still 180 currencies circulating throughout the world? With the political and economic collapse of the United States comes the financial failure of the world's markets. This includes the disintegration of fiat currencies the world currently depends on to conduct business.

The sequence of events is as follows: The Rapture of the Church will impact the entire world, but will gut the United States; the downfall of the United States will cause the global financial markets to implode. This crisis provides the opportunity for global leaders to reorganize into regional governments to survive the catastrophe, which gives the Antichrist (an unknown entity) the ability to quickly rise through the ranks and ascend to the top. He will introduce a technological solution to the world's economic problems; this solidifies his political authority. His political authority will engender instability amongst nations that do not want to be under his thumb, which leads to a third world war.

World war leads to global economic ruin (that's what wars usually do), except for those people who are profiting from the war. The Antichrist will then use this crisis to consolidate his financial and commercial control over the world's economic systems much in the same way Hitler attempted to do across Europe with his Four-Year Plan.[19]

Think of this as the Antichrist's "Seven-Year Plan." In theory, this will create not only greater wealth, but greater control over the population as private ownership disappears and every form of commerce becomes digitized (thus trackable and controlled by the surveillance state). In reality, this system will grind down hundreds of millions in order to prop up a few. Mass starvation and scarcity will become the real "new normal," as people are forced into accepting the "Mark" system in order to buy or sell.

Takeaways:

- Antichrist will implement a failsafe form of identity protection and commerce via this new technology. This mark (presumably a type of biomedical device) will serve as a form of identification, a system of credit, and a way to demonstrate loyalty to this final kingdom.[20]

- The mark will also serve as a form of worship in this new system; by taking it, one swears allegiance to the Beast. This allegiance makes the bearer unredeemable (Revelation 14:9–10), which means it seemingly alters or corrupts the bearer's DNA/RNA genetically.
- Those who refuse to take the mark are increasingly shut out of the system and face ruin, execution, and/or starvation.

FOURTH SEAL JUDGMENT

When He opened the fourth seal, I heard the voice of the fourth living creature saying, "Come and see." So I looked, and behold, a pale horse. And the name of him who sat on it was Death, and Hades followed with him. And power was given to them over a fourth of the earth, to kill with sword, with hunger, with death, and by the beasts of the earth. (Revelation 6:7–8)

The rider (Death) on the pale horse signifies an escalation of the previous horses, through power of the sword, hunger, death, and beasts of the earth (from wild animals to viruses and bacteria). These four horsemen wipe out a fourth of the earth's population.

Takeaways:

- By this time, war, famine, and pestilence will have killed a quarter of the earth's population. If we were using 2021's population of 7.8 billion, this would be equivalent to the deaths of 1,950,000,000 people.
- Antichrist will use this crisis to further consolidate his religious control. The False Prophet (the Antichrist's public-relations chief) will begin to turn worship away from the ecumenical Mystery Babylon (see Revelation 17) and towards the Antichrist himself by the midpoint.

FIFTH SEAL JUDGMENT

When He opened the fifth seal, I saw under the altar the souls of those who had been slain for the word of God and for the testimony which they held. And they cried with a loud voice, saying, "How long, O Lord, holy and true, until You judge and avenge our blood on those who dwell on the earth?" Then a white robe was given to each of them; and it was said to them that they should rest a little while longer, until both the number of their fellow servants and their brethren, who would be killed as they were, was completed. (Revelation 6:9–11)

After the Rapture, a minority of left-behind survivors will realize what just happened because, during the years leading up to the Rapture, many online and traditional ministries will have been speaking of it and preaching about it. Although the number of those speaking and preaching about the subject has decreased in recent years, there will still be enough residual information available that, as soon as the Rapture occurs, many will seek this information out and realize it for what it was: the Church's deliverance. These people will also learn that to take the mark of the Beast is to commit spiritual suicide and secure eternal damnation.

Because the Beast's (the ten heads) ascendancy in a post-Rapture world will be so overwhelming and unstoppable, this minority, the emerging remnant, will refuse to participate, and will be killed mercilessly. Revelation 13:7 states:

It was granted to him [the Antichrist] to make war with the saints and to overcome them. And authority was given him over every tribe, tongue, and nation.

Many will be slain for their turn to Christ, yet, their questioning of how much longer is interesting. Since Revelation 13 is an overview of the rise of the Beast, the Antichrist, and the False Prophet, the war he makes against the Tribulation saints denotes that it begins in Revelation chapter 6, or possibly even before. Note God's response to the souls of the martyrs; He tells them to wait until a specific number of them are killed, as they were.

Takeaways:

- The False Prophet (the Antichrist's right-hand man) also takes advantage of emerging technology with artificial intelligence, augmented reality, and holography to broadcast the Antichrist's image everywhere and to display his seemingly supernatural power.
- This religious fervor will cause Antichrist's followers to increasingly and mercilessly persecute anyone who does not worship the Beast or take his mark of loyalty. It will make what we see today with ISIS and other Islamic *jihadi* movements seem tame by comparison.

SIXTH SEAL JUDGMENT

I looked when He opened the sixth seal, and behold, there was a great earthquake; and the sun became black as sackcloth of hair, and the moon became like blood. And the stars of heaven fell to the earth, as a fig tree drops its late figs when it is shaken by a mighty wind. Then the sky receded as a scroll when it is rolled up, and every mountain and island was moved out of its place.

And the kings of the earth, the great men, the rich men, the commanders, the mighty men, every slave and every free man, hid themselves in the caves and in the rocks of the mountains, and said to the mountains and rocks, "Fall on us and hide us from the face of Him who sits on the throne and from the wrath of the Lamb! For the great day of His wrath **has come**, and who is able to stand?" (Revelation 6:12–17, emphasis added)

The opening of the sixth seal will trigger a massive earthquake, which presumably produces so much dust and smoke that it blots out the sun during the day and causes a blood moon to occur at night. We know that a regular blood moon cannot coexist with a solar eclipse, due to the position of the earth in relation to either the sun or the moon.

Also coinciding with this is a massive meteor shower that blankets the earth. The earth then will be shaken so much that every mountain and island will be moved out of its place (such as when the Great Sendai Earthquake/tsunami in 2011 moved Japan by eight feet) and the sky will recede as a scroll. Presumably, if this a meteor shower, its entry into earth's atmosphere will appear as a burning sky. The rich and poor alike will then hide themselves for fear and recognize that the wrath of the Lamb has come.

> The verb ēlethen ("has come") is aorist indicative, referring to a previous arrival of wrath, not something that is about to take place. Men see the arrival of this day at least as early as the cosmic upheavals that characterize the sixth seal (6:12–14), but upon reflection they probably recognize that it was already in effect with the death of one-fourth of the population (6:7–8), the worldwide famine (6:5–6), and the global warfare (6:3–4). The rapid sequence of all of these events could not escape notice, but the light of their true explanation does not dawn upon human consciousness until the severe phenomena of the sixth seal arrive.[21]

Thus, the argument from many proposing a mid-Trib or pre-wrath Rapture (who advocate that wrath really doesn't begin until the trumpet judgments) are either lacking in their understanding of what wrath is, or simply in denial of it. Christ Himself initiates the wrath in the opening of the first seal.

Takeaways:

- Fearful sights and great signs will appear from the heavens.
- Great earthquakes will occur in various places.
- God will push back in a warning; the earth dwellers will hide in

fear. Note the mention of military leaders and great men hiding in caves and bunkers at the celestial turbulence (see also Luke 21:25–26).

SEVENTH SEAL JUDGMENT:

When He opened the seventh seal, there was silence in heaven for about half an hour. (Revelation 8:1)

Throughout Scripture, Heaven (where God resides) is always described as being a place of continuous praise and worship of God almighty by His angels. For there to be silence means something ominous is about to begin. There is also a literary jump in the text here; we're taken from the sequential ordering in the seal judgments of chapter 6 to the sequential ordering of trumpet judgments in chapter 8, skipping over chapter 7.

Takeaways:

- Scripture (Revelation 4–5) tells us that Heaven is always filled with the unceasing praise by the living creatures, the elders, and angels who continually praise God and His holiness. At the seventh seal, however, there is silence, which indicates the intensifying sense of foreboding about the things that are coming upon the earth.
- Chapter 7 primarily deals with the sealing of the 144,000 male virgins from the twelve tribes of Israel and a return discussion to the martyrs coming out of the Tribulation. Technically, there are thirteen tribes, with Joseph's two sons (Ephraim and Manasseh) usually rotating in to replace Levi in the Old Testament. The missing tribes not included in this divine sealing are Dan and Ephraim, which may either relate to their past apostasies (in the time of the judges) or to some future one related to the coming of the Antichrist.

(Note: For more information about the seal judgments, please see the article, "Seals, Trumpets, and Bowls" by Pete Garcia, in Appendix A.)

CLARISSA WATCHED THE UNFOLDING EVENTS UPON THE EARTH AS Christ opened seal after the other. She knew that from earth's perspective, these seemingly random events appeared to be happening because of the Great Disappearing. However, from her heavenly perspective, she could see the horsemen ride down to earth and carry out their apocalyptic rides of terror across the face of the earth because of what Christ had done.

She could see the slaughter of all those who had become believers because of the Rapture and would not bow to the rising Beast system. By the sixth seal, the world and its leaders were hiding from all the terrible cosmic disturbances and the greatest earthquake to date.

But when they got to the seventh seal, all of Heaven fell silent. There was a profound sense of foreboding, as the seven angels lined up and received their trumpets. Even though a quarter of mankind had died during the seal judgments, what the trumpet judgments offered was far more severe.

She watched as God the Holy Spirit sealed 144,000 Jewish male virgins on the forehead, even though they were scattered throughout the earth. These were young boys between the ages of four and five who had been born in the years after the Rapture but before the official start of the Seventieth Week. Although they had not reached adolescence, she understood they would enter into the Kingdom this way, as children. This reminded Clarissa of something Jesus had said in His ministry on the earth, "Let the little children come to Me, and do not forbid them; for of such is the kingdom of heaven." These would follow Jesus wherever He went, and they would, in fact, inherit the Kingdom. Only then would they continue to grow into their mature, glorified bodies.

In the meantime, they would need the divine protection for what was now coming upon the earth.

10

THE TRUMPET JUDGMENTS

Whereas most of the seal judgments are focused on both the geopolitical terraforming and culling of the global population, the trumpet judgments are focused initially on physically terraforming the earth. Not only this, but the severity has increased, destroying not just man, but nature as well.

(Authors' note: Since much of Revelation is drawn from the Old Testament and has a very Jewish flavor, it should be no surprise that we begin to see similarities between the plagues that rocked Egypt during the days of the Exodus and here at the end. We will compare the two events only insomuch as the kind of judgments; clearly, the Egyptian plagues were limited to Egypt during Moses' day.)

THE TRUMPET JUDGMENTS

When He opened the seventh seal, there was silence in heaven for about half an hour. And I saw the seven angels who stand before God, and to them were given seven trumpets. Then another angel, having a golden censer, came and stood at the altar. He was given much incense that he should offer it with the prayers of all the saints upon the golden altar which was before the throne. And the smoke of the incense, with the prayers of the saints, ascended before God from the angel's hand. Then the angel took the censer, filled it with fire from the altar, and threw it to the earth. And there were noises, thunderings, lightnings, and an earthquake. So the seven angels who had the seven trumpets prepared themselves to sound. (Revelation 8:1–6)

FIRST TRUMPET JUDGMENT

The first angel sounded: And hail and fire followed, mingled with blood, and they were thrown to the earth. And a third of the trees were burned up, and all green grass was burned up [seventh Egyptian plague correlation].

According to nature.com, a recent scientific study found that the earth currently contains around 3.04 trillion trees. While that might sound like a lot (it was more than they originally believed), the presumably *unbiased* researchers go on to theorize that it is roughly half the number of trees they believe existed since humans started walking upright (their opinion).

According to Scripture, during the first trumpet judgment, one-third of all the trees on the earth will be burnt up through fire and hail (Revelation 8:7). Purely going off the number of trees, this study shows that almost a third of three trillion trees are located in the Western Hemisphere. If we were to add up the total number of trees in the Western Hemisphere's three largest nations (Canada, 318 billion; Brazil, 302 billion; United States, 228 billion), we get 848 billion trees. That is 152 billion trees short of one trillion. However, if we add in the rest of the nations in our hemisphere (Mexico, Argentina, Chile, etc.), it should reasonably fill out the rest of the one trillion trees that are consumed inside the Seventieth Week of Daniel.

Does this mean that the Western Hemisphere is destroyed by some supernatural, cataclysmic event? We do not know, but the numbers are intriguing.

SECOND TRUMPET JUDGMENT

> Then the second angel sounded: And something like a great mountain burning with fire was thrown into the sea, and a third of the sea became blood. And a third of the living creatures in the sea died, and a third of the ships were destroyed.

There are several theories floating around about this particular judgment. The first is that it is a massive comet or meteor strikes the earth. The second is that a massive volcanic eruption, perhaps based on the previous massive earthquake (Revelation 6:12), causes a mountain in or near the Atlantic to be thrown into the ocean (Coast Mountains, Canary Island, etc.). The third theory is based on the Two Witnesses calling down this judgment based on what Jesus stated in Mark 11:23:

> For assuredly, I say to you, whoever says to this mountain, "Be removed and be cast into the sea," and does not doubt in his heart, but believes that those things he says will be done, he will have whatever he says.

All we know for certain is that John is shown what appears to be something as large as a mountain, on fire, being thrown into the sea. Now, some have speculated that for an object this size to hit the earth and do the damage it does, it should be (if in the near future) visible to either NASA or even amateur astronomers years ahead of its arrival. But, there have been near misses in the past that no one had been tracking. In early June of 2020, an asteroid more than one hundred meters wide (three hundred feet) passed between the moon and the earth. No one even knew about it until it had already passed.[22]

(Authors' note: The Tunguska event, which was the meteor that struck Siberia, Russia, in 1908, was believed to be only 330 feet across, and the explosion flattened 80 million trees in an area of 830 square miles.)

While modern astronomy and space agencies (Space Command, NASA, International Space Station, etc.) pride themselves on their prediction capabilities, this competency is based on technology available today. We may have significantly reduced capabilities after the seal judgments and all the damage done on the earth at that point in the future (i.e., after the four horsemen's arrival, the occurrence of the great earthquake, and the receding of the sky, etc.). It is very likely they may not see it coming at all.

As far as location, could this be referencing the Mediterranean Sea? Most biblical references to the "great sea" are speaking of the Mediterranean, as much of the Western Hemisphere at that point had not yet been discovered. If it is, what would the blood oceans accomplish? Of note here, the sea does not become "like" blood, but it, in fact, "becomes" blood. This means that ships and other seafaring boats would not be able to traverse its red waves. There are three strategic choke points in the Mediterranean: the Suez Canal, the Turkish Strait of Bosporus, and the Strait of Gibraltar. If the waters of any of these three were turned to blood, it could effectively shut down a majority of all seafaring traffic in the Mediterranean. However, if this is referencing the Atlantic Ocean, which makes up a third of the earth's oceans, it could permanently divide or cut off those in the Western Hemisphere from those in the Eastern Hemisphere.

THIRD TRUMPET JUDGMENT

Then the third angel sounded: And a great star fell from heaven, burning like a torch, and it fell on a third of the rivers and on the springs of water. The name of the star is Wormwood. A third of the waters became wormwood, and many men died from the water, because it was made bitter. (Revelation 8:10–11)

The common name "wormwood" (*Artemisia absinthium*) comes from the silvery-green perennial herb that contains the volatile and psychoactive oil thujone. Wormwood has been used for millennia as both a medicine and a form of gall (either wormwood or myrrh mixed with wine to dull the senses; later refined into the popular liquor absinthe), which in small doses is purported to cause hallucinations.[23]

"Wormwood" is mentioned only once in the New Testament—here in Revelation—but eight times in the Old Testament. Each time, it is associated with bitterness, poison, and death. It is then assumed that this second heavenly body to strike the earth contains some pollutant that makes the fresh waters turn toxic.

Takeaways:

- "Over 68 percent of the fresh water on Earth is found in icecaps and glaciers, and just over 30 percent is found in ground water. Only about 0.3 percent of our fresh water is found in the surface water of lakes, rivers, and swamps. Of all the water on Earth, more than 99 percent of Earth's water is unusable by humans and many other living things!"[24]
- With the fresh water becoming contaminated, mankind will be forced to turn to the desalination of sea water to find suitable drinking water. "Israel is considered the pioneers in seawater and briny wells," through evaporation and reverse osmosis. Currently, the nations who rely on desalination processes for the majority of their drinking waters are: Saudi Arabia, United Arab Emirates, Kuwait, Qatar, Bahrain, and Libya.[25]
- More than 50 percent of the desalination plants are located in the Middle East, with Africa (6.2 percent), Asia (10.6 percent), Europe (10.1 percent), North America (17 percent), South America (0.6 percent), and Australia (0.4 percent) making up the rest.[26]

Again, this judgment (along with the first trumpet judgment) seems to be canalizing the world's population back to the Middle East. It would seem that nations that have long depended on seawater desalination would be better prepared to survive this judgment than nations who never have.

FOURTH TRUMPET JUDGMENT

> Then the fourth angel sounded: And a third of the sun was struck, a third of the moon, and a third of the stars, so that a third of them were darkened. A third of the day did not shine, and likewise the night.

Takeaways:

- As in a reverse form of what happened at Babel, instead of scattering, God may be coagulating the earth's population. The first through fourth trumpets may indicate God confining mankind to one geographic location on the earth by making up to a third or a fourth of the planet uninhabitable. One-fourth of the earth's land mass is found in the Americas (North, Central, South, and Greenland).
- If a third of the celestial bodies is darkened, then it must be from smoke, dust, or some other form of obscuration that blocks our view of the sky from the earth. A scenario like the Yellowstone Supervolcano erupting could do that.
- If this is the case, then the Antichrist will have a short time between the Rapture and the first trumpet judgment to get the people, equipment, and weapons he needs from the Americas over to Europe to consolidate his power. Then it will become the world's greatest migratory movement of people, as well as its greatest wealth transfer ever.

And I looked, and I heard an angel flying through the midst of heaven, saying with a loud voice, "Woe, woe, woe to the inhabitants of the earth, because of the remaining blasts of the trumpet of the three angels who are about to sound!" (verse 13)

FIFTH TRUMPET JUDGMENT (FIRST WOE)

Then the fifth angel sounded: And I saw a star fallen from heaven to the earth. To him was given the key to the bottomless pit. And he opened the bottomless pit, and smoke arose out of the pit like the smoke of a great furnace. So the sun and the air were darkened because of the smoke of the pit. Then out of the smoke locusts came upon the earth. And to them was given power, as the scorpions of the earth have power. They were commanded not to harm the grass of the earth, or any green thing, or any tree, but only those men who do not have the seal of God on their foreheads. And they were not given authority to kill them, but to torment them for five months. Their torment was like the torment of a scorpion when it strikes a man. In those days men will seek death and will not find it; they will desire to die, and death will flee from them.

The shape of the locusts was like horses prepared for battle. On their heads were crowns of something like gold, and their faces were like the faces of men. They had hair like women's hair, and their teeth were like lions' teeth. And they had breastplates like breastplates of iron, and the sound of their wings was like the sound of chariots with many horses running into battle. They had tails like scorpions, and there were stings in their tails. Their power was to hurt men five months. And they had as king over them the angel of the bottomless pit, whose name in Hebrew is Abaddon, but in Greek he has the name Apollyon. One woe is past. Behold, still two more woes are coming after these things. (Revelation 9:1–12)

The book of Revelation has suffered more ridicule at the hands of liberal theologians and skeptics than any other book of the Bible except for maybe Genesis. Yet, even the hardest passages to take in light of this veritable age of reason and information we live in are not as far-fetched as some might think.

In dealing with all the revisionist changes the Bible has suffered under the increasingly apostate "Christian" theological circles, we are reminded of the Sadducees in Jesus' day. It would seem that they put the Pentateuch by Moses above all other OT books. They also rejected the resurrection of the dead and the existence of angels (Acts 23:8). Most theologians today would like to simply explain away Revelation as symbolic apocalyptic literature, and reduce it to just a sentence that states: "In the end, God wins."

However, that isn't what God gave us. He provides specific details about a period of time scheduled to happen here on planet earth in the not-too-distant future. Even in these details, some things are still a mystery to us. For those of us who take the Bible seriously and hold to a literal, grammatical, and historical hermeneutical view of God's Word, we still wrestle with passages such as Revelation 9:11.

Many scholars have come to these passages and tried to interpret them in light of our modern weaponry, such as helicopters or robotic drones. While it's tempting to try to superimpose our understanding onto these passages, it simply doesn't do God's Word the justice it deserves. However, that doesn't mean we can't know anything about it. So here is what we know and can reasonably determine (or speculate) thus far. First, here is a quote from John Phillips that is apropos:

> Picture what the world would be like if we were to open the doors of all the penitentiaries of earth and set free the world's most vicious and violent criminals, giving them full reign to practice their infamies upon mankind. Something worse than that lies in store for the world. Satan, cast out of heaven, is now permitted to summon to his aid the most diabolical fiends in the abyss to act as his agents in bringing mankind to the footstool of the Beast.[27]

The Locust King

> The locusts have no king, yet they all advance in ranks. (Proverbs 30:27)

> Then the fifth angel sounded: And I saw a star fallen from heaven to the earth. To him was given the key to the bottomless pit. And he opened the bottomless pit, and smoke arose out of the pit like the smoke of a great furnace. So the sun and the air were darkened because of the smoke of the pit. (Revelation 9:1–2)

The book of Revelation is symbolic in many areas, but the symbolism itself is not abstract or nonsensical; its meanings can be found in other parts of the Scripture itself. So when we come to passages that can't be taken either literally or physically, as a star could not physically land on the earth, we look at the Bible to interpret itself, and then the improbable comes into clear focus. These passages refer to angels and Satan in figurative terms, but clearly there is a real meaning behind the symbolism (Job 38:7; Isaiah 14:12; Luke 10:18; Jude 1:13; Revelation 1:20, 12:4). A "star falling to earth" refers to an angelic being coming to the earth, as the being is referred to as a "him," and he was in possession of the "key to the bottomless pit."

The late Chuck Missler was the first theologian we are aware of to note that a bottomless pit could easily reside within the center of the earth. Since the earth is a sphere, at the center, every direction from there would be "up," it would, by that very nature, have no bottom to it. Moreover, as we've seen a dramatic increase in the number and intensity of volcanic eruptions in the last twenty years, it isn't hard to imagine that smoke and ash from a large one (or multiple ones) could darken the skies and blot out the sun and moon for weeks on end all around the globe.[28]

> Then out of the smoke locusts came upon the earth and to them was given power, as the scorpions of the earth have power. They

were commanded not to harm the grass of the earth, or any green thing, or any tree, but only those men who do not have the seal of God on their foreheads. And they were not given authority to kill them, but to torment them for five months. Their torment was like the torment of a scorpion when it strikes a man. **In those days men will seek death and will not find it; they will desire to die, and death will flee from them.** (Revelation 9:2–6, emphasis added)

So, right off the bat, we realize that these are not normal locusts, as normal locusts don't originate from smoke-filled pits that resemble great furnaces. Locusts eat vegetation (Joel 1:4), but these were instructed not to eat the grass or any vegetation, but to inflict torment on those who did not have the seal of God on their foreheads. When Moses was instructed by God to stretch out his rod and summon forth the plague of locusts against the Pharaoh, note the precise description of the event:

They were very severe; previously there had been no such locusts as they, **nor shall there be such after them.** For they covered the face of the whole earth, so that the land was darkened; and they ate every herb of the land and all the fruit of the trees which the hail had left. So there remained nothing green on the trees or on the plants of the field throughout all the land of Egypt. (Exodus 10:14–15, emphasis added)

(Note: The global plague mentioned in Exodus could also be a lead contributor to the end of the Bronze Age, with agriculture famine decimating areas around Egypt, depending on how we date the Exodus.)

So not only are these *not* regular insects, but they're not mechanical or modern weaponry, either. They are intelligent, sentient beings who, as we will see later, act under the authority of their leader, Abaddon.

Also of interest is that John notes that men will aggressively "seek death," but cannot find it. Does this mean that they will not be able to die? We imagine that if there were any truth to a "zombie apocalypse," as it has been commonly called, it would be during this period. If people put a gun in their mouth and pull the trigger, will they continue on grotesquely disfigured? We don't know, but perhaps part of the selling point of taking the mark of the Beast in the first place is the premise that it does something to the body that prevents death. So the specific purpose of the torment of these "locusts" directly correlates to something the mark does to the body.

> The shape of the locusts was **like** horses prepared for battle. On their heads were crowns of something **like** gold, and their faces were **like** the faces of men. They had hair **like** women's hair, and their teeth were **like** lions' teeth. And they had breastplates **like** breastplates of iron, and the sound of their wings was **like** the sound of chariots with many horses running into battle. They had tails **like** scorpions, and there were stings in their tails. *Their power was to hurt men five months.* (Revelation 9:7–10, emphasis added)

If you want to see what is symbolic in Revelation and what is not, just look for the word "like." A first-century apostle, John, is attempting to put into words what he is seeing, and to him, this is how they appear. Because they look so bizarre, modern theological scholars have struggled with what exactly these might represent. They have human faces, breastplates of iron, and wings that sound like chariots when they move. Many have tried to apply a twenty-first-century perspective to a first-century description. The only problem is these beings are not human. The closest we can come to anything like these creatures is found in mythology.

If something like this does exist in military weaponry, it is buried deep within the bowels of some secret DARPA complex. However, that still does not explain how robotic or mechanical equipment followed and were led by a fallen angel and came out of a bottomless pit. I believe, for the time being, we will just have to take John's word for it as he saw them.[29]

And they had as king over them the angel of the bottomless pit, whose name in Hebrew is Abaddon, but in Greek he has the name Apollyon. (Revelation 9:11)

There was a time in man's history when fallen angels intermingled with man in an attempt to corrupt man's bloodline so much that a Messiah could not come from the line of man (Genesis 3:15). These fallen angels were punished severely for crossing God's divine boundaries:

And the angels who did not keep their proper domain, but left their own abode, He has reserved in everlasting chains under darkness for the judgment of the great day. (Jude 1:6)

For if God did not spare the angels who sinned, but cast them down to hell and delivered them into chains of darkness, to be reserved for judgment. (2 Peter 2:4)

We know, according to biblical and extrabiblical texts, that there were supposedly two hundred "watchers" that intermingled with the seed of man. It would appear—at least according to the strict reading of the text—that those angels are still confined and will be until the Day of Judgment. What we don't know is how many *other* fallen angels (or other heavenly beings or their offspring) either prior to the Flood or afterwards crossed some other divine barrier and were thus confined by God to the Abyss for such a day as this. We know according to Scriptures that there were angels confined to the Abyss, because Luke 8:30–32 records it.[30]

Abaddon, or Apollyon (the Destroyer)—along with the fallen angels—will be released from the Abyss during the fifth trumpet judgment. Remember that in a single night, one angel wiped out 185,000 Assyrians (2 Kings 19:35–36). But now (during the fifth trumpet judgment) they no longer have their might as angels, but are released as locust-like beings. These cursed beings no longer have the power or authority to kill, but only to torment for five months. Why five months as opposed to six or seven? Their limited time seems to be in preparation for the sixth trumpet judgment, because the text tells us that "one woe is past," and that the sixth trumpet judgment is prepared for an army and supernatural beings "who had been prepared for the hour and day and month and year, were released to kill a third of mankind" (Revelation 9:13–21).

Takeaways:

- Although we are given a great physical visualization of what these demonic locusts look like, we're not told that the people they inflict can see them. The late Clarence Larkin, a pastor, Bible teacher, and author, believed them to be disembodied demonic spirits who possess and torment those who do not have the seal of God on them. That may very well be true. If men could see them, they probably would have died of heart attacks long before they were stung.
- It is very likely that the members of this group were a portion of the fallen angels who rebelled with Lucifer and have been kept under lock and key for this particular time since before Creation. The Abyss is such a dreaded and terrible place that the demons Jesus encountered in Luke 8 (Legion) begged not to be sent there early. If these demonic scorpion locusts do manifest in physical bodies, their arrival on earth will be a dreadful sight.
- Joel 2:1–9 seems to fit their actions very closely. Joel also distinguishes between normal locusts and what these demon-locusts are in 2:25. Also, normal locusts do not have kings (Proverbs 30:27).

SIXTH TRUMPET JUDGMENT (SECOND WOE)

Then the sixth angel sounded: And I heard a voice from the four horns of the golden altar which is before God, saying to the sixth angel who had the trumpet, "Release the four angels who are bound at the great river Euphrates." So the four angels, who had been prepared for the hour and day and month and year, were released to kill a third of mankind. Now the number of the army of the horsemen was two hundred million; I heard the number of them. And thus I saw the horses in the vision: those who sat on them had breastplates of fiery red, hyacinth blue, and sulfur yellow; and the heads of the horses were like the heads of lions; and out of their mouths came fire, smoke, and brimstone. By these three plagues a third of mankind was killed—by the fire and the smoke and the brimstone which came out of their mouths. For their power is in their mouth and in their tails; for their tails are like serpents, having heads; and with them they do harm. (Revelation 9:13–19)

According to the excellent research done by Tim Chaffey in his book, *Fallen: The Sons of God and the Nephilim,* the Lord's judgment at the Tower of Babel was far worse than what was originally believed. After the Flood, God instructed man regarding a number of matters. One was to be fruitful, multiply, and fill the earth. Instead, the sons of Noah (Shem, Ham, and Japeth) and their descendants (the seventy nations; see Genesis 10) migrated to the plains of Shinar (modern-day Iraq) and settled there. Over a brief period, Nimrod rose up and began to take over as their would-be leader. They began to build a tower whose height reached into the heavens.

At this point in human history, mankind was still united by means of a common language. They decided (wickedly) to disobey God by not spreading out and filling the earth; instead, they coagulated in one location and built a giant tower for ill-intended purposes. Then, God went down (perhaps with members of His divine council) and saw the ruinous path they were undertaking. He not only separated them by language and genetics, but He also placed certain angels—presumably from this divine council—in charge of the respective nations (as a form of punishment), with the exception of Israel, whom the Lord keeps for Himself (see Psalm 89, 1 Kings 22, Daniel 4:17, etc.).

When the Most High gave to the nations their inheritance,
when he divided mankind,
he fixed the borders of the peoples
according to the number of the sons of God.
But the Lord's portion is his people,
Jacob his allotted heritage. (Deuteronomy 32:8–9)

These angels are later charged with failing to uphold their duties (Psalm 82) and leading their nations astray. This makes more sense when we consider those passages in Daniel in which the angel Gabriel references the "Prince of Persia" and the "Prince of Grecia" (Daniel 10:20). Furthermore, now we see in Revelation 9 that these four angels (presumably former territorial angelic princes) are bound as a form of punishment at Euphrates. This would include the modern nations of Iraq (formerly Babylon), Iran (Persia), Turkey, and Syria. The passage does not indicate that they kill anyone, but rather, that they stir up their human forces (the two hundred million).

Takeaways:

- Certainly these four who are bound at Euphrates are fallen angels, because holy angels are not bound; their sole purpose is to kill a third of mankind. Their loosening sends forth an army of two hundred million horsemen bent on war.
- Whereas the demonic locusts from the Abyss were only allowed to torment those who did not have the seal of God on them, these demons are allowed to kill. Whether this is a supernatural army or a human military force we cannot be certain. Regardless, by adding the previous fourth of the population killed (by the fourth seal judgment) to this third, half of the world's population to date will have died.
- Even as horrific as these judgments are, mankind is still refusing to repent for their demon worship, murders, sorceries, sexual immorality, and theft.

Seven Thunders

I saw still another mighty angel coming down from heaven, clothed with a cloud. And a rainbow was on his head, his face was like the sun, and his feet like pillars of fire. He had a little book open in his hand. And he set his right foot on the sea and his left foot on the land, and cried with a loud voice, as when a lion roars. When he cried out, seven thunders uttered their voices. Now when the seven thunders uttered their voices, I was about to write; but I heard a voice from heaven saying to me, "Seal up the things which the seven thunders uttered, and do not write them."

The angel whom I saw standing on the sea and on the land raised up his hand to heaven and swore by Him who lives forever and ever, who created heaven and the things that are in it, the earth and the things that are in it, and the sea and the things that are in it, that there should be delay no longer, **but in the days of the sounding of the seventh angel, when he is about to sound, the mystery of God would be finished, as He declared to His servants the prophets.** (Revelation 10:1–7, emphasis added)

Takeaways:

- If we include the seven thunders in the lineup, there are now twenty-eight judgments (7 x 4).
- Since these judgments are sealed up until they happen, we have no way of knowing what they are, but we can only speculate that they are some type of transition judgments between the trumpet judgments and the bowl judgments that further decimate the Antichrist's kingdom (Revelation 10:4).
- The seventh trumpet signals the transition to the even more severe bowl/vial judgments, which are set to begin.
- Transition: The sealing of the 144,000 and the arrival of the martyrs to Geaven.

SEVENTH TRUMPET JUDGMENT

Then the seventh angel sounded: And there were loud voices in heaven, saying, "The kingdoms of this world have become the kingdoms of our Lord and of His Christ, and He shall reign forever and ever!" (Revelation 11:15)

The angel takes up the task of proclaiming the everlasting gospel since the Church was removed at the Rapture, the 144,000 are missing, and the Two Witnesses have been killed by the Beast who ascended out of the Abyss (Abaddon; see Revelation 11:7). In this prophetic shot-calling, akin to Babe Ruth's famed called shot in Game 3 of the 1932 World Series, the angels proclaim what will happen as having already happened with 100 percent certainty.

And the twenty-four elders who sat before God on their thrones
fell on their faces and worshiped God, saying:
"We give You thanks, O Lord God Almighty,
The One who is and who was and who is to come,
Because You have taken Your great power and reigned.
The nations were angry, and Your wrath has come,
And the time of the dead, that they should be judged,
And that You should reward Your servants the prophets and
    the saints,
And those who fear Your name, small and great,
And should destroy those who destroy the earth."

Then the temple of God was opened in heaven, and the ark of His covenant was seen in His temple. And there were lightnings, noises, thunderings, an earthquake, and great hail. (Revelation 11:16–19)

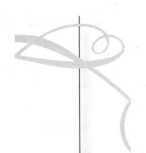

Marcie had gotten arrested somewhere around the eighth year after the Rapture—the "Great Disappearance" as she now knew it. The way she'd figured it, there had been three and a half years from the Rapture until the start of the Seventieth Week (the major peace agreement), and she'd made it to just past the halfway point when she got apprehended by the Beast forces. She'd been scratching out a living scavenging in between Ohio, Kentucky, and Missouri, and doing so fairly successfully by using abandoned vehicles and moving only at night. She even found a new home in southeastern Missouri, in the Mark Twain National Forest. It was a well-equipped underground bunker that she used as her base of operations. From what she gathered, moonshiners had once used this location to brew their illegal homemade whiskey out of sight from the authorities. And, judging by all the gadgets, weapons, and food stores, they had been fairly successful.

For the most part, the Americas (North, Central, and South) had been abandoned, save a half dozen major urban areas along the East and West Coast. Most of the Beast's New World Order forces were tied up in the Mediterranean, the Middle East, and Europe. However, the regional governments (under careful control by the global government) had turned to using armies of drones (aerial, aquatic, terrestrial, and subterranean) to monitor and patrol the more ungovernable areas. These lethal autonomous weapon systems (LAWS) used a combination of low-earth-orbit satellites, artificial intelligence, and thermal and infrared imaging to monitor the vast wastelands that used to be "America's breadbasket." With this type of technology, they could see in the day, at night, through solid objects, and across large areas of land without actually having to put "boots on the ground."

Apparently, drones had tagged her geolocation one night as she was exiting the road that led to her bunker; local security forces had been dispatched from the nearest enforcement center in Oklahoma City to arrest her.

They had interrogated Marcie at first, attempting to find out how many others like her were still hiding underground. But she couldn't tell them what she didn't know—which was the truth. They then tried to get her to take the mark, but she refused. She'd remembered what Clarissa had said about it, as well as what she'd read in Revelation. No way. She'd rather die than be damned for all eternity. The local forces didn't press her much beyond some light torture (waterboarding and electroshock). For them (as part of the Beast network) the mark was a badge of honor, equaling full-throated citizenship. The mark gave you access to everything: food, water, Internet, transportation, housing, clothing, entertainment—anything and everything you could want. Thus, if she didn't want it, they weren't going to make her take it; however, they were ordered to execute her for being an enemy of the state.

She'd been locked up in a super-max facility outside of what used to be Oklahoma City for several months. They'd been executing people with an efficiency matched only by the Nazis during the height of the Holocaust, but had recently stopped, due to their body-burning furnaces malfunctioning. Then one day, all the guards disappeared. Marcie and about forty other death-row inmates were all that remained of the prison population, and they had, apparently, been abandoned to languish in the cells to die of dehydration and starvation. However, on the third day after the security staff had left, their magnetically locked cell doors automatically opened. Apparently, the electrical grid in the area had failed, overriding all the system fail-safes. The doors had simply clicked open.

Marcie had later found out that the entire Atlantic Ocean had turned to blood, so the Beast (their leader) had recalled all of his forces back to

New Babylon. She wasn't entirely sure who had caused the electrical grid to fail, but she would like to think God had something to do with it. She had read in the book of Acts about a similar account when the Apostle Peter had been miraculously freed from his chains in prison.

She was worried, though. She had already read through the Bible twice now, had committed much of it to memory, and knew what was coming—the bowl judgments. She wasn't sure how she would survive that. Just then, a thought comforted her:

Blessed are those who are persecuted for righteousness' sake, for theirs is the kingdom of heaven. (Matthew 5:10)

Marcie longed for the Kingdom to come, and had hoped she might be able to make it long enough to see it ushered in. For now, she would make her way back to her bunker and see if old Rocky had survived in her absence.

Meanwhile, in Heaven

It's hard to gauge time in Heaven, Clarissa thought. It felt like she had only been there for a few hours, but apparently, they were already moving into the bowl judgments, which she knew occurred during the second half of the seven-year Tribulation.

For Clarissa, Bible prophecy was one of those sweet delights she had cherished above all her other academic studies, so, she thought she was prepared. However, watching the brutality of the Beast kingdom was something else altogether. They ruthlessly slaughtered people for refusing the mark of the Beast that, admittedly, even in her glorified state, made her stomach turn bitter. But she knew why they were watching it, because it proved God's twenty-eight judgments as both just and necessary to curb the ferocious atrocities of this final, wicked kingdom.

She couldn't explain how she knew, but she knew her friend Marcie had been born again. Perhaps it had something to do with those who take the mark being erased from the Lamb's Book of Life. Consequently, she had been keeping a watchful eye on each of the massive groups of martyrs who were brought into Heaven out of the Tribulation. She was torn. Although she wanted to see Marcie again, she didn't want it to come at the expense of her martyrdom. But better that than her friend take the mark and be damned forever.

So far, she hadn't seen her yet, and she didn't know how much longer she could hold out. The bowl judgments would bring a new, more severe level of judgment upon the earth. These judgments were seemingly targeted at the foundational necessities of life on planet earth—water, heat, and light. She didn't know how much longer her friend could make it. Still, with God, all things are possible, so there was hope.

(Note: For more information about the trumpet judgments, please see the article, "Seals, Trumpets, and Bowls" by Pete Garcia, in Appendix A.)

11

THE BOWL JUDGMENTS

While the seal judgments focus on unleashing the disastrous Beast kingdom upon the earth, God will not let the Antichrist steal all the credit. Jesus caps off the seal judgments in the sixth with an awesome, earth-shaking seismic event followed by a terrifying display of cosmic signs and wonders. This judgment so rattles the nerves of the world leaders and so-called mighty men that they hide in caves and mountains, rightfully noting to whom this wrath belongs.

The trumpet judgments move the "suck factor" up three pegs, bringing the "misery index" on earth to right below "unbearable." These judgments now begin terraforming the earth and limiting the Beast's reach and maneuverability as well as adding the very literal demonic elements to unleash *Hell on earth*. Whereas the seventh seal judgment introduces silence in Heaven—presumably for the first time ever—the seventh trumpet introduces the victorious conquest of the Lord of Heaven.

Shortly after the vicious murder of the Two Witnesses and their very public resurrection/rapture event near the midpoint of the seven years, there comes a very powerful, yet localized earthquake in Jerusalem; then the seventh trumpet is sounded. The proclamation declares ahead of time, with 100 percent certainty, that the kingdoms of the earth are now the kingdoms of His Majesty, King Jesus. The heavenly hosts and saints now invoke Him through praise and worship to unleash even more judgment (His wrath) upon the earth to destroy those who will not repent of their murders, sorceries, immorality, and blasphemies.

Now the third woe begins.

(Administrative comment: Let us also note again the correlations to the Egyptian plagues, but this time ask the question, why? Why is there a correlation?

The divine judgments, as found in both Exodus and Revelation, serve as an *inclusio* [divine bookends] on human history. One would think these judgments of increasing severity would cause men to repent, but rather, it causes them to curse God and further harden their hearts [as the judgments did to Pharaoh]. Men's incorrigible wickedness proves these judgments are just, and thus further validates God's righteousness in executing them.)

BOWL JUDGMENT 1

Then I heard a loud voice from the temple saying to the seven angels, "Go and pour out the bowls of the wrath of God on the earth." So the first went and **poured out his bowl upon the earth**, and a foul and loathsome sore came upon the men who had the mark of the beast and those who worshiped his image. (Revelation 16:1–2, emphasis added)

Sixth Egyptian Plague

So the Lord said to Moses and Aaron, "Take for yourselves hand-fuls of ashes from a furnace, and let Moses scatter it **toward the heavens** in the sight of Pharaoh. And it will become fine dust in all the land of Egypt, and it will cause boils that break out in sores on man and beast throughout all the land of Egypt." Then they took ashes from the furnace and stood before Pharaoh, and Moses scattered them **toward heaven**. And they caused boils that break out in sores on man and beast." (Exodus 9:8–10, emphasis added)

- The mark of the Beast, which required the unregenerate to insert some form of biotech into their bodies as a form of economic/financial access, and as an act of worship, has now become an abhorrent reminder of their fateful choice.

BOWL JUDGMENT 2

Then the second angel **poured out his bowl on the sea**, and it became blood as of a dead man; and every living creature in the sea died. (Revelation 16:3, emphasis added)

- If the Atlantic was the first third that was turned to blood in the second trumpet judgment, then it would seem this judgment poisons the rest of the world's oceans.
- This absolutely cripples the shipping industry and naval movement, and kills every living thing in the ocean. Boats do not sail well through blood, and the world's commercial and military ocean will come to a complete halt, forcing all movement to take place over land.
- Desalination would no longer be an option for drinking water.
- Those who are still in the Americas, Australia, the Indo-Pacific, and so forth, would be isolated until the angels gather them (Matthew 24:31).

BOWL JUDGMENT 3

Then the third angel poured out his bowl on the rivers and springs of water, and they became blood. And I heard the angel of the waters saying:

"You are righteous, O Lord,
The One who is and who was and who is to be,
Because You have judged these things.
For they have shed the blood of saints and prophets,

And You have given them blood to drink.

For it is their just due."

And I heard another from the altar saying, "Even so, Lord God Almighty, true and righteous are Your judgments." (Revelation 16:4–7)

First Egyptian Plague

Then the Lord spoke to Moses, "Say to Aaron, 'Take your rod and stretch out your hand over the waters of Egypt, over their streams, over their rivers, over their ponds, and over all their pools of water, that they may become blood. And there shall be blood throughout all the land of Egypt, both in buckets of wood and pitchers of stone.'" (Exodus 7:19)

- With the seas—and now the fresh water—turned to blood, options are extremely limited.
- Of interest is the phrase "the angel of the waters." It would appear that, just like there are angels who are appointed over territories, nations, and the different types of living beings on the earth, so, too, there are angels over nonliving things like rivers and such.

BOWL JUDGMENT 4

Then the fourth angel **poured out his bowl on the sun**, and power was given to him to scorch men with fire. And men were scorched with great heat, and they blasphemed the name of God who has power over these plagues; and they did not repent and give Him glory. (Revelation 16:8–9, emphasis added)

- Trumpet judgment 4 diminishes one-third of the sun, moon, and stars.

- First God takes away the rest of the oceans, then He takes away the fresh waters, now He scorches men with great heat.
- Although scientists say that our sun does not have enough mass to supernova, our God is the God of the impossible. The angel pours out the bowl **on the sun**, presumably causing it to have a supernova-like effect.
- John MacArthur makes a good point in that this superheating of the earth would melt the polar ice caps, raising the depth of the world's oceans by as much as two hundred feet. This will flood all coastal cities and flood plains (including the Fertile Crescent) with bloody waters.[31]

BOWL JUDGMENT 5

Then the fifth angel **poured out his bowl on the throne of the beast**, and his kingdom became full of darkness; and they gnawed their tongues because of the pain. They blasphemed the God of heaven because of their pains and their sores, and did not repent of their deeds. (Revelation 16:10–11, emphasis added)

Ninth Egyptian Plague

Then the Lord said to Moses, "Stretch out your hand toward heaven, that there may be darkness over the land of Egypt, **darkness which may even be felt**." So Moses stretched out his hand toward heaven, and there was thick darkness in all the land of Egypt three days. (Exodus 10:21–22, emphasis added)

- In a traditional supernova, the sun superheats and expands, then explodes and dies, which would mean total darkness. We are not told that the sun completely dies, but that the "throne of the beast, and his kingdom" is engulfed in darkness. So it seems that either the sun partially dies (as if a percentage of the sun darkens) or there is a supernatural darkness superimposed over Babylon.

BOWL JUDGMENT 6

Then the sixth angel **poured out his bowl on the great river Euphrates**, and its water was dried up, so that the way of the kings from the east might be prepared. And I saw three unclean spirits like frogs coming out of the mouth of the dragon, out of the mouth of the beast, and out of the mouth of the false prophet. For they are spirits of demons, performing signs, which go out to the kings of the earth and of the whole world, to gather them to the battle of that great day of God Almighty.

"Behold, I am coming as a thief. Blessed is he who watches, and keeps his garments, lest he walk naked and they see his shame."

And they gathered them together to the place called in Hebrew, Armageddon. (Revelation 16:12–16, emphasis added)

Takeaways:

- If the earth was superheated (melting the polar ice caps), and also assuming that this excess water isn't dried up in the process, not only would the Euphrates be overflowing, but much of modern-day Iraq would be under water (being a flood plain); there is a supernatural path clearing for these massive armies coming from the east.
- With the sun going supernova and burning the earth, it would, presumably, destroy and incinerate all satellites and disable all of the technological grids and capabilities (telecommunications, global-positioning satellites, weather tracking technologies, surveillance, intercontinental ballistic weapons systems, etc.) the Beast kingdom used to have control over, which may signal to the other nations that their time has come to overthrow the Beast.

- Three sets of unclean spirits that appear froglike stir or possess the world's leaders to gather their armies at the valley of Megiddo (Armageddon) for one final battle. With all that has transpired, it appears that Satan is rallying mankind to destroy Israel so Christ cannot return or fight Christ as He returns.

TRANSITION: BOWL JUDGMENT 7

Then the seventh angel poured out his bowl into the air, and a loud voice came out of the temple of heaven, from the throne, saying, "It is done!" And there were noises and thunderings and lightnings; and there was a great earthquake, such a mighty and great earthquake as had not occurred since men were on the earth. Now the great city was divided into three parts, and the cities of the nations fell. And great Babylon was remembered before God, to give her the cup of the wine of the fierceness of His wrath. Then every island fled away, and the mountains were not found. And great hail from heaven fell upon men, each hailstone about the weight of a talent. Men blasphemed God because of the plague of the hail, since that plague was exceedingly great. (Revelation 16:17–21)

Seventh Egyptian Plague

And Moses stretched out his rod toward heaven; and the Lord sent thunder and hail, and fire darted to the ground. And the Lord rained hail on the land of Egypt. So there was hail, and fire mingled with the hail, so very heavy that there was none like it in all the land of Egypt since it became a nation. (Exodus 9:22–24)

- Not only would one-hundred-pound hailstones decimate civilian structures, but they would also do devastating damage to any exposed military equipment and facilities, such as missiles, tanks, planes, radars, and runways. This may in fact limit man's only option for moving to Armageddon to land, foot, and horseback.

- Since (if our theory is correct) the Americas are no longer in play, armies are moving primarily from the south, the north, and the east towards Israel. Note that Daniel 11 excludes the west (as a cardinal direction) from the armies listed in how they move against Israel.

- By this point, the militaries of the world cannot utilize the oceans for a water-borne assault since they will have been turned to blood. Neither will they be able to use the air for an aviation assault on Israel. The supernatural heat wave, darkness, and massive hailstones will make airborne operations untenable.

- Hal Lindsey makes a great point in noting that one-hundred-pound hailstones (made of ice melt) will create divots in the earth, particularly in the Valley of Megiddo. Ice melts, when mixed with blood, could create the bloody waters that rise to the bridle of the horses.

BOWL JUDGMENT COMMENTARY

First, we have the ominous and much-expanded correlation with the Egyptian first, sixth, seventh, and ninth plagues, as well as with the fourth trumpet judgment. Then we have the water being removed as either a viable source of life (critical to life on planet earth) or as a source of transportation. Next, we have the heat being turned up, followed by the lights going off.

Now, when part of the earth goes dark naturally (nighttime in the rotating hemispheres), temperatures are cooler than the previous day. This is why we know this darkness (whether or not it's caused by the supernova event) is supernatural. With the entire earth going dark, it should be moving quickly into subzero temperatures. However, the text does not mention that. In fact, the subsequent chapters show us the "kings of the east," along with their massive armies, moving west over the dried-up Euphrates

towards Israel. If the earth were plunged into norma
ness through atmospheric obscuration (overcast skies,
eclipses, etc.) the temperature would decrease in the ar
darkness. However, it appears that the unbearable hea

We noted how many of these judgments are similar to those of the
Egyptian plagues, with the exception that they were no longer confined to
Egypt, but they affected the entire world. In the case of the supernatural
darkness, Moses was told that it would be so dark it could be felt. The
darkness in Egypt, although supernatural, could be explained by some
natural phenomenon like a prolonged eclipse, similar to the unnatural
darkness at Christ's crucifixion (Luke 23:44). All of these judgments have
one thing in common: there is a similarity to the hardening of men's hearts
(just like with Pharaoh). In misery and anger, men blasphemed God and
would not repent of their sins. [32]

(Note: For more information about the bowl judgments, please see
the article, "Seals, Trumpets, and Bowls" by Pete Garcia, in Appendix A.)

Since her recent prison experience, Marcie began to venture out more during the daytime, since she knew the Beast had largely abandoned the ruins of what used to be the United States. Whatever criminal elements that were left seemed to have also abandoned the former state of Missouri for more profitable areas. What remained was a ragtag handful of survivors, largely believers like herself, who formed small, loose-knit communities. Her community included around fifteen people, all of whom lived within a few miles of each other.

Each group (aside from Marcie, who lived alone with her aging dog Rocky) was made up of two to three people. All groups were assigned provisions to produce. Two groups had chickens and goats; others had small gardens. Still others continued to scrounge around the area for any items they could find that could be of use.

Marcie's job, as head of this particular community, was information-gathering. Whoever had built the bunker she originally found and occupied had left behind a rather sophisticated communications array. There was a hand-cranked, emergency radio, a ham radio with a powerful base station, which gave her some access to a local repeater tower. She also had a satellite-based Internet system; however, since she moved in, it continually degraded to the point that it rarely worked anymore. Most of the information she was able to pick up was over the AM/FM radio. Even that came in less frequently since the Beast forces had retreated.

So, Marcie's job was to monitor the radio and keep the group informed of what was happening elsewhere in the world. Because the biblical judgments had wreaked havoc on the modernity of the Beast system (5G networks, Wi-Fi, satellites, etc.), AM/FM radios were still the most reliable way to listen to information. Although the Americas (North, Central, and South) had largely been abandoned, there were still some government forces operating along the East Coast. Even so, she believed that her radio systems and her ability to keep getting information were more supernatural miracles than anything.

Once a day, twice a week, they would meet up with several other groups who would trade everything from food (mostly tomatoes, eggs, and goat milk) to information about what was going on. They also held small Bible studies, primarily focusing on the book of Revelation. In truth, Marcie had done more to earn her keep than just relay information. She helped the others build their bunkers or help fortify what they were currently living in. But most importantly, her small group of survivors respected her and trusted her—trust was a commodity that was in short supply in those days.

Breaking news reported that a massive military buildup was happening now in Israel. Armies from all over the world were collectively moving toward the Valley of Megiddo, which could only mean one thing: Armageddon.

12

THE ARMAGEDDON CAMPAIGN

So now, we have arrived at the end.

It is not the end of all things, but definitely the end of a rebellious humanity running the show on planet earth. All of the evil. All of the wickedness. All of the corruption, violence, and idolatry that has run roughshod on terra firma for nearly six thousand years is about to come to its divinely appointed end.

While Armageddon is the ultimate assemblage of military forces in human history, with some estimating more than one billion soldiers gathered, there is no actual fighting in the Valley of Megiddo itself. It is simply the place where the Antichrist's forces assemble to go and attempt to wipe out the nation of Israel for the last time. The fighting will take place along a nearly two-hundred-mile stretch, beginning in Bozrah down to the Red Sea.[33]

There is another common misnomer associated with the word "Armageddon," in that it is said to be the greatest battle in human history. Not true. It is the greatest *defeat* in all of history. The minute Christ tears open the sky and rides into view with the host of the heavenly armies behind Him, the battle will already be over. He'll simply speak a word and all before Him will melt from the inside out.

The fleeing forces of the Antichrist will spread out over 1,600 furlongs (a furlong is about an eighth of a mile). Thus, the carnage will be so extensive that the blood from the bodies of a billion soldiers will form a river nearly two hundred miles long (Revelation 14:20). That, along with the previous judgment of one-hundred-pound hailstones (which are melting by this point into a watery mess) and the rivers (freshwater) that have turned to blood, creates a river of blood up to the horses' bridle (around four feet high). This will most likely flow from the Kidron Valley (Jehoshaphat) down to the Jordan River Valley, down south through the Dead Sea to the Red Sea.

However, let's back up and give the full story. We need to catch you up to speed to how we will get to this point in human history.

RECAP: FROM A STRATEGIC/OPERATIONAL PERSPECTIVE

After the divine defeat of the Gog and Magog coalition (Ezekiel 38–39) just after the Rapture and the subsequent arrival of the Two Witnesses (Revelation 11), Israel decides it is finally the right time to build the Third Temple on the Temple Mount. Even though the Dome of the Rock and al-Aqsa Mosque will have been destroyed during the attempted Gog invasion, this still will not go over well in the court of international opinion. In fact, despite how crazy the Magog defeat will have been, and frankly, how terrified the other nations will be of Israel, there will still be an overwhelming political pushback against erecting a Third Jewish Temple.

However, a Gentile world leader will come forward and intervene. He is not the head of the new, regionalized, world government, but a rising star in its ranks, and a convincing voice nonetheless. He helps champion Israel's right to build a Third Temple. The other nations of the world will be jealous of Israel's seemingly preferential treatment; they do not have to follow the rules that the rest of them seemingly are being forced to do. Along with their powerful Two Witnesses, Israel will seem like it's finally arrived at the coming of their long-prophesied Messiah (Malachi 4:5–6).

The ten general-kings begin to raise their concerns and voice their objection to their leader, the Beast (as the Antichrist now is personifying this new government) regarding this perceived preferential treatment. He is now facing unrest from the outer provinces (like from the kings of the east). The Beast agrees and turns on Israel in a vicious, 180-degree turn of political subterfuge.

He first subdues the Two Witnesses, killing them publicly and leaving their bodies in the street to rot for three days. He then issues a decree to kill all Jews, causing many to flee the city in a panic. After this, he flagrantly and blasphemously desecrates the Third Temple by erecting a visage of himself in the Holy of Holies. On the third day, the Two Witnesses, who, having laid dead in the streets of Jerusalem for three days, stand up on their feet. A voice from Heaven commands them to come up, and they are immediately *caught up* (raptured) with the entire world watching. This must be salt in the wound for all who believed the great lie about the Disappearance being caused by aliens or some other nonsense. At this time, there will be no question as to what really happened on *that day*.

This brings us to the halfway point (three and a half years into the Tribulation).

Within an hour of the Two Witnesses' miraculous resurrection and rapture, a massive earthquake will strike the city, causing a tenth of it to fall. The Jews who haven't fled from the city are killed, while the remnant who do escape, head southeast towards Petra. The Antichrist will give chase to those who flee, but a weather phenomenon, in the form of torrential rains and flooding, will prevent him from pursuing. This remnant group of Jews will be protected, seemingly, by supernatural forces. This further infuriates the Antichrist, and he and his False Prophet will begin the worldwide persecution against those who will not bend the knee to him and take his mark. Meanwhile, he'll also rally the armies of the world and summon them to the Valley of Megiddo.

After the death of the Two Witnesses, unseen to human eye are activities going on in Heaven: the appearance of Christ with the 144,000 unblemished male virgins, the mighty angel, the little book, and the issuing of the sealed seven thunders. Finally, we come to the angel blowing the seventh trumpet, issuing his decree that the kingdoms of the world are now the kingdoms of Christ. From Heaven's perspective, the battle is already won.

> After these things I looked, and behold, the temple of the tabernacle of the testimony in heaven was opened. And out of the temple came the seven angels having the seven plagues, clothed in pure bright linen, and having their chests girded with golden bands. Then one of the four living creatures gave to the seven angels seven golden bowls full of the wrath of God who lives forever and ever. The temple was filled with smoke from the glory of God and from His power, and no one was able to enter the temple till the seven plagues of the seven angels were completed. (Revelation 15:5–8)

ON EARTH

Now, while the bowl judgments are being poured out from Heaven into the physical realm, these judgments transition from the eternal realm to our temporal realm in ominous silence. For example, as the angel pours out the first bowl, the subsequent action appears as boils on all who bear the mark of the Beast. It is our belief that the fullness of sin stored up in these bowls, is the exact measure of wrath man has stored up for himself (Revelation 15:1, Romans 12:19). Furthermore, as with all the judgments, their execution (opening the seals, blowing the trumpets, issuing the thunders, and now pouring out the bowls) may happen successively in Heaven, but may be time-proportionate on the earth.

After the midpoint of the Tribulation, the Dragon, the Antichrist, and the False Prophet all begin issuing decrees to summon all military forces to Israel. These issuances, while they appear to be commands, are actually froglike demons that go forth deceiving the leaders of the world to come and fight one last, glorious battle. They are being deceived into believing they can actually wage war against Heaven and win. It is beyond insanity, which is why they must be deceived into leading their armies against such overwhelming odds.

As the trumpet and bowl judgments are being exacted upon the earth, the military forces, which will have been called forth to fight, are being stranded in various parts of the earth. The naval forces of the Beast kingdom will have largely been stranded out at sea, as a third of the oceans will have been turned to literal blood (second trumpet judgment). Soon after, all the seas and oceans will be turned to blood (second bowl judgment). The blood oceans, along with the scorching heat, will unleash massive amounts of microorganisms (blood-borne pathogens) from all of the sea creatures dying off, producing untold and even unknown bacteriological and viral outbreaks. The pounding of the waves and natural evaporation processes that take place within the hydrological cycle will quickly aerosolize these microorganisms into the atmosphere.

The air will then have become as treacherous as the oceans, considering the danger of flying with a third of the light having been turned to darkness (fourth trumpet judgment). In addition, with the demonic army unleashed in the fifth trumpet judgment, pilots will likely be grounded after being afflicted by terrible stings and demonic possessions, thus crippling the Beast's aerial forces. The scorching heat (fourth bowl judgment) will also quickly overheat almost any vehicle and weapon system, causing troops to be forced to move either by foot or by horse. This later intensifies with hundred-pound hailstones striking the earth from the skies (seventh bowl judgment), destroying aircraft on the ground, in their hangars, and in the air. Anything that is not bunkered underground will presumably be destroyed. Even those, however, will remain grounded because of destroyed runways.

All of New Babylon will be plunged into supernatural darkness, forcing the armies of the Beast to slowly move by land to the west. The oppressive heat, having already scorched the polar ice caps, will cause the seal levels to rise significantly; flood plains will be submerged under the overflow of these oceans of blood. The smell from it will be both putrid and suffocating. This will, in effect, have a reverse-migration effect, causing those near the coastlines to move farther inland. Those who remain or can't leave the hot, bloody bodies of water will gag and suffocate due to the putridity. The horrible smell, though, won't be the only problem; the air will also quickly fill up with blood-borne microorganisms.

The forces of the Beast will have to wait for the miserable heatwave to lessen and then come up with a new plan to move out of New Babylon in total darkness. Still, through all this, mankind will not repent. Instead, they'll blame God for the affliction and attempt to wage war against Him.

Word, by then, will have spread that the kings of the east are coming to join the fray. Although they will have been summoned, the Beast will worry that the kings of the east will seek to dethrone him, coming in such overwhelming numbers. He knows they will not be satisfied in just taking Jerusalem. They're coming to stay for good and will be problematic for his rule moving forward. Mysteriously, the mighty Euphrates dries up, which further adds to his concern, seeing as they will now have nothing to slow them down as they descend like a barbarian horde upon the tiny nation of Israel. The Beast knows this massive assemblage of forces will not fit in or around Jerusalem; the terrain won't support it. They will need to assemble in the Valley of Megiddo, from Bozrah to Jehoshaphat (Isaiah 63:1–6)—the world's most perfect battlefield.

The following is a general timeline for the events surrounding the war of Armageddon and the Second Coming of Christ.

1. The satanic trinity gathers the armies of the world to Har Megiddo:

> Then the sixth angel poured out his bowl on the great river Euphrates, and its water was dried up, **so that the way of the kings from the east might be prepared**. And I saw three unclean spirits like frogs coming out of the mouth of the dragon, out of the mouth of the beast, and out of the mouth of the false prophet. For they are spirits of demons, performing signs, which go out to the kings of the earth and of the whole world, **to gather them to the battle of that great day of God Almighty**. (Revelation 16:12–14, emphasis added)

In both the books of Daniel and Revelation, the ten kings are represented as ten horns, with the Antichrist rising up as the eleventh, and subduing three. After gaining the majority control, he'll demand obedience from the rest of the seven. While it is not evident during the first half of the seven-year Tribulation, at the midpoint (3.5 years into it), the Antichrist will turn on Israel. He, the False Prophet, and Satan himself will call forth the armies of the world to gather for war in Israel.

> The ten horns which you saw are ten kings who have received no kingdom as yet, but they receive authority for one hour as kings with the beast. These are of one mind, and they will give their power and authority to the beast. These will make war with the Lamb, and the Lamb will overcome them, for He is Lord of lords and King of kings; and those who are with Him are called, chosen, and faithful. (Revelation 17:12–13)

2. Religious Babylon is destroyed. Near the midpoint of the Tribulation, the False Prophet, the Antichrist, and the rest of the ten kings will overthrow the world's ecumenical, politically correct, Nazi-esque religion (the harlot). They will have used her at first to rid the world of all the competing religious systems left in the wake of the Rapture. Now, the Antichrist wants all the worship to himself. He does not like to share his glory with another.

> So he carried me away in the Spirit into the wilderness. And I saw a woman sitting on a scarlet beast which was full of names of blasphemy, having seven heads and ten horns. The woman was arrayed in purple and scarlet, and adorned with gold and precious stones and pearls, having in her hand a golden cup full of abominations and the filthiness of her fornication. And on her forehead a name was written:
> MYSTERY, BABYLON THE GREAT, THE MOTHER OF HARLOTS AND OF THE ABOMINATIONS OF THE EARTH.

Then he said to me, "The waters which you saw, where the harlot sits, are peoples, multitudes, nations, and tongues. And the ten horns which you saw on the beast, these will hate the harlot, make her desolate and naked, eat her flesh and burn her with fire. For God has put it into their hearts to fulfill His purpose, to be of one mind, and to give their kingdom to the beast, until the words of God are fulfilled. And the woman whom you saw is that great city which reigns over the kings of the earth." (Revelation 17:3–5, 15–18)

3. Commercial Babylon is destroyed. While the military forces are beginning to ready their forces to move towards Israel, the Antichrist and his forces will begin to plan their attack on Jerusalem. Presumably, this will be around the midpoint of the Tribulation, right after the Antichrist kills the Two Witnesses and commits the "abomination that causes desolation" (Matthew 24:15, 2 Thessalonians 2:4, Revelation 13:6).

At this point, the Antichrist might be splitting his time between his headquarters in Babylon and Jerusalem, whose distance is around 660 miles (if using Baghdad, Iraq, as a point of reference). After the midpoint of the Tribulation and likely near the end of the bowl judgments, the Beast's headquarters in Babylon will be utterly and supernaturally destroyed.

The kings of the earth who committed fornication and lived luxuriously with her will weep and lament for her, when they see the smoke of her burning, standing at a distance for fear of her torment, saying, "Alas, alas, that great city Babylon, that mighty city! For in one hour your judgment has come." (Revelation 18:9–10)

3. Half of Jerusalem is captured. It's interesting to note that from 1948–1967, half of Israel was already under Gentile domination (British/ Jordanians). Since Israel's victory in the Six Day War, there has been an intense, fifty-plus-year struggle to wrest Jerusalem back out of the hands of Israel. At some time after the midpoint, the Antichrist will finally achieve

taking back a portion of Jerusalem, likely, the portion with the Temple Mount and the newly built Third Temple.

> Behold, the day of the Lord is coming,
> And your spoil will be divided in your midst.
> For I will gather all the nations to battle against Jerusalem;
> The city shall be taken,
> The houses rifled,
> And the women ravished.
> Half of the city shall go into captivity,
> But the remnant of the people shall not be cut off from the city. (Zechariah 14:1–2; see also Zechariah 12:1–9 and 14:1–2, Micah 4:11–5:1)

4. Antichrist moves against Petra and the remnant there. After he has taken Jerusalem, the Antichrist will be furious that many have escaped. His hatred for the Jews will eclipse even that of Reich Marshal Hermann Göring and Führer Adolf Hitler's at the height of the power of the Third Reich. He will rally his forces to chase after the Jews in the same fashion that Pharaoh chased after the Hebrews in the Exodus. His flood of forces will meet a fate that will be in similar fashion to the parting of the Red Sea, except instead of being deluged by the ocean, the Antichrist's forces will be swallowed up by the earth like Korah (Numbers 26:10).

> Now when the dragon saw that he had been cast to the earth, he persecuted the woman who gave birth to the male Child. But the woman was given two wings of a great eagle, that she might fly into the wilderness to her place, where she is nourished for a time and times and half a time, from the presence of the serpent. So the serpent spewed water out of his mouth like a flood after the woman, that he might cause her to be carried away by the flood. But the earth helped the woman, and the earth opened its mouth and swallowed up the flood which the dragon had spewed out of

his mouth. And the dragon was enraged with the woman, and he went to make war with the rest of her offspring, who keep the commandments of God and have the testimony of Jesus Christ. (Revelation 12:14–17; see also Zechariah 13:8; Daniel 9:27; Isaiah 33:13–16; Jeremiah 49:13, 14; Micah 2:12; Matthew 24:15–31; Revelation 12:6, 14)

5. Israel is regenerated. In Matthew 23:37–39, Jesus states:

O Jerusalem, Jerusalem, the one who kills the prophets and stones those who are sent to her! How often I wanted to gather your children together, as a hen gathers her chicks under her wings, but you were not willing! See! Your house is left to you desolate; for I say to you, you shall see Me no more till you say, "Blessed is He who comes in the name of the Lord!"

So it has been for nearly two millennia, Israel has nationally rejected Jesus as the One, True Messiah. Here, after the murder of the Two Witnesses (and their subsequent rapture), the desecration of their new Temple, the sacking of Jerusalem by the Antichrist, and their fleeing to Petra, the Jewish remnant, in their desperation, will finally have the veil lifted (2 Corinthians 3:15–16; see also Leviticus 26:40–42; Deuteronomy 4:29–31; 36:6–8; Jeremiah 3:11–18; Hosea 5:15; Joel 2:28–32; Isaiah 53:1–9; Isaiah 64; Zechariah 12:10; Matthew 23:37–39; Romans 1:25–27).

6. Christ will return in the Second Coming. After the remaining portion of Israel turns to Jesus Christ as their Messiah, this triggers a devastating and culminating response from Heaven. Jesus Himself will step forward and move out from eternity toward earth. The first time He came to earth, He was an infant. The second time He comes to earth, He will return as its rightful King. From Revelation 19:11–6:

Now I saw heaven opened, and behold, a white horse. And He who sat on him was called Faithful and True, and in righteousness

He judges and makes war. His eyes were like a flame of fire, and on His head were many crowns. He had a name written that no one knew except Himself. He was clothed with a robe dipped in blood, and His name is called The Word of God. And the armies in heaven, clothed in fine linen, white and clean, followed Him on white horses. Now out of His mouth goes a sharp sword, that with it He should strike the nations. And He Himself will rule them with a rod of iron. He Himself treads the winepress of the fierceness and wrath of Almighty God. And He has on His robe and on His thigh a name written:

KING OF KINGS AND LORD OF LORDS.

The sky will open as if it were a veil being torn in two. The air pushes ahead of Him with the power of a straight-line hurricane knocking down everything in front of Him. A blinding light will pierce through the dark night like a bolt of lightning. The sound of an army of horses galloping will be heard in the distance, their thunderous hooves sounding like the roar of many rushing waters. Then He will be there, splendidly arrayed in a dazzlingly white robe, its ends dipped in blood. His eyes will be aflame like bright burning fires; His hair white as snow. All who gaze upon Him will feel their knees buckle. Their bowels will loosen, their hands will shake and tremble. The battle will be lost before it begins. Christ, the Alpha and Omega, the First and the Last, is too powerful and overwhelming for all the armies of the earth.

7. The final campaign takes place. Beginning at Bozrah, Jordan (Isaiah 34:6, 63:1–6), the skies tear open, and Christ and His armies will begin working their way up the two hundred-mile stretch up the Jordan River Valley to the Kidron Valley (Jehoshaphat).

Then I saw an angel standing in the sun; and he cried with a loud voice, saying to all the birds that fly in the midst of heaven, "Come and gather together for the supper of the great God, that you may eat the flesh of kings, the flesh of captains, the flesh of mighty men, the flesh of horses and of those who sit on them, and the flesh of all people, free and slave, both small and great."

And I saw the beast, the kings of the earth, and their armies, gathered together to make war against Him who sat on the horse and against His army. Then the beast was captured, and with him the false prophet who worked signs in his presence, by which he deceived those who received the mark of the beast and those who worshiped his image. These two were cast alive into the lake of fire burning with brimstone. And the rest were killed with the sword which proceeded from the mouth of Him who sat on the horse. And all the birds were filled with their flesh. (Revelation 19:17–21; see also 2 Thessalonians 2:8; Joel 3:12, 13; Zechariah 14:12–15)

8. Jesus descends to the Mount of Olives. After He crushes the armies of the Antichrist, He then casts these two reprobates (the Antichrist and the False Prophet) alive into the Lake of Fire. These two are the first and only inhabitants of this most dreadful place for the first thousand years. After their armies are destroyed, Jesus will descend out of the sky and step foot on the Mount of Olives (where He gave His Olivet Discourse), splitting the mount in half. This may in fact coincide with the seventh bowl judgment (Revelation 16:17–18).

> Then the Lord will go forth
>   And fight against those nations,
>   As He fights in the day of battle.
>   And in that day His feet will stand on the Mount of Olives,
>   Which faces Jerusalem on the east.
>   And the Mount of Olives shall be split in two,
>   From east to west,
>   Making a very large valley;
>   Half of the mountain shall move toward the north
>   And half of it toward the south.

Then you shall flee through My mountain valley,
For the mountain valley shall reach to Azal.
Yes, you shall flee
As you fled from the earthquake
In the days of Uzziah king of Judah.
Thus the Lord my God will come,
And all the saints with You. (Zechariah 14:3–5; see also Joel
3:14–16; Matthew 24:29; Revelation 16:17–21).

Marcie and the rest of the group of survivors hadn't heard much about Armageddon other than it was beginning. After that, it was radio silence for days. Thankfully, God had provided them with water to drink and food to eat, because everything was failing them. The sun was a third dimmer, the freshwater sources and the seas had all turned to blood. Hundred-pound hailstones had pummeled the earth. Finally, a massive earthquake shook the ground so hard that they even felt it in eastern Missouri.

The skies had grown really dark, especially towards the east. Then they saw it. They saw *Him*, rather. Jesus and His armies. Marcie couldn't explain how she saw it, due to the curvature of the earth and the distance, but she could see the light in the horizon, and then it was as if her eyes could pan in and see His face. They had all been sitting around a small campfire, staving off the cold, when it happened. They were then all on their knees, praising God for finally ending this horror show.

Then Clarissa appeared, with two angels escorting her. Although Marcie recognized her friend immediately, Clarissa looked different—like an upgraded version of herself. She was taller, more vibrant. Her once brown eyes now seemed to burst with flashes of brilliant blue and gold, as if reflecting her time spent in the heavenly realms. Marcie shuddered to think of what she must look like to Clarissa—a gaunt shadow of her former self. Thirty pounds lighter at least, and weathered from surviving not just the worst of humanity, but the judgments themselves, to a degree. The two women embraced as sisters. Their earthly humor still resonated through the supernatural divide.

"I'm here to take you home! Glad you finally got right with the Lord," Clarissa said.

"Yeah, me too. It only took the Rapture and the world ending to figure that out," Marcie replied, mixing her remorsefulness with her characteristic wit.

"Things are going to be looking up for you and the rest of the redeemed survivors, I promise—and very soon."

"Good, I can't wait."

13

THE MILLENNIAL AGE

Immediately after the tribulation of those days the sun will be darkened, and the moon will not give its light; the stars will fall from heaven, and the powers of the heavens will be shaken. Then the sign of the Son of Man will appear in heaven, and then all the tribes of the earth will mourn, and they will see the Son of Man coming on the clouds of heaven with power and great glory. And He will send His angels with a great sound of a trumpet, and they will gather together His elect from the four winds, from one end of heaven to the other. (Matthew 24:29–31)

After the victorious Armageddon campaign, Jesus will throw the Antichrist and the False Prophet alive into the Lake of Fire (Revelation 19:20). He will then proceed to the Mount of Olives, whereby simply setting foot at the top of the mountain causes it to split in half from east to west (Zechariah 14:4). The angels will then gather the remnant elect from Heaven and earth and bring them to Jerusalem, where Jesus will conduct the judgment of the nations, or what has come to be referred to simply as the "Sheep and Goat Judgment."

When the Son of Man comes in His glory, and all the holy angels with Him, then He will sit on the throne of His glory. All the nations will be gathered before Him, and He will separate them one from another, as a shepherd divides his sheep from the goats. And He will set the sheep on His right hand, but the goats on the left. Then the King will say to those on His right hand, "Come, you blessed of My Father, inherit the kingdom prepared for you from the foundation of the world....Then He will also say to those on the left hand, "Depart from Me, you cursed, into the everlasting fire prepared for the devil and his angels." (Matthew 25:31–34, 41)

Here, in the context of the passage, good works (feeding and clothing the hungry and poor) do not gain these automatic salvation, but rather, entrance into the Kingdom. Those who don't help the poor and hungry (presumably all those who will have taken the mark and persecuted the remnant on the earth) will be sent off to everlasting punishment.

Authors' note: Salvation is and only ever was through the person of Jesus Christ; that has NEVER changed. However, because of the unfolding nature of God's economy (i.e., the dispensations), when spiritual regeneration occurred (à la New Testament salvation), some things had changed. For example, the Old Testament (OT) saints who lived and died before Jesus came to earth the first time were not saved as Paul lays out in Romans 10:9–13, because, no OT saint knew who Jesus was; they for sure did not know His name. They were also struggling with how and when the Kingdom would come. Even John the Baptist (who knew Jesus personally) struggled to see how this plan of ushering in the Messiah and the Kingdom would play out (Matthew 11:3).

As far as OT saints knew, the Messiah would be named *Immanuel* (Isaiah 7:14), and He would be like Moses, physically and politically delivering the nation of Israel from their Gentile oppressors. However, Immanuel (the name) was describing what this Messiah would be, rather than simply what He would be called. Thus, salvation in the OT could not be based on calling on the name of Jesus because they would not have known who He was until after He came.

Those Old Testament saints had righteousness imputed to them based on their faith in God (Romans 4:11) and in their belief that He would provide a Redeemer for mankind. This belief even goes back as far as the first written book of the Bible, in Job 19:25. The OT saints would have to wait in Paradise until Christ could come and redeem them personally, which He did after His death on the cross. Since those who died before Jesus' atoning sacrifice on Mt. Calvary could not go straight to Heaven, they went to the Paradise side of Sheol (Abraham's Bosom) to await the coming of the Messiah. When Jesus died on the cross, He went down to redeem those who had come before Him (Ephesians 4:7–9). Therefore, they were saved in the end, but there are nuances to this that are instrumental in God's overarching plan for mankind.

During the Church Age (from the first Pentecost after His death, burial, and resurrection to the Rapture), believers (both Jew and Gentile) were regenerated into the Body of Jesus Christ at the moment of their belief. They became part of the singular, corporate, universal Body of Christ known as the Church (Ephesians 5:22–32). Jesus said He would build this Church, and no one could snatch them from Him (Matthew 16:18–20, John 10:28). These New Testament (or covenant) believers were then SEALED by the Holy Spirit FOR the day of redemption, which was the Rapture of the Church (Ephesians 4:30).

Now, Old Testament believers could lose and regain their imputed righteous "status," because the Holy Spirit did not seal them. For many of them, the Holy Spirit could either fill them or leave them, depending upon their actions (e.g., Samson, Saul). They were not spiritually regenerated into new creations as were New Testament believers while they were still living, and thus could fall away from the faith (2 Corinthians 5:17).

Those who come to faith in Christ after the Rapture will be redeemed—but again, they are not sealed by the Holy Spirit as the Church was. With the exception of the 144,000 from the twelve tribes of Israel (Revelation 7:1–8), the Bible does say God "seals" anyone else during this time. We could assume since there are many who become martyrs during this time (Revelation 6:9–11, 7:9–17), they are able to die with a saving faith and the regeneration by the Holy Spirit. We say this not to dispute the Holy Spirit's role in sealing them, but they appear to play a slightly different role than the Church once they arrive in Heaven (Revelation 7:14–17). Those who come to faith in Christ during the Tribulation will have to die (or live) as those did in the Old Testament times—by grace through faith. Again, the notable distinction between the Age of the Church and the time of the Seventieth Week of Daniel is that of sealing by the Holy Spirit.

Thus, entrance into this long-promised, finally delivered Kingdom will be for those who both survive the Tribulation and who are worthy to enter. Although this idea of being found worthy has been troubling for the New Testament-era believers, largely because we are a "salvation by grace through faith" bunch, it isn't troubling when we keep things in their proper perspective.

For example, when we look at the Sermon on the Mount, and most notably, the Lord's Prayer (Matthew 6:9–13), we should keep in mind that the offer of the Kingdom was still on the table for Israel at that time before they (as a nation) officially rejected Him. Let us reread the Lord's Prayer, but now imagine a Tribulation believer reciting it, rather than a group of fifth graders in a Baptist Sunday school class.

> [The Lord's Prayer] is a part of the "Sermon on the Mount." It asks that "The Kingdom" may come, not that the "Church" may increase and prosper. There is no petition for "Salvation from sin" in it. It asks that "God's will may be done in earth, as it is done in heaven." It is a prayer for those who shall be living in the "Tribu-lation Period" who in their persecutions will long for the return of the King, that the Kingdom may be set up, and God's will be done, as it will be done then, on earth as it is done in Heaven. At that time the "Beast" (Antichrist) will be in power and no one shall be able to "buy" or "sell" except he that hath the "Mark of the Beast," and this explains the petition "Give us this day our

DAILY BREAD," for unless food is supplied **miraculously** they will perish. And it will be a time when they shall particularly need to be delivered, not from evil, but the **EVIL ONE** Satan, who will tempt them to recant and worship the Beast.[34]

THE KINGDOM

In Daniel 2, we read that King Nebuchadnezzar has a troubling dream. His dream is of an imposing, multi-metallic statue of a man, rising high and inspiring both dread and awe. Daniel is given the interpretation of this dream, which reveals the successive human kingdoms through the end of the age that would come to dominate the world and age in which they live. In Daniel 7–8, God gives this same vision to Daniel, but instead of it being an imposing statue, these kingdoms are shown as four hybrid, wild beasts. Nebuchadnezzar sees them from man's perspective; Daniel sees them from God's perspective. In Revelation, the final world power structure (the iron-clay toes of the statue in Daniel 2), shows up as the Beast in Revelation chapter 13. However, these beasts are no longer separate, successive, kingdoms; they will have morphed into a singular, hybrid kingdom.

Aside from the potential for immortality, the promise of an everlasting Kingdom has been one of the most sought-after, alluring dreams in man's long history on planet earth. Every human kingdom that has arisen and fallen has at least aspired to be it. The Egyptians, the Assyrians, the Babylonians, the Persians, the Greeks, the Romans, the Holy Roman Empire, the Turks, the British, the Germans, the Soviets, the Americans, and the Beast have all sought to establish themselves as the preeminent power on planet earth, and for a time, they were. Each came to believe their regional or global dominance was proof positive of their own version of *manifest destiny*.

However, they all failed. They all failed, because they suffer from the same maladies—sin, corruption, human weakness, and Satan.

In Daniel 2, the multi-metallic statue was utterly crushed and destroyed by a rock that cut without human hands. The rock came to fill the entire earth not gradually, but suddenly. In Revelation, the Rock is none other than Jesus Christ. He tears open the sky and destroys the final kingdom in a two-hundred-mile campaign of carnage so devastating that it forms a river of blood two hundred miles long. There is only one true King and one true Kingdom, and it will not be shepherded by mere mortals, but by the God-Man Himself—Jesus Christ.

After the battle:

> Then I saw an angel coming down from heaven, having the key to the bottomless pit and a great chain in his hand. He laid hold of the dragon, that serpent of old, who is the Devil and Satan, and bound him for a thousand years; and he cast him into the bottomless pit, and shut him up, and set a seal on him, so that he should deceive the nations no more till the thousand years were finished. But after these things he must be released for a little while. (Revelation 20:1–3)

Right after the Armageddon campaign, Satan will be caught, chained up, and tossed into the Abyss. His reign of terror on earth is put on a thousand-year hiatus to show mankind what life on earth is like without him. However, he will be released at the end to also prove that, even in a perfect world, with Christ physically ruling and reigning, corruptible man (those natural humans who survive and enter the Kingdom) still have their sin natures. We're not told how long this "a little while" lasts, but it could be months to years. Those sin natures will be tested with Satan's last-ditch effort to stir up rebellion and war against Christ and His people.

> And I saw thrones, and they sat on them, and judgment was committed to them. **Then** I saw the souls of those who had been beheaded for their witness to Jesus and for the word of God, who had not worshiped the beast or his image, and had not received his mark on their foreheads or on their hands. And they lived and

reigned with Christ for a thousand years. But the rest of the dead did not live again until the thousand years were finished. This is the first resurrection. Blessed and holy is he who has part in the first resurrection. Over such the second death has no power, but they shall be priests of God and of Christ, and shall reign with Him a thousand years. (Revelation 20:4–6, emphasis added)

What often gets lost in interpretation is the distinction between the words *before* and *after* the word "then." First John sees thrones and "they" (plural) sat on them, and judgment was committed to them. So who are "they"? Well, there will be three categories in the ranks of the righteous: the Church (in the New Jerusalem), Old Testament saints (in the earthly Jerusalem), and the Tribulation saints. We're not told that the Tribulation saints rule anything, but they are shown in the temple of God and never leave it (Revelation 7:15).

The Church (*ekklesia*) is the universal, corporate, singular Body of Christ of all who have lived and died and were resurrected from the first Pentecost after Christ's ascension until the Rapture. They are also those who are alive at the Rapture, who will be translated alive from mortality to immortality. The Church will rule and reign with Christ in the New Jerusalem. Having become like Christ (1 John 3:1–3), we will no longer be bound by the constraints of time and space, as we will have become immortal beings taking after (but not becoming) the likeness of Christ (Revelation 1:6; 5:10). The New Jerusalem will not touch down on earth, as it would throw the earth off balance as well as appear extraordinarily absurd (standing some 1,500 miles high). Rather, it, as many experts have suggested, it might circle the earth in a low-level, geo-stationary orbit always reflecting the glory of God upon the earthly Jerusalem.

For the Old Testament saints who will be snatched up out of Paradise upon Christ's resurrection and taken to Heaven, we suspect they'll rule and reign with Christ as well (in similar glorified bodies) but will do so in the physical Kingdom on earth, with Christ sitting on David's throne

(Luke 1:32). The Third Temple (the one that will be desecrated) is sanctified during the additional 1,335 days in a series of ritual cleansing (Ezekiel 40–48). Once Christ ascends the newly rebuilt throne of David, He will demonstrate that He is in fact the perfect embodiment of both the Law and the Prophets (Matthew 5:17). Not only will that, but the final division of the land will be perfectly apportioned to each of the twelve tribes as per the instructions given to Abraham and Moses. Here, the nations will stream forward to pay tribute to Him (Isaiah 2; 11).

> Now it shall come to pass in the latter days
> That the mountain of the Lord's house
> Shall be established on the top of the mountains,
> And shall be exalted above the hills;
> And all nations shall flow to it.
> Many people shall come and say,
> "Come, and let us go up to the mountain of the Lord,
> To the house of the God of Jacob;
> He will teach us His ways,
> And we shall walk in His paths."
> For out of Zion shall go forth the law,
> And the word of the Lord from Jerusalem.
> He shall judge between the nations,
> And rebuke many people;
> They shall beat their swords into plowshares,
> And their spears into pruning hooks;
> Nation shall not lift up sword against nation,
> Neither shall they learn war anymore. (Isaiah 2:1–4)

Life on earth at this time will be Heaven on earth, perfectly contrasting the Tribulation's Hell on earth. This is when the wolf lies down with the lamb and the child plays with the asp, which is now completely harmless. Men will beat their swords into plowshares, as there will be no more war. The human lifespan will go back to the way it was prior to the Flood, with people living for many centuries. If someone chooses not to worship Christ, he or she will die as if still a child at one hundred years of age (Isaiah 65:20). The world itself will no longer be groaning under the curse of sin, but will yield its maximum bounty in everything. The waters will be pure, the animal life peaceful, and, for the second time in history (Genesis 1–2), the earth will be exactly as it was designed.

> Now when the thousand years have expired, Satan will be released from his prison and will go out to deceive the nations which are in the four corners of the earth, Gog and Magog, to gather them together to battle, whose number is as the sand of the sea. They went up on the breadth of the earth and surrounded the camp of the saints and the beloved city. And fire came down from God out of heaven and devoured them. The devil, who deceived them, was cast into the lake of fire and brimstone where the beast and the false prophet are. And they will be tormented day and night forever and ever. (Revelation 20:7–10)

As mentioned previously, at the end of the thousand years, Satan is released for a little time. We're not sure how long this lasts, but it's long enough to gather such a massive army so as to try and overthrow Christ's reign on the earth. You would think that people who have been living in such idyllic conditions would never dream of doing such a thing, but such is the unrepentant human heart: incurably wicked. These will have zero excuse for attempting such a blasphemous feat.

Christ will be physically ruling on the earth. The Second Coming will have been seen by everyone, demonstrably proving not only the truth of Scripture, but the reality that He is the rightful King of Kings, and Lord of Lords. Yet, these people want to sin, and they don't like being under the authority of God. Thus, when Satan is released for this short season, they'll seize the opportunity to rally against Christ. Of course, this doesn't turn out well for them, as they'll be immediately destroyed and Satan will be cast head first into the Lake of Fire to spend all eternity in misery, pain, and torment forever. He, the False Prophet, and the Antichrist will be the first three inhabitants of this terrible place.

> Then I saw a great white throne and Him who sat on it, from whose face the earth and the heaven fled away. And there was found no place for them. And I saw the dead, small and great, standing before God, and books were opened. And another book was opened, which is the Book of Life. And the dead were judged according to their works, by the things which were written in the books. The sea gave up the dead who were in it, and Death and Hades delivered up the dead who were in them. And they were judged, each one according to his works. Then Death and Hades were cast into the lake of fire. This is the second death. And anyone not found written in the Book of Life was cast into the lake of fire. (Revelation 20:11–15)

We've now arrived at the Great White Throne Judgment. This is where all of the wicked from the Old Testament, the Church Age, and the Tribulation, as well as the righteous and the wicked from the Millennium will be judged according to their works. Apparently, while still absolutely terrifying, there will be degrees of horror upon horror the wicked will suffer inside the Lake of Fire.

Remember, the Church will have already been judged at the Bema Judgment (1 Corinthians 3, 2 Corinthians 5), which will take place after the Rapture but before the end of the Seventieth Week of Daniel (the Tribulation). The Church will already have been glorified and raised up with Christ. Therefore, the Church will NOT go through the Great White Throne Judgment.

While we know there are degrees of reward for the righteous at the Bema Judgment, it is likely (our opinion) that there will also be degrees of suffering for the wicked. For example, the Old Testament wicked (from Cain until the time of Christ) will be brought up from Sheol (the torments side of Hades), and will be judged according to their works. Since they lived and died before Christ came, their suffering in the Lake of Fire (while still terrible), will not be as terrible as those who follow them.

The wicked from the time of Christ through the Rapture will suffer even more for rejecting Christ than those who came before them. For example, the Pharisees who rejected Jesus to His face will undergo a greater degree of horror inside the Lake of Fire, because even though they saw Him, they still rejected Him. Jesus warned them of their rejection in Matthew 10:15 by stating:

Assuredly, I say to you, it will be more tolerable for the land of Sodom and Gomorrah in the day of judgment than for that city!

As for those who come after Christ's death, burial, resurrection, and ascension, they've had a threefold witness—the Holy Spirit, the Church, and the Word of God—to testify to the truth. Jesus further expounds upon the responsibility of knowing in this passage from the Gospel of Luke.

But he who did not know, yet committed things deserving of stripes, shall be beaten with few. For everyone to whom much is given, from him much will be required; and to whom much has been committed, of him they will ask the more. (Luke 12:48)

The wicked from the Tribulation will have had the Rapture as evidence, as well as the twenty-one-plus judgments, the angels in Heaven proclaiming the everlasting gospel, the Two Witnesses, and an abundance of signs and wonders to convince them. Yet, they will still reject Christ; thus, their level of punishment will be increased accordingly.

Finally, we get to the righteous and the wicked from the Millennial Kingdom. The names of the righteous will be found in the Book of Life, and they will enter the eternal state with Christ. The wicked from the

Kingdom era will have zero excuses, and will receive the harshest of all the degrees of severity (except for Satan, the Antichrist, the False Prophet, and the fallen angels). The names of the wicked (from all the ages since Cain) who will not be found in the Lamb's Book of Life will be eternally separated from Him forever. They will be cast into the Lake of Fire, which burns eternally. Furthermore, Christ will also put death and Hell (possibly fallen angelic beings representing these domains, as well as the domains themselves) into the Lake of Fire.

14

RULES FOR REMNANT

Whenever a prophet foretold the future, it was to awaken the people to their responsibilities in the present. Bible prophecy isn't entertainment for the curious; it's encouragement for the serious.[35]
—Warren Wiersbe

So what do you do with all you've just read about in this book?

Well, if you're a redeemed believer in Jesus Christ, you should occupy until He returns. Use the gifts God has given you to be the salt and light in your community (or wherever God has placed you). If you are not a born-again, blood-bought believer, then you need to take advantage of salvation today, before it's too late! Nevertheless, here are some practical and eternally important rules to follow if you find yourself still on earth after the Rapture.

1. **Believe: Do place your faith** in the finished work of Jesus Christ's death, burial, and resurrection.

   A—*Admit* you're a sinner and need a Savior (Romans 3:23, 6:23).
   B—*Believe* in your heart that the Lord Jesus Christ died for your sins, was buried, and God raised Him from the dead (John 3:16, Romans 5:8).

C—Call upon the name of the Lord, *trusting* on the Lord Jesus
Christ for salvation (Romans 10:9–13).[36]

Because the world will lose all believers in one stunning instant of
Disappearing, the world will be immediately turned on its head. Those
who remain will have neither the capacity, the knowledge, nor the desire
to call things as they are. If millions of people have suddenly gone missing,
please understand it wasn't because of aliens or Gaia, it was the Rapture
of the Church.

Whatever is left of the religious system hereafter will be 100 percent
complicit in helping promote the lie that the Rapture was something other
than God rescuing His people. They have to lie, because it is proof positive that they were completely wrong, and they will now have to save face.
They (the government, the media, and the apostate church) will believe
the lie. Actually, this lie may manifest itself in the form of a person, who
will pretend to be the Messiah/God, but who really is the Antichrist.

1. **Resist: Do NOT take the mark of the Beast.** This means you
   will not be able to buy or sell, work or play, rent or buy a home,
   or anything else in society. You will likely become homeless and
   in some form of vagrant status. You will increasingly be shut out
   of the world's surviving global system. You may starve or even die
   because you cannot buy food or find a place to live, but if you take
   the mark, you will be damned forever. It's better to struggle for a
   few years than to suffer for all eternity in the Lake of Fire (Revelation 14:9–11).

2. **Embrace martyrdom: The truth is, if you miss the Rapture, you
   will probably be martyred.** Revelation 13:7 states: "It was granted
   to him to make war with the saints and to overcome them. And
   authority was given him over every tribe, tongue, and nation."
   The weapons of the Beast's systems will be vast: artificial intelligence, global surveillance, and robotic weapons systems, as well
   as supernatural forces (demons) aiding them.

Yes, you most likely will die. However, if you place your faith in Jesus Christ, **do not fear** the first death (physical), you will immediately be with God in Heaven. **Do fear** the second death (spiritual). The first death is not the end, only the beginning of a glorious future with Christ. If you die spiritually as well (the second death), you will spend eternity in the Lake of Fire.

3. **Endure:** Endure to the end *if* you are not martyred. Run, hide, pray. If you survive the seven years, you will be some of the precious few to physically enter the Millennial Kingdom, which will literally be "Heaven on earth." The fictional character Marcie in our book was portrayed as having survived the Tribulation. The truth is, the earth's population (either through judgments or persecution) will be reduced in number by over three-quarters. Literally more than six billion people will perish in those short few years. Those who do make it to Armageddon will see their population reduced even further due to all the armies of the Antichrist and the world being utterly destroyed. However, there will be physical survivors who will make it and will enter the Millennial Reign of Christ.

TIMELINE RECAP

THE RAPTURE

This just happened. The Church is rescued and evil is no longer restrained on the earth.

The Time Gap

We don't know how long this gap will last; perhaps it will be months or even a few years. But there is a window of time between the Rapture and the official start of the Tribulation. During the gap, there are some things we think will likely happen:

1. Part I: The Muslim nations surrounding Israel will take advantage of the global chaos and launch an attack, and will be defeated, greatly expanding Israel's current borders (Psalm 83). Part II: Russia, Turkey, Iran, Libya, and Sudan will go to war against the nation of Israel. God will supernaturally defeat them (Ezekiel 38–39). *These two events will fundamentally destroy Islam as a belief system.* Israel will then begin to rebuild the Third Temple on the Temple Mount.

2. The world will reorganize into ten regional powers. This global system will be known as the "Beast."

3. Out of the ten regional governments, three will be overthrown and one man (the Antichrist) will rise to power. He will be aided by another known as the False Prophet. He will be able to do supernatural signs and wonders. A mark will be implemented for buying and selling that is put on either the hand or forehead. *DO NOT TAKE THIS MARK.* Remember, these two men will not appear to be evil at first (Revelation 6, 13).

4. Two Witnesses will also arrive during this time. They will have supernatural powers, and will preach from Jerusalem for three and a half years. They cannot be killed or destroyed until the three and a half years are completed (Revelation 11).

THE TRIBULATION (REVELATION 6:18)

The official name for the Tribulation is the "Seventieth Week of Daniel" (Daniel 9:27). It is a seven-year period during which God will unleash twenty-one divine judgments upon the earth. Over half of the world's population will die as a result of these judgments, which include the seas being turned to blood, fresh drinking water being turned to blood, and the sun and moon ceasing to give light. A contract between the Antichrist and the nation of Israel will begin these judgments.

The seven seals (Revelation 6): One-fourth of the world's population will die.

1. The white horse (Antichrist; false peace)
2. The red horse (war)
3. The black horse (drought/famine/economic disaster)
4. The pale horse (plague/disease)
5. Martyrdom of those who refuse to worship the Beast (slaughter of the Tribulation saints)
6. A great earthquake that causes such a geological disturbance that the dust and smoke obscure the sun, stars, and moon
7. Silence in Heaven

The seven trumpets (Revelation 8–11): One-third of the world's population will die.

1. Hail and fire mixed with blood
2. A great mountain cast into the sea
3. Wormwood—a meteor that poisons (makes bitter) a third of the drinking water
4. A third of the sun, moon, and stars darkened (great cold, darkness)
5. Fifth trumpet (demonic locusts plague those who take the mark)
6. Sixth trumpet (one-third of mankind killed by a demon army)
7. Seventh trumpet (lightning, voices, thunder, an earthquake and great hail)

The seven vials/bowls (Revelation 16):

1. Grievous sores on those who take the mark of the Beast
2. The rest of the seas turned to blood
3. Rivers and fountains turned to blood
4. Great heat
5. Great darkness over seat of Beast kingdom
6. Euphrates River dries up
7. Massive earthquake and vast earth changes

THE BATTLE OF ARMAGEDDON (REVELATION 19)

At the end of the seven years, the Beast's armies, along with the kings of the east, gather in the Megiddo Valley (Israel) try to destroy what remains of the Jewish people. The skies are rolled back, and Christ returns in power and glory, followed by the armies of Heaven. He destroys the armies gathered there. The Beast and the False Prophet will be cast alive into the Lake of Fire.

THE JUDGMENT OF THE NATIONS (MATTHEW 25)

Christ will judge the remaining nations. Those who will have aided Israel during this Seventieth Week will be allowed entrance into the earthly, Millennial Kingdom, over which Christ rules as the undisputed King. Those who will have attacked or who will have done ill towards the nation of Israel (and its inhabitants) will be cast into outer darkness to await judgment.

THE MILLENNIAL REIGN OF CHRIST (REVELATION 20)

Christ will reign upon the earth for one thousand years. The world will be released from the curse of sin and it will become a Paradise. People will be given unnaturally long life spans. People who do not choose to follow Christ will die at the age of one hundred. At the end of the thousand years, Satan will be released for a season and cast into the Lake of Fire.

THE GREAT WHITE THRONE JUDGMENT (REVELATION 20:10–14)

The unsaved/unredeemed dead from all ages will be brought before Christ and judged according to their works. Everyone here will ultimately be cast into the Lake of Fire, because their works cannot save them. What is determined here is how severe their torment will be for all of eternity. Death and Hell will also be cast into the Lake of Fire.

ETERNITY FUTURE (REVELATION 21–22)

A New Heaven and a New Earth will be created, as the former ones will pass away. For the redeemed, eternity future will be a magnificent adventure filled with the worship of God (while being in His glorious presence); exploration (seeing all what God has been working on these past two thousand years); a never-ending period of peace, joy, comfort, happiness, contentment, and love forever.

CLOSING THOUGHTS

In the meantime, our world is increasingly aligning itself to become the final world government the Bible describes. It is becoming increasingly hostile to both the Jew and the born-again Christian. The decline of our civilization, by way of the rapid deterioration of morality and objective truth, is removing all those who would simply ride the fence and not take sides. The last-days events are the ultimate sifting of wheat in that we are increasingly placed in either/or scenarios. Either you get on board with the current "Antichrist zeitgeist" (anti-Christian, anti-Semitism, anti-conservative, pro-humanist, pro-hedonist, etc.), or you'll be increasingly shut out from the public arena of ideas.

The recent 2016 election and the ensuing Trump presidency exposed just how corrupt the American government (and the world governments) have become. The 2020 pandemic exposed just how far the world governments would go to politicize a crisis. We should have known they (the one-world proponents) would never let President Trump receive his hard-earned victory. It got us thinking back on everything that has since happened, and we (as born-again believers) realized that we were angry. Not throwing-things-around or shaking-our-fist-at-the-TV angry, but the kind of anger that lies just beneath the surface. We found ourselves reflecting on it and asking God "why?"—why Biden? Why let Trump go when, clearly, he's been good for the nation, good for the Christian, and good for Israel? Why let the Democrats get away with such a brazen theft of the

American population's will? Why did Mike Pence all of a sudden lose his backbone?

The response was immediate.

If not now, when?

What happens when 2024 rolls around and the Democrats put up an even more egregious attempt to overthrow the election? We know they aren't going to quit until they can permanently seal our nation into a one-party system.

Why delay?

Indeed. Why delay?

It is our position that we think our deliverance is going to come a lot sooner than many expect. Nevertheless, for all the good things Trump did, there were also missteps, one of which was listening to theologians and preachers who either do not understand Bible prophecy or who purposely confuse it. An example of this prophetic malfeasance, mostly by conservatives in the religious spectrum, is the thinking that, somehow, the US is going to come out on top in the end.

The Bible does not say that anywhere. In fact, there is no mention of any nation that even remotely resembles the United States in Scripture.

Many of these prophetically confused religious leaders come from either the post-millennialist camp (who believe the Church is responsible for Jesus' return), or the amillennial/preterist camps (who believe we are the Kingdom now). They believe (as many did) that they should fight for revival in this nation. There's nothing wrong with revival; we are to occupy until He comes (Luke 19:13).

However, there are two streams of thought going on right now regarding where we are as a nation. In one stream, we realize we have to live in this nation, whatever it becomes, until Christ returns. Do we want to live under an increasingly socialist/communist regime that persecutes Christians and increasingly promotes an Anti-God agenda? No. We want to live under the constraints of a constitutional republic. Therefore, we work, vote, and promote systems that enable them, while avoiding or boycotting things that work against our Constitution.

The other stream recognizes that God's Word comes true no matter what we think. God's will is laid out in the pages of the Bible, and it states the what, when, how, and why things happen. Some people chose to eisegete (add to) the text what they want to happen. However, we are called to exegete (take from) the text what it says, using a literal, grammatical, and historical interpretation.

The Bible clearly states that, as the end times draw closer, things will go from bad to worse. In fact, things will get so bad that Christ Himself must return to save mankind before all flesh is destroyed (Matthew 24:22).

We as born-again believers have to get our priorities realigned and realize our political alliances are not with the Democrats or the Republicans. As Christians, we should be monarchists. Our allegiance is to Christ the King. He will come back and fix all this; we do not need to allow anger to fester in our hearts like a disease. We're not even supposed plant roots in this life. Our home is a heavenly one. Our reality is an eternal reality.

Brethren, join in following my example, and note those who so walk, as you have us for a pattern. For many walk, of whom I have told you often, and now tell you even weeping, that they are the enemies of the cross of Christ: whose end is destruction, whose god is their belly, and whose glory is in their shame—who set their mind on earthly things. For our citizenship is in heaven, from which we also eagerly wait for the Savior, the Lord Jesus Christ, who will transform our lowly body that it may be conformed to His glorious body, according to the working by which He is able even to subdue all things to Himself. (Philippians 3:17–21)

Our time here on earth is fleeting, at best. We are like blades of grass— here one day and gone the next (Psalm 103:14–16). And while we have to live here for the balance of time remaining in our life, or until the Lord comes for us at the pre-Tribulation catching up, we must try our best to make do with what the Lord has entrusted to us. That is all any of us can do.

Yes, things are so upside down, topsy-turvy these days. Black is white, male is female, good is bad, and bad is good. But the chaotic and wicked nature of our generation shouldn't cause us to despair. As Jan Markell is fond of saying, "Things are not falling apart, they are falling into place."

Our hope is not in DC.

Our hope is not in world governments.

Our hope is not in the United Nations.

Our hope is not in man's ability to overcome adversity.

Our hope is in Christ.

Meanwhile, our freedoms may dwindle.

However, our freedom is in Christ, and that is forever.

We are freed from the bondage of sin and death. No one can take that from us. We cannot even do it to ourselves, because when we are born again (John 3:16), we are permanently changed. We go from being spiritually dead to being spiritually alive. Moreover, because we cannot do that by our own power, it has to be by the power of Christ and His shed blood that redeems us 100 percent. He did not pay for some of our sins, He paid for ALL of our sins; even the ones we haven't yet committed.

> Therefore we also, since we are surrounded by so great a cloud of witnesses, let us lay aside every weight, and the sin which so easily ensnares us, and let us run with endurance the race that is set before us, looking unto Jesus, **the author and finisher of our faith**, who for the joy that was set before Him endured the cross, despising the shame, and has sat down at the right hand of the throne of God. (Hebrews 12:1–3, emphasis added)

Furthermore, once we are born again, God seals us with His Holy Spirit (Ephesians 1:11–14, 4:30). We cannot unseal ourselves any more than we could seal ourselves by our own works. Our salvation is not dependent upon our works—it is not our good deeds, our tithes, our baptism, our church attendance, etc. Our salvation lies squarely in the faultless sacrifice of God's own Son, at Mt. Calvary, perfectly fulfilling the

Law's demand and taking God's full wrath upon Himself on our behalf.

Therefore, don't worry that the world is increasingly shutting us out of the public arena. Jesus tells us that even though we have little strength, the door will remain open (Revelation 3:8–10). Satan knows he cannot steal our salvation, but he loves to crush our hope and spirit. He loves to cause us to be depressed, angry, or anxious. Do not let him. Ephesians 6 gives us the tools to fight the fiery darts of the enemy. The days may turn sour in the here and now, but just remember we have far better days ahead.

> Therefore we do not lose heart. Even though our outward man is perishing, yet the inward man is being renewed day by day. For our light affliction, which is but for a moment, is working for us a far more exceeding and eternal weight of glory, while we do not look at the things which are seen, but at the things which are not seen. For the things which are seen are temporary, but the things which are not seen are eternal. (2 Corinthians 2:16–18)

One day, that will all change.

On a day known only to God the Father, He will send the Son to bring His Church home to be with Him (John 14:1–3).

On that special day, the world will be left reeling in chaos and horror, as they'll be about to enter the "hour of temptation" (Revelation 3:10), which will come upon the entire earth. Thus, if you are reading this after the Great Disappearing, you need to know what awaits you.

> But concerning the times and the seasons, brethren, you have no need that I should write to you. For you yourselves know perfectly that the day of the Lord so comes as a thief in the night. For when they say, "Peace and safety!" then sudden destruction comes upon them, as labor pains upon a pregnant woman. And they shall not escape.
>
> **But you, brethren, are not in darkness, so that this Day should overtake you as a thief.** You are all sons of light and sons

of the day. We are not of the night nor of darkness. Therefore let us not sleep, as others do, but let us watch and be sober. For those who sleep, sleep at night, and those who get drunk are drunk at night. But let us who are of the day be sober, putting on the breastplate of faith and love, and as a helmet the hope of salvation. For God did not appoint us to wrath, but to obtain salvation through our Lord Jesus Christ. (1 Thessalonians 5:1–9)

Even so, Maranatha!

APPENDIX A

SEALS, TRUMPETS, AND BOWLS

By Pete Garcia

Someone recently asked me to explain why God uses seals, trumpets, and bowls as the symbols for the earth's final judgments. Since no one had ever asked me that before, I found it intriguing and worthy of investigation. In my brief searching through both my books and online, I discovered that hardly anyone else had bothered to discuss it, either. In fact, we are overwhelmed with what these judgments are, but hardly anyone discusses why these particular symbols are used. I was able to find some descriptions in Clarence Larkin's book on the book of Revelation, so I will lean some on his work. So here we go.

WHY SEALS?

Books in ancient times came in the form of scrolls. It wasn't until the time of Julius Caesar (circa 30 BC) that books were put into different forms resembling what we come to think of as the rectangular-shaped books we have today. However, this particular scroll (book) contains the Title Deed to the earth. It was the inheritance that Adam forfeited when he sinned against God. Adam had been given dominion over the earth (Genesis 1:26, 28), but when he willingly disobeyed God, he forfeited that over to Satan (Genesis 3:17–19, Luke 4:5–6).

Thus, the sealed scroll represents the Title Deed to the earth that Adam lost and God regained, and that now, in Revelation 5, will be opened by its rightful owner. This is why we see the angel ask, "Who is worthy to open the book and loose its seals?" As Revelation 5 goes on to show, only Jesus was worthy to do so. Jesus is both God and Man, and accordingly, is the only capable *Kinsman Redeemer* in all of existence (Leviticus 25:23–34, Ruth 4:1–12). Regarding this worthiness, the great Clarence Larkin wonderfully points out:

> In the Gospels four titles are given to Jesus. He is the Son of David; the Son of Abraham; the Son of Man; and the Son of God.
> 1. As the Son of David, He has title to the Throne of David.
> 2. As the Son of Abraham, He has title to the Land of Palestine, and all included in the Royal Grant to Abraham.
> 3. As the Son of Man, He has title to the Earth and the World.
> 4. As the Son of God, He is the Heir of All Things.

The Scroll has seven seals on it. As many have pointed out, the number seven represents completeness and perfection throughout the Bible. The Bible itself is broken into seven major divisions: The Law, the Prophets, the Psalms, the Gospels and Acts, the General Epistles, the Pauline Epistles, and the book of Revelation. The angel Gabriel gave Daniel God's remaining prophetic timeline for the nation of Israel (Daniel 9:24–27) as seventy weeks of seven years (or 490 years). The sixty-ninth week ended with the crucifixion of Christ, and the seventieth week is still future, since **nothing** historically corresponds with its fulfillment.

In the book of Revelation alone, the number seven is used forty-nine times (7 x 7). This includes only the explicit uses of seven, and not the duplicates in the same verse. These groups of seven are: *churches, spirits, candlesticks, stars, lamps, seals, horns, eyes, angels, trumpets, thunders, thousand men, heads, crowns, plagues, vials (or bowls), mountains, and kings.*[37]

Therefore, we can conclude that these seven seals, plus the seven trumpets and the seven bowls (equaling twenty-one judgments, or 7 x 3) represent God's perfect or complete series of judgments upon planet earth. What is hidden still is what or how the seven thunders (Revelation 10:3–4) figure into the judgments.

The first four seals unleash what we commonly refer to as the four horsemen, since these judgments come in the form of riders on different colors of horses. But all of the seal judgments seem to find a corresponding description in the Jesus' Olivet Discourse found in the synoptic Gospels (Matt, Mark, Luke). However, this discourse is not a strict timeline, as it seems to cover all of the overarching components of the twenty-one judgments.

Seal 1: *White Horse (arrival of final world tyrant—the Antichrist)*
　　　Matthew 24:4–5 (false Christs)
Seal 2: *Red Horse* (peace is taken from the earth)
　　　Matthew 24:6–7 (wars)
Seal 3: *Black Horse* (global famine and scarcity)
　　　Matthew 24:7
Seal 4: *Pale Horse* (one-fourth of the earth dies)
　　　Matthew 24:7–8
Seal 5: The cry of the martyrs
　　　Matthew 24:9–13
Seal 6: Cosmic disturbances, great earthquake—the wrath of the Lamb recognized
　　　Matthew 24:29–30
Seal 7: Silence in Heaven for about a half hour (Heaven is never silent)

Nevertheless, the seventh of each judgment works to introduce the next series of judgments.

WHY TRUMPETS?

Trumpets are used for many things in the Bible. They were used as a call to war, a call to worship, for the convocation of the people, and to proclaim the festivals of the Year of Jubilee and the Feast of Tabernacles, and also for Judgments (Ex. 19:16. Amos 3:6. Joshua 6:13–16. Zeph. 1:14–16). These "Seven Angels" prepared themselves to sound.[38]

Whereas most of the seal judgments are focused on both the geopolitical terraforming and culling of the global population, the trumpet judgments seem to focus initially on physically terraforming the earth. This may have not just be about judgment, but also about channelizing, or limiting, Satan's options as time progresses forward. Thus, the severity of the judgments is increased and diversified in destroying not just man, but nature as well.

There is much confusion today for many who subscribe to either the mid-Trib or pre-Wrath Rapture positions who liken the seventh trumpet judgment as the timing of the Rapture (*harpazo*, "catching up"). The problem with this is there is nothing in Revelation 11:15–19 that speaks to, or addresses, the catching-up of believers, a translation from mortality to immortality, or a resurrection of the dead in the corresponding passages.

One must conclude that if the Church (*ekklesia*—"called-out assembly") is caught up at the **last trump** (1 Corinthians 15:52), there must also have been a corresponding **first trump** of equal or like nature (if we are comparing apples to apples). It would make no sense to use the first trumpet blast of Joshua's march around Jericho as being equal to the last trumpet spoken of in 1 Thessalonians 4:16. This has the same inequality as comparing 1 Corinthians 15:52 Rapture with the seventh trumpet judgment. These are two very different things.

Thus, if the purpose of the Rapture of the Church is the ingathering of all believers from the first Pentecost after Christ's ascension until today (both alive and dead) to meet the Lord in the air, then we must find a corresponding first gathering of a *called-out assembly*.

The first mention of a trumpet blast in Scripture is found in Exodus 19:16–20, when the Israelites were gathered together for the first time as a nation at the foot of Mount Sinai. The last trumpet blast, correspondingly, gathers the Church of all ages together for the first time to meet the Lord in the air.

Note the similarities:

THE FIRST TRUMPET

Then **it came to pass on the third day,** in the morning, that there were thunderings and lightnings, and a thick cloud on the mountain; and **the sound of the trumpet was very loud,** so that all the people who *were* in the camp trembled. [17] And Moses **brought the people out of the camp to meet with God,** and they stood at the foot of the mountain. [18] Now Mount Sinai *was* completely in smoke, because the Lord descended upon it in fire. Its smoke ascended like the smoke of a furnace, and the whole mountain quaked greatly. [19] And when the blast of the trumpet sounded long and became louder and louder, Moses spoke, and God answered him by voice. [20] **Then the Lord came down** upon Mount Sinai, on the top of the mountain. And the Lord called Moses to the top of the mountain, **and Moses went up.** (Exodus 19:16–20, emphasis added)

THE LAST TRUMPET

For **the Lord Himself will descend** from heaven with a shout, with the voice of an archangel, and **with the trumpet of God.** And the dead in Christ will rise first. [17] Then we who are alive *and* remain **shall be caught up together with them in the clouds to meet the Lord in the air.** And thus we shall always be with the Lord. (1 Thessalonians 4:16–17)

In both passages:

- A trumpet blasts
- The Lord descends
- Man goes up

I believe the "third day" reference is equally compelling, both as symbolism pointing to the death, burial, and resurrection of Christ, as well as to God's prophetic overview in dealing with the nation of Israel in Hosea 6:1–3 passage. Nevertheless, we see the judgments increasing both in scope and severity.

Trumpet 1: One-third of vegetation struck
Trumpet 2: One-third of the seas struck
Trumpet 3: One-third of fresh waters struck (Wormwood)
Trumpet 4: One-third of heavens struck
Trumpet 5: Demonic locusts from bottomless pit torment mankind for five months
Trumpet 6: Angels from the Euphrates released—kill one-third of mankind
　　　~Seven thunders proclaimed—not written down
Trumpet 7: Kingdoms proclaimed

WHY BOWLS (VIALS)?

The last series of seven judgments are the full measure of God's wrath being poured out on an increasingly recalcitrant mankind. These judgments must either be of a short duration, or they occur right before the very end, since some are so severe mankind could not long survive. Why does God use bowls instead of say, barrels or buckets? Like the seals and the trumpets, bowls are of those most basic of human tools common throughout all of man's epochs.

There has always been some form of seal to cover the contents of a parchment since there have been either leather or papyrus parchments. There has always been some form of metal horn (Genesis 4:21–22) used to announce and to make music. Similarly, the bowl, or vial, is one of those most basic of human tools common to every age, culture, and nation. This is also why God doesn't use an iPad, an electric keyboard, and a blender for these symbols, as they would have only made sense in this last generation. Everyone can picture a bowl overflowing, and here, we get a glimpse of God's wrath overflowing from these bowls to pour out upon the earth.

Bowl 1: Loathsome sores appear on those who bear the mark of the Beast.

Bowl 2: The rest of the seas turns to blood.

Bowl 3: All fresh water sources turn to blood.

Bowl 4: Men are scorched by the sun and its heat.

Bowl 5: Painful darkness descends upon the Beast's kingdom.

Bowl 6: The Euphrates River dries up, opening the way for the kings of the east to join in on Armageddon.

Bowl 7: The greatest earthquake in history utterly shakes the earth and drastically alters earth's geography; Jerusalem is divided into three parts; every island disappears into the seas of blood; one-hundred-pound hailstones pummel the earth.

That is the basic overview of why God uses the seal, trumpet, and the bowl to convey His great displeasure and wrath with the wickedness of a fallen creation. Glory be to God that we (the Church) will not be here to experience it. Jesus stated that the final seven years will be the worst period of time in all of human history, and if He didn't personally intervene, there would be no flesh left to save.

Even so, Maranatha!

APPENDIX B

LIVING IN BIBLICAL TIMES

By Pete Garcia

There has been a lot of discussion over the past century on whether or not we can know when the Rapture happens. And if we remove all the crazy date setters and wild-eyed speculators out there from the equation, what remains are essentially two camps of watchers: those who think we can't know, and those who think we can. Let us see what the Bible says on the subject.

> ...not forsaking the assembling of ourselves together, as is the manner of some, but exhorting one another, and so much the more as you see the Day approaching. (Hebrews 10:25)

According to the writer of Hebrews, watching believers should be able to see "the Day" approaching. But what does that mean exactly? If the Rapture is a signless event (it is), then how can we see it approaching? How does Matthew 24:36 factor into it?

> But of that day and hour no one knows, not even the angels of heaven, but My Father only.

At this point, we have a verse saying we will see (with our own eyes) "that Day" approaching, and we have another verse stating we can't know exactly when Christ will return. If Matthew 24:36 were Christ's final or only words on the subject, I would tend to agree that we can't know.

However, these are not Christ's final or only words on the subject of His return. Nearly sixty years later, Christ tells the Apostle John on the island of Patmos to address seven letters to seven churches. Of note, here is a portion of Christ's words to the church at Sardis:

> Remember therefore how you have received and heard; hold fast and repent. Therefore if you will not **watch**, I will come upon you as a thief, and *you will not* ***know*** *what hour I will come upon you.* (Revelation 3:3)

So now, Christ adds both the seeing (watching) and connects it with the knowing. If taken through its logical conclusions, if we will not watch, then we will not know what hour He comes upon us. Conversely, if we will watch, then we should know what hour He will come. This seems to correspond more with the passage in Hebrews 10 as being able to see "that Day" approaching than it does with the Matthew 24:36 passage.

It was to the Apostle Paul who was given the task of explaining the mystery of the Rapture to a growing Gentile church. In fact, Paul writes more about the Rapture of the Church than any other writer in Scripture. Paul clarifies this line of thinking regarding knowing vs. not knowing when he writes these verses to a small church in Thessalonica:

> But concerning the times and the seasons, brethren, you have no need that I should write to you. For *you yourselves* ***know perfectly*** that the day of the Lord so comes as a thief in the night. For when they say, "Peace and safety!" then sudden destruction comes upon them, as labor pains upon a pregnant woman. And they shall not escape. But you, brethren, **are not in darkness**, so that this Day should overtake you as a thief. (1 Thessalonians 5:1–4)

Being "in darkness" is a colloquialism for being blind (or not being able to see). Here, Paul links those who are not in Christ and are of the world to being in darkness. He also links those who are in Christ and are watching to being "sons of the day." Paul links being able to see (being of the day) with knowing perfectly when the Day of the Lord is at hand.

As I have written in previous articles, there are two different usages of the phrase the "Day of the Lord" (DoTL) used in Scripture. There is a general usage of this term DoTL throughout the New and Old Testament that speaks to the whole seven years. There are also numerous passages that speak to specific usage of this term, speaking directly to the Second Coming itself. However, I believe Paul is addressing the general usage of the DoTL phrase here in 1 Thessalonians 5.

In conclusion, we who are watching will be able to know "that Day" is approaching, because we are seeing the things (geopolitical, technological, financial, religious, etc.) come to pass that are necessary for the Seventieth Week of Daniel to happen. Like we know Thanksgiving is near when we see the decorations for Christmas going up, we also know the Rapture is near when we see the things pertaining to the Seventieth Week going up. Although we cannot know the specific day or hour (or the exact moment) of the Rapture, we can know the season.

HARVESTS, FEASTS, AND SEASONS

While the earth remains, seedtime and harvest, cold and heat, winter and summer, and day and night shall not cease. (Genesis 8:22)

Speaking of times and seasons, Jesus often referred to parables when speaking of His return. In His most famous parable on the subject, He links His return to a specific time of year. While we cannot be dogmatic about it, clearly, Jesus knew every word He spoke and was recorded in Scripture would be scrutinized to the nth degree. Therefore, it is my opinion He used this example very strategically.

Then He spoke to them a parable: "Look at the fig tree, and all the trees. When they are already budding, you **see** and **know** for yourselves that **summer** is now near. So you also, when you see these things happening, know that the kingdom of God is near. Assuredly, I say to you, this generation will by no means pass away till all things take place. Heaven and earth will pass away, but My words will by no means pass away." (Luke 21:29–33)

Although most of us are not farmers, we know that the Israelites were given instructions in the Old Testament on how and when to harvest their crops. First, they were to gather the "first fruits" as an offering to the Lord. Second, they would then conduct the main harvest (minus the corners of the field). Depending on the crop, there would be an early and late harvest. Last, the poor could be allowed to come in once the main harvest was complete, and they would be allowed to go through the gleanings of the field (Leviticus 19:9–10). Perhaps one of the greatest examples of this is found in the story of Ruth (a gentile bride), which is celebrated during the Feast of Weeks (Shavuot or Pentecost), which puts it in late spring, early summer.

The times and seasons also corresponded with the feasts of the Lord. There were four feasts in the spring, then a long summer break, and then three feasts in the fall. We know that, in the life of Christ, He fulfilled the first three with His death, burial, and resurrection. We also know that the Church was conceived at Pentecost some fifty days later. What remains are the fall feasts, and we believe that these will also be fulfilled literally during the Seventieth Week of Daniel. The question remains: Where does the Rapture of the Church fall into this pattern (if at all)?

FEASTS OF THE LORD

And the Lord spoke to Moses, saying, "Speak to the children of Israel, and say to them: 'The feasts of the Lord, which you shall proclaim *to be* holy convocations, these *are* My feasts.'" (Leviticus 23:1–2)

SPRING FEASTS

1. Feast of Passover (Fulfilled)
   (24 hours later)
2. Feast of Unleavened Bread (Fulfilled)
   (2–6 days later)
3. Feast of First Fruits (Fulfilled)
   (50 days later)
4. Feast of Weeks (Shavuot/Pentecost) (Fulfilled)
   (135 days later)

FALL FEASTS

5. Feast of Trumpets
   (10 days later)
6. Feast of Atonement
   (5 days later)
7. Feast of Tabernacles
   (73 days later)
8. Hanukah
(Dates courtesy of Robert Breaker's White Board!)

Now, the Church was conceived (not born) at Pentecost, and what we have been waiting for these past two thousand years during our gestation period (i.e., the Church age) is the Rapture (our birth). This is the long-awaited birth of all the singularly corporate, body of believers from that first Pentecost until the Rapture (Romans 8:18–25). Every born-again believer of both the living and the dead will meet Christ in the air for the greatest reunion the world has ever seen. What we can't know is whether or not this reunion and transformation (from mortality to immortality) happens as part of the *Feasts of the Lord*, or is a completely unconnected event. It would seem though, that given our conception being originally connected with Pentecost, must in some way, find its birth also with Pentecost (to close the loop, so to speak).

Now, some have pointed out that the last trump must be connected with the Feast of Trumpets, but I do not think this is the case. As I have pointed out on numerous prior occasions, if there is a *last trumpet*, there must also be a *first trumpet*. The first trumpet blast gathered the nation of Israel together for the first time at the foot of Mt. Sinai (Exodus 19). It only makes sense that the last trumpet gathers all of the Church together in the air at the Rapture (1 Thessalonians 4:13–18; 1 Corinthians 15:51–56). Thus, this explains the significance of the "last trump" as being connected with the gathering of a body of believers, rather than a feast.

SIGNS

Then God said, "Let there be lights in the firmament of the heavens to divide the day from the night; and let them be for signs and seasons, and for days and years." (Genesis 1:14)

The Bible is replete with references to the heavens, and we know, historically, the Mazzeroth held significance to earlier Bible people. Correspondingly, many in our own day have pointed to various astronomical events such as the *Blood Moon Tetrads* or the *Revelation 12 sign* as having prophetic significance. Whether they are significant or not, I cannot say with authority. We know that, two millennia ago, God used the "Star of Bethlehem" as a sign for the Gentile wise men to follow and worship the child, Jesus. We also know that inside of the Seventieth Week of Daniel (the seven-year Tribulation) there will also be major astronomical signs in the sun, moon, and stars (Acts. 2:19–20) that herald the Day of the Lord. However, we cannot say with any specificity whether or not the things we are seeing now in the heavens point to anything specific.

If we are in the dispensation of the Church (I believe we are), then we do not derive our authority from the signs and wonders that accompanied the Old Testament times and/or will find fulfillment inside the Tribulation.

Rather, we preach Christ crucified, which is a stumbling block to the Jews and foolishness to the Greeks (1 Corinthians 1:23). Therefore, anything we see today is either not for the Church to apply to our own deliverance or serves as a sign pointing Israel to the lateness of the hour, since they have rejected the message of Christ crucified.

> For since, in the wisdom of God, the world through wisdom did not know God, it pleased God through the foolishness of the message preached to save those who believe. For Jews request a sign, and Greeks seek after wisdom. (1 Corinthians 1:21–22)

As I've said on numerous occasions, I don't dismiss out of hand things like the Revelation 12 sign or other events, I just don't think we can pin any of our specific hopes on them. The proof of this is that they have happened, and we are still here, so whatever they meant is beyond us. What we can know, though, is that creation is moaning and groaning, and we are seeing our universe becoming increasingly hostile to the burden of sin placed upon it. This means an uptick in both natural calamities, such as earthquakes, volcanic activity, and hurricanes, as well as cosmic disturbances. If there are any signs we as the Church can see and point to as the lateness of the hour, it is the birth pangs. The fact that we are seeing such a dramatic increase in both the frequency and intensity of the natural and cosmic disturbances is a testament to the lateness of the hour.

But it is not just the universe winding down that points to our end coming soon. There are many other signs happening simultaneously that are also heralding the end of our age. These are the growing apostate nature of Christendom (not the true Church), the geopolitical alignment of nations against Israel (e.g., Gog-Magog), the revival of the old Roman Empire, technological advancements in military weaponry, genetics, artificial intelligence, information processing, and the implementation of these things into the human body. The old order of geopolitics is falling apart and the New World Order is rising. Across the board, evil is being called good, and good, evil. Because of this, we are feeling the effects of the *wrath of abandonment* in this once-blessed nation. Violence and wickedness are on the rise everywhere. Lastly, we are seeing the nations of the world setting the stage for the coming ten-nation confederacy by using "governance by crisis" as test runs with global mandates and lockdowns.

CLOSING

People have been saying for many years now that Christ's coming must be soon because of this sign or that. Some pointed to the rise of Hitler or the year 2000 as proof. To be fair, what are a few decades in light of eternity? So "soon" or "at hand" are relatively subjective terms. In light of what we have discussed already, and instead of saying that Christ is coming soon (this term is rather vague), let us consider a few key points as we close out this study by looking at things in reverse order.

1. We know Christ's Second coming will be tied to a specific time, rather than to some random moment. We know this because Christ's First Coming was tied to something known as the "fullness of times" (Galatians 4:4–5). Presumably, this meant that all the conditions necessary for the Messiah to come the first time had been met. So, whatever conditions are necessary for Christ's Second Coming must also be met in order for us to know when that might occur.

2. We know that, at the Second Coming, Christ's triumphant return in the air with the armies of Heaven in tow meet the Antichrist and his global forces in Israel at Armageddon. We know that Antichrist will have recently recaptured Jerusalem from the Jews and desecrated their Temple. In order for this to have happened, the Jews must be living back in Israel and their Third Temple must be standing.

3. We know that the Antichrist will need to have the technology available to control all buying and selling in the world. He will

need the technology to control all the governments in the world, as well as their armies.

4. We know that Russia, Turkey, Iran, and the "many other nations" will align themselves to come against Israel. In their overtly divine destruction, Israel decides it's time to rebuild their Third Temple.

5. We know the world is united behind a false religion known as "the whore." We know this new religion will masquerade as Christianity, but will promote all the blasphemous things God hates.

6. We know the world will be forced to unite over a major global crisis we assume to be the Rapture of the Church, which will decimate the United States and realign the global power structure.

7. We know the world is quickly approaching the two-thousandth anniversary of Christ's death, burial, and resurrection (2032). We know that the Seventieth Week of Daniel lasts approximately seven years. We know that, to God, a day is as a thousand years and a thousand years is as a day. We also know that God promised to raise Israel up on the third day (Hosea 6:2).

I guess, at this point, you just need to ask yourself if you can see anything on this short list as already existing? Is it already in play? Is it already being implemented? What's left to happen? If you can see it, then as "sons of the light" and "sons of the day," you should know that our salvation (deliverance) is at hand.

Now when these things begin to happen, look up and lift up your heads, because your redemption draws near. (Luke 21:28)

The Environmental Impacts
of the Tribulation
upon the Earth

By Pete Garcia

For the past hundred years, we have had an endless train of climate prophets promoting their environmental *armageddonism* and climate alarmism regarding a coming global threat of "_____." I leave that particular *threat* blank, because frankly, the *threat* keeps morphing to fit the current political narrative, rather than the facts on the ground. Nevertheless, these purveyors of climate doom and gloom have repeatedly and consistently gotten it wrong almost every time they open their mouths. What is truly amazing is that anyone still listens to them, much less gives them both an Academy Award (*An Inconvenient Truth*) as well as a Nobel Prize. (See https://cei.org/blog/wrong-again-50-years-of-failed-eco-pocalyptic-predictions/.)

Just like the failed prophecies of Balaam, when these false climate prophets say it's going to be global cooling, then the world heats up. If they say it's going to be global warming, then things begin to cool down. God is purposely making them look foolish to show them the height of their folly. This explains why they have (as of a few years ago) changed the political narrative to the generic catch-all, "climate change."

As previously mentioned, world leaders are hell bent on reordering the world system to adjust to the coming global government that they are trying to create. Now, these human political puppets don't truly understand what is coming per se (because they reject the biblical worldview), but the demonic forces behind their thrones do. Satan and his forces are the ones actively pulling their strings to prepare for what is coming. They know judgment that is coming, and they also know the ecological, terrestrial, and geological impacts these judgments will bring to the earth. I mean to say, they were there for the Noahic Flood, the destruction of Sodom and Gomorrah, the Tower of Babel, and the Exodus plagues. They know what God is capable of and willing to do. Thus, they are attempting to corral mankind into some kind of preemptive defensive position long before it does.

Below is **my theorized summarization** of the twenty-one judgments and their environmental impacts on earth. Everything underlined are judgments that appear to have some kind of ecological/terrestrial/ geological impact upon the earth as well as the area surrounding the earth. While I acknowledge the other judgments and their horrific impacts upon mankind, the effects of those are currently outside the scope of this brief and will not be addressed.

THE SEVEN SEALS (REVELATION 6): ONE-FOURTH OF THE WORLD'S POPULATION DIES

1. The First Seal—*the White Horse (Antichrist)
Typically speaking, the rise of political power doesn't necessarily mean ecological catastrophe. However, the coming Ten Nation/Region Confederacy will likely use and strengthen current environmental policies (Paris Climate Accord, Kyoto Protocols, Green New Deal, etc.) as a means to cement their global authority over the nations. (See Agenda 2030, Sustainable Development Goals, etc.)

2. The Second Seal—*the Red Horse (War)
Given the draconian nature of the globalist power grabs, war will be inevitable as rogue nations such as Russia and China revolt. War always introduces tremendous ecological damage to whatever environment it takes place. Whether we are talking about burning ships, cities, bombs (esp.

nuclear weapons), biological weapons, and just the overall wear and tear caused by giant mechanical vehicles, the earth takes a beating during times of war. If these coming war(s) are global in nature, you can expect environmental damage to occur at World War II levels.

3. The Third Seal—*the Black Horse (Scarcity)

We know that the rider on the black horse introduces incredible economic calamity to the earth. Presumably, this occurs thru the Ten Nation/Region Confederacy (the Beast) attempt at forcing the whole world into this new economic mark of the Beast system, which intentionally causes widespread famine and economic disparity. Famine is usually either caused by governmental malfeasance or environmental drought or pestilence. We can assume that in this particular seal judgment, it is the former.

4. The Fourth Seal—*the Pale Horse (Death)

The obvious implications of the black horse lead to the activation of the consequences of the pale horse. IF part of the judgment of the black horse is the global rise in temperatures, then we should expect to see the polar ice caps melting. In so doing, this melting could unleash some potentially very bad viruses and/or bacteria that have lain dormant under the ice for millennia. This could also be a furious unleashing of new variants in present viruses that either make them much more transmissible or untreatable.

5. The Fifth Seal—Martyrdom of those who refuse to worship the Beast (slaughter of the Tribulation saints)

6. The Sixth Seal—*the Great Earthquake

The sixth seal unleashes an earthquake of such magnitude, it causes massive disturbances in both the earth and the atmosphere. The atmospheric disturbances appear to cause the dust and smoke to obscure our neighboring solar objects, causing the sun to appear black and the moon to appear blood red.

This mega earthquake seems to occur in conjunction with a major cosmic disturbance (such as an extreme solar storm or Coronal Mass Ejection [CME]). A massive CME has the potential to wipe out all of earth's satellites, thus triggering a global Internet and global communications blackout as information platforms collapse around the world. It seems the world leaders appear to know this cosmic storm is coming ahead of time as they hide in DUMBs (Deep Underground Military Bunkers) around the world and try and wait it out.

This may also explain why the earth dwellers hide from the "Wrath of the Lamb" as environmental judgments appear to happen both subterranean as well as atmospherically, simultaneously. Another thought is that these earth dwellers are led to believe (potentially as part of the great delusion) that this sixth seal judgment is "Judgment Day," and after surviving it (thinking the worst is behind them), they set out to rebuild the New World Order.

7. Silence in Heaven

THE SEVEN TRUMPETS (REVELATION 8–11): ONE-THIRD OF THE WORLD'S POPULATION DIES

1. The First Trumpet Judgment

Hail and fire mixed with blood strike the earth, burning up one-third of the world's vegetation. It is unknown whether this is hail fire is a global storm, or if it only strikes a targeted area. My theory on this is it hits and environmentally decimates the Americas. The Western Hemisphere (North, Central, and South America) make up one-third (28.4 percent) of the earth's land mass. My reasoning for this is that God begins to channelize the world's population back to the boundaries of the *Old World*.

In terms of why blood is mingled in with the hail, a) I believe it is real blood (or else it would have been described "like" blood); and b) this blood is part of the judgment for the loss of all the innocent lives on earth and is similar to what we also see in the Gog-Magog destruction (Ezekiel 38:22).

2. The Second Trumpet Judgment

A *great mountain* cast into the sea kills a third of the ocean life and turns those seas/oceans into blood. The obvious implications would be, this would completely shut down all marine traffic in the affected areas, as well as causing a horrific stench to arise (as all the sea life in those areas dies) and float to the surface. My theory is that this judgment takes place in the Atlantic Ocean (which makes up a third of all the bodies of water—29 percent) and is one of the most heavily trafficked oceans in the world. This would absolutely shut down trans-oceanic travel between the Old World and the New.

Again, the purpose is to channelize and limit the Antichrist's ability to maneuver and control all the world. Granted, he probably wouldn't want the Americas either (if my theory is correct) after these first two trumpet judgments occur.

What exactly is this great mountain? First, we should note that the text says "**something like** a great mountain" was thrown into the sea. It could easily be a great meteor or comet that strikes the Atlantic Ocean, causing some form of contamination. A more naturalistic explanation would require something like a volcanic eruption (La Palma Volcano, Canary Island, for example) triggering a massive mountain to fall into the ocean. This would presumably cause an enormous tsunami that somehow poisons the Atlantic. Arguably, this latter explanation seems more implausible than something striking it from space.

3. The Third Trumpet Judgment

As the second trumpet judgment strikes the salty seas, this cosmic Wormwood (meteor or comet) ends up poisoning (makes bitter) a third of the drinking water. Again, a third part of the world's fresh waters (rivers, lakes, and springs) are found in the Americas. If my theory is correct, God is making the Western Hemisphere completely untenable and inaccessible to the Beast kingdom.

4. Fourth Trumpet Judgment

A third of the sun, moon, and stars darkened, as was a third of the day and a third of the night. Somehow, a great atmospheric disturbance blots out the light from the solar sources (sun, moon, and stars). Now, one theory is that this would introduce great cold (a mini ice age) and plummet temperatures due to the obscuration from the sun. Another thought could be that we get the darkness, but the heat increases. This would obviously defy natural law and seemingly impose some supernatural law as a preview of Hell on earth.

5. Fifth Trumpet—First Woe (demonic locusts plague those who take the mark)

6. Sixth Trumpet—Second Woe (one-third of mankind killed by a demonic army, death of Two Witnesses, earthquake in Jerusalem)

7. Seventh Trumpet—Third Woe

Essentially, this judgment introduces all of what we see in the cataclysmic seven bowl judgments as all being part of and wrapped up in this third woe. Here is what some of the most respected Christian eschatologists have said regarding the third woe.

Dwight Pentecost in *Things to Come* (Grand Rapids: Zondervan, 1958) states:

- "The seventh trumpet and the third woe judgment (11:15) brings about the return of Christ to the earth and the subsequent destruction of all hostile powers at the conclusion of the Armageddon program" (362).

Arnold G. Fruchtenbaum in The *Footsteps of the Messiah: A Study of the Sequence of Prophetic Events* (Tustin, CA: Ariel Ministries, 2003) states (emphasis added):

- "The seventh trumpet that **contains** the seven Bowl Judgments is the third woe (239)."

John F. Walvoord, "Revelation," in T*he Bible Knowledge Commentary: An Exposition of the Scriptures*, edited by J. F. Walvoord and R. B. Zuck (Wheaton, IL: Victor Books, 1985) states:

- "The seventh trumpet chronologically reaches to Christ's return. Therefore the seventh trumpet introduces and includes the seven bowl judgments of the wrath of God revealed in chapter 16 (2:956-957)." (https://hermeneutics.stackexchange.com/questions/5787/what-is-the-third-woe-in-the-book-of-revelation)

THE SEVEN BOWL JUDGMENTS (REVELATION 16):

1. The First Bowl: Grievous sores on those who take the mark of the Beast

2. The Second Bowl
Let's assume for a second that the second trumpet judgment did only affect the Atlantic Ocean. Now, we have the second bowl impacting the rest of the world's oceans. The economic impacts would be massive as global sea trade grinds to a halt. This could also mean, presumably, a limit to the Antichrist's military forces. If previous judgments impacted air travel (lightning, diminished natural light, atmospheric obscurations, etc.), then the Antichrist and the rest of the world forces are increasingly bound by land travel. Furthermore, this would cripple many nations that

have come to depend on desalinization (turning seawater into drinking water) as their primary source of drinking water.

3. The Third Bowl
Great thirst begins to fill the world as the rest of the rivers and freshwater are turned to blood. Presumably, this happens fairly close to the Armageddon campaign, as the human race could not long survive without water. However, there is a passage speaking to men wanting to die, but not being able to, which may play into this somehow (Revelation 9:6).

4. The Fourth Bowl
Adding salt to the wound of the increasingly thirsty earth dwellers is the great heat that fills the kingdom of the beast.

5. The Fifth Bowl
A terrifying picture is beginning to develop of *Hell on earth*—great unquenchable thirst, blistering heat, and now, a supernaturally dark darkness fills the kingdom of the beast. My understanding of this is that these three judgments (3rd, 4th, and 5th) force those who were living here out very quickly as they flee for other areas not as impacted by the judgments.

6. The Sixth Bowl
Euphrates River dries up, allowing for the kings of the east to march westward to the land of Israel. We can assume that if the previous three judgments target the kingdom of the beast, and that kingdom now lies somewhere in the vicinity of modern-day Iraq/Saudi Arabia/Syria, the heat could be the primary factor for the Euphrates drying up and why these forces have to travel by land (rather than flying or sailing).

7. The Seventh Bowl

> Then the seventh angel poured out his bowl into the air, and a loud voice came out of the temple of heaven, from the throne, saying, "It

is done!" And there were noises and thunderings and lightnings; and there was a great earthquake, such a mighty and great earthquake as had not occurred since men were on the earth. Now the great city was divided into three parts, and the cities of the nations fell. And great Babylon was remembered before God, to give her the cup of the wine of the fierceness of His wrath. Then every island fled away, and the mountains were not found. And great hail from heaven fell upon men, each hailstone about the weight of a talent. Men blasphemed God because of the plague of the hail, since that plague was exceedingly great. (Revelation 16:17–21)

- **Noises, thunderings, and lightnings**: Serve to unnerve mankind and display God's power. There are appears to be an escalation or intensification of this as we progress through the book of Revelation. G. K. Beale, in his book, *The Book of Revelation*, notes the intensification:
  Rev. 4:5: lightnings, rumblings, thunders
  Rev. 8:5: lightnings, rumblings, thunders, earthquake
  Rev. 11:9: lightnings, rumblings, thunders, earthquake, hail
  Rev. 16:18–21: lightnings, rumblings, thunders, great earthquake, great hail
- **Great hailstones**: One hundred-pound hailstones would absolutely decimate any standing structures they land upon (see Job 38:22–23; Exodus 9:22–26; Joshua 10:11).
- **World's greatest earthquake (megathrust)**: Levels all the cities of the world, as well as sinking and displacing every island, and levels the world's mountain ranges.

The greatest earthquake in recorded history was the 9.5 earthquake that struck Valdivia, Chile, in 1960. The magnitude of the earthquake is not just in how strong it shakes, but also in how long it shakes. For this seventh-bowl earthquake to do what the Bible says it's going to do, it would have to be well north of a magnitude 10.0.

Now, I certainly would not want to test God's ability to make a 10.0+ earthquake happen, but apparently, everywhere I've read said it's impossible. The experts base their reasoning on the length of fault lines we currently know about, but I have a sneaking feeling that God is going to make it happen with or without fault lines. However, I don't put too much stock into what the "experts" say, as these are also the same folks who would say that the parting of the Red Sea or walking on water was impossible as well. All we know is that there is a mega-quake coming, which is so strong, it causes the islands to sink and the mountain ranges to flatten. How strong that earthquake is, or how it happens exactly, is beyond our ability to understand it at the present. We just know it is coming.

CONCLUSION

If the US collapses after the Rapture (it will) then it only makes sense that God is channelizing people back to the Old World. Perhaps the reason He is doing this is that it will force the Beast kingdom to align and function according to their ancient boundaries—that being primarily around the Mediterranean and Israel. This channelizing into denser populations also serves to intensify the effects of the judgments upon the remaining populations. The twenty-one-plus divine judgments also seem to serve the purpose of both, purging, as well as terraforming, the earth ahead of the impending Kingdom Age.

> And another angel came out from the altar, who had power over fire, and he cried with a loud cry to him who had the sharp sickle, saying, "Thrust in your sharp sickle and gather the clusters of the vine of the earth, for her grapes are fully ripe." So the angel thrust his sickle into the earth and gathered the vine of the earth, and threw *it* into the great winepress of the wrath of God. (Revelation 14:18–19)

We know creation is presently groaning under the burden of the Adamic sin curse. We also know the earth is drowning in all the blood that has been shed on her ground since Cain slew Abel (Romans 8:20–22; Genesis 4:10–11). With the fires, the pestilences, the oceans and rivers turning to blood, comets, cosmic storms, the mega-quakes, and the massive hailstones pummeling the earth, this purging-terraforming seems to be addressing every spectrum of life from the largest cosmic body to the smallest microscopic particle. In a sense, God is turning creation inside out while He is pouring out the full measure of His wrath upon a Christ-rejecting world (Jeremiah 30:7–11).

Ultimately, we know that after the Millennial Reign of Christ, the heavens and the earth will be destroyed by fire and then, God creates a "new heaven and a new earth" (Revelation 21). It is here where we will live our eternal life in a supercharged reality that is superior in every possible way to our world today. Now, if we live in a world today that has some breathtakingly beautiful scenery, imagine what this new heaven and new earth will hold. Physically, we will be able to explore and experience this new reality with zero fear or limitations. If we want to fly into space, we can. If we want to explore the deepest portions of this new earth, we can. We won't be limited by oxygen or altitude pressure, by water or by fire. Even better still is that we will live harmoniously with all of nature as God always intended it.

Now, with this in mind, if we can just keep our gaze fixed on the world to come, rather than on this fallen planet that is currently collapsing around us, it will preserve our joy and our hope in the reality to come. I know it is difficult to see the world today and think there is any light at the end of that tunnel, and you're correct. There is no saving this planet (in its current form), and even if you could, would you? So much blood, violence, and wickedness have been committed here that this current form of the earth must be purged in order for us to move on. And if we are seeing the signs of the end now, and those signs are escalating at a pace and intensity that is scaring you (and me), it is now we lean into Christ and trust in His strength to carry us through. If I can paraphrase C. S. Lewis on this matter, we look ahead because far better things are ahead than any we leave behind.

> Therefore, since all these things will be dissolved, what manner of persons ought you to be in holy conduct and godliness, looking for and hastening the coming of the day of God, because of which the heavens will be dissolved, being on fire, and the elements will melt with fervent heat? Nevertheless we, according to His promise, look for new heavens and a new earth in which righteousness dwells. (2 Peter 3:11–13)